THE SCRIPTURE AND HERMENEUTICS SEMINAR

THE SCRIPTURE AND HERMENEUTICS SEMINAR

RETROSPECT AND PROSPECT

Craig G. Bartholomew, David J. H. Beldman,
Amber L. Bowen, and William Olhausen, editors

ZONDERVAN
ACADEMIC

ZONDERVAN ACADEMIC

The Scripture and Hermeneutics Seminar

Requests for information should be addressed to:
Zondervan, *3900 Sparks Dr. SE, Grand Rapids, Michigan 49546*

Zondervan titles may be purchased in bulk for educational, business, fundraising, or sales promotional use. For information, please email SpecialMarkets@Zondervan.com.

Library of Congress Cataloging-in-Publication Data

Names: Bartholomew, Craig G., 1961- editor. | Beldman, David J. H., 1977- editor. | Bowen, Amber, 1987- editor. | Olhausen, William, editor.

Title: The Scripture and hermeneutics seminar: retrospect and prospect / Craig G. Bartholomew, David J. H. Beldman, Amber Bowen, and William Olhausen, editors.

Other titles: Scripture and hermeneutics seminar.

Description: Grand Rapids : Zondervan, 2022. | Series: The scripture collective series

Identifiers: LCCN 2022014480 (print) | LCCN 2022014481 (ebook) | ISBN 9780310144816 (hardcover) | ISBN 9780310109655 (paperback) | ISBN 9780310109662 (ebook)

Subjects: LCSH: Bible—Hermeneutics. | Scripture and hermeneutics seminar. | BISAC: RELIGION / Biblical Studies / Exegesis & Hermeneutics | RELIGION / Biblical Criticism & Interpretation / General Classification: LCC BS476 .S39 2022 (print) | LCC BS476 (ebook) | DDC 220.601—dc23/eng/20220513

LC record available at https://lccn.loc.gov/2022014480

LC ebook record available at https://lccn.loc.gov/2022014481

Cover design: Emily Weigel
Cover art: © www.heqiart.com
Interior design: Sara Colley

Printed in the United States of America

22 23 24 25 26 27 28 29 30 31 32 /LSC/ 14 13 12 11 10 9 8 7 6 5 4 3 2 1

Contents

Preface

Shortly after his conversion, Johann Georg Hamann (1730–88), one of the greatest Christian philosophers, who is unfortunately far too little known, wrote his *Londoner Schriften* (London Writings), an extended reflection on the Bible. He begins by expressing a sense of awe and excitement that God should be an author! What condescension! Even as we hand over this volume, prepared during the pandemic that continues to ravage far too many lives, we share Hamann's sense of excitement and awe. Above all else, through the Bible we hear the address of God and come to participate in his life. This ongoing and ever new possibility has motivated the Scripture and Hermeneutics Seminar (SAHS) for the past twenty-five years, and it continues to inspire our work today.

Hermeneutics concerns itself with the task of hearing afresh the communicative word – the wonder and mystery of language in and through time. Hermeneutics involves attentive listening, which Jean-Louis Chrétien evocatively describes as the "first act" of "hospitality."[1] When it comes to biblical hermeneutics, we are concerned with extending this hospitality to the biblical texts. For the SAHS, this hospitality is above all to the Word made flesh disclosed in the witness of the texts of Scripture, which *Dei Verbum* rightly calls the "pure and everlasting source of spiritual life."[2]

The SAHS was established in order to address what we perceived as a crisis in biblical interpretation. So much rigorous work was being done on the Bible but rarely in the spirit of hospitality described earlier, and little of it was performed in a way that remained rigorous but also deepened and supported the life and work of the church. Where could resources be found that would

1. Jean-Louis Chrétien, *The Ark of Speech*, trans. Andrew Brown (London and New York: Routledge, 2013), 9.

2. Vatican II Council, "Dogmatic Constitution on Divine Revelation: *Dei verbum*" (Solemnly promulgated by His Holiness Pope Paul VI on 18 November 1965), VI.21. https://www.vatican.va/archive/hist_councils/ii_vatican_council/documents/vat-ii_const_19651118_dei-verbum_en.html.

address this situation? Furthermore, in 1960 Hans-Georg Gadamer published his hugely influential *Wahrheit und Methode* (*Truth and Method*),[3] generating an explosion of work in philosophical hermeneutics. As the title indicates, Gadamer challenged an excessive dependence on method in understanding and interpretation, thereby opening up fresh avenues for understanding how we read and engage with a text.

Hermeneutics is related to *postmodernism*, which gathered momentum prior to and during the decade of our annual, international seminars. Through its critique of modernity, postmodernism opened the door, in principle at least, for Christian faith to play an integral role in academic biblical interpretation. We hoped that close attention to philosophical hermeneutics in an interdisciplinary Christian context would provide a matrix for retaining the rigour of biblical interpretation while directing it towards listening for God's address. As a result, the SAHS's primary distinctive in its early years was a sustained attempt to engage the field of biblical hermeneutics from the perspective of philosophical hermeneutics, Christian theology, and interdisciplinarity. Very few were approaching biblical interpretation in quite this way, so to this extent the Seminar was an early expression of a renewed, self-conscious theological turn in biblical interpretation.

The SAHS was first convened in 1997 in Cheltenham, England, by Craig Bartholomew and colleagues at the University of Gloucestershire and the Bible Society. Over the intervening years, it has grown into a much larger community of both established and younger scholars. Now, in 2022 the Seminar is celebrating its twenty-fifth birthday! This present volume is a celebration of twenty-five years as we look back to some of the high points of the journey so far and, in turn, begin to identify new questions and challenges for biblical hermeneutics.

In his introductory chapter (**Part I**), Craig Bartholomew recounts some of the seminal moments of the Seminar and lays out the questions that the Seminar sought to explore within the context of the wider field of philosophical and biblical hermeneutics. **Part II** provides a window into the eight volumes in the Scripture and Hermeneutics Series (2000–2007). Here is a list of the volumes with their publication years:

Vol. 1 *Renewing Biblical Interpretation* (2000)
Vol. 2 *After Pentecost: Language and Biblical Interpretation* (2001)
Vol. 3 *A Royal Priesthood? The Use of the Bible Ethically and Politically: A Dialogue with Oliver O'Donovan* (2002)

3. Hans-Georg Gadamer, *Wahrheit und Methode: Grundzuge einer philosophischen Hermeneutik* (Tubingen: Mohr, 1960). The first English edition was published in 1975.

Vol. 4 *"Behind" the Text: History and Biblical Interpretation* (2003)
Vol. 5 *Out of Egypt: Biblical Theology and Biblical Interpretation* (2004)
Vol. 6 *Reading Luke: Interpretation, Reflection, Formation* (2005)
Vol. 7 *Canon and Biblical Interpretation* (2006)
Vol. 8 *The Bible and the University* (2007)

In this part we highlight a number of the standout essays, written by leading scholars, that are representative of some of the most important themes and contributions in the field of biblical hermeneutics. We also briefly introduce the volume from which each essay is taken, along with its focus and significance. Our hope is that these essays will alert new and established scholars as well as students to the importance of this work, lead them back into the eight volumes, and act as an inspiration for further research.

Part III of this volume contains essays that not only dialogue with the earlier work of the Seminar but also address new questions along with queries that have been sharpened by the development of the Scripture and Hermeneutics Seminar into the Scripture Collective. As part of the Kirby Laing Centre for Public Theology in Cambridge (KLC), the SAHS now sits alongside three other Seminars: Scripture and Doctrine, Scripture and Church, and Scripture and the University, all part of what we call our Scripture Collective. We are particularly excited to be able to include an essay written by the celebrated French Catholic philosopher Jean-Louis Chrétien, translated into English for the first time by Andrew Sackin-Poll.

We always knew that a renewal of biblical interpretation would need to counteract the individualism of modernity and nurture a community of scholars. Nowadays few things embody the rich community that has emerged as our Annual Meal, held each year on the Saturday evening of the SBL Annual Meeting. **Part IV** of this volume expresses this community through a collection of stories and testimonies from participants in both the original consultations and the SAHS's more recent expressions. This communal ethos is captured well by the mission statement of the KLC, which is committed to "Christian scholarship and public theology, rooted in spirituality and practised in community, for the glory of God and the flourishing of the church in the world." These stories are a celebration of this special and distinctive ethos. A sensitivity to the best in the hermeneutic tradition has wonderfully fostered a community of Christian scholars from across diverse traditions.

This volume is the first in a new series of carefully choreographed, multiauthor volumes emerging from the work of the Scripture Collective and the KLC. This is, therefore, an important landmark in the Seminar's history and an exciting anticipation of what we trust will be the good fruits to come. We are grateful to Zondervan Academic for a partnership that includes this new series, and offer our thanks to Katya Covrett, Stan Gundry, and the Zondervan team.

Finally, we are very grateful to all our contributors, to the Bible Society, and to our many other partners and contributors to the Scripture and Hermeneutics Seminar over its twenty-five year history. We give a special thanks to Istine Swart, whose hard work, attention to detail, and perseverance were vital to the production of this volume – her work (quiet and behind the scenes) is evident on every page.

William Olhausen and David J. H. Beldman
October 2021

PART 1

Introduction

CHAPTER 1

On Not Refusing – Indeed Welcoming! – the One Who Is Speaking[1]

The History of the Scripture and Hermeneutics Seminar

Craig G. Bartholomew

INTRODUCTION

> Who could ever harm us resting on this breast
> from which all of light has come forth?
> – *Georges Bernanos, to his fiancée*[2]

This question from Bernanos evokes in exquisite fashion the telos of the Bible. In John's Gospel the beloved disciple reclines on Jesus's breast, an action which becomes in Bernanos's question a metaphor for the role of Scripture. In his extraordinary *Under the Gaze of the Bible*, Jean-Louis Chrétien similarly notes that

1. An allusion to Hebrews 12:25.

2. Quoted by Erasmo Leiva-Merikakis, *Fire of Mercy, Heart of the Word: Meditations on the Gospel According to St. Matthew*, vol. 1 (San Francisco: Ignatius, 1996), 7.

> When I read the Bible this way[3] and receive it as a missive in which my name is traced with the sympathetic ink of grace, the today of my living attention enters the temporal dimension of which this writing itself speaks, that is, the sacred story. As small and narrow as may be the door of my reading, which causes me to enter into that which it speaks of, as insignificant as may be the flame of my today, it is still into the sacred story that I am placed, and to it henceforth that I belong as long as I listen.[4]

Central to the Scripture and Hermeneutic Seminar (SAHS) from its inception has been this sense of the grace, power, and importance of the Bible as the living Word of God, a theme that finds rich expression in the previous quotes and in the Epistle to the Hebrews. Equally central to the SAHS was a sense of the gap between this approach to the Bible and that of the academy.

Thomas Oden structures his book *Requiem* around the metaphor of "the feast." In his preface to Oden's book, which he heads "An Invitation to the Feast," Richard John Neuhaus says,

> More and more "young fogeys" like Oden are discovering the truth that is "ever ancient, ever new" (Augustine). It is called the catholic faith, and it is a feast to which he invites us. It is a movable feast, still developing under the guidance of the Spirit. Oden is like cinema's "Auntie Mame," who observed that life is a banquet and most poor slobs are starving to death. Origen, Irenaeus, Cyril of Alexandria, Thomas Aquinas, Teresa of Avila, Martin Luther, John Calvin, John Wesley – the names fall trippingly from Oden's tongue like a gourmet surveying a most spectacular table. Here are arguments you can sink your teeth into, conceptual flights of intoxicating complexity, and truths to die for. Far from the table, over there, *way* over there, is American theological education, where prodigal academics feed starving students on the dry husks of their clever unbelief.[5]

As Scripture, clearly the Bible is at the heart of this feast. Why then does so much academic biblical scholarship do so little to help us and invite us to feast at the Lord's table?

3. Chrétien is not referring to the quote from Bernanos but to reading the Bible "today" in the sense of the Epistle to the Hebrews.

4. Jean-Louis Chrétien, *Under the Gaze of the Bible*, trans. John Marson Dunaway (New York: Fordham University Press, 2015), 2–3.

5. Richard J. Neuhaus, "An Invitation," in Thomas C. Oden, *Requiem: A Lament in Three Movements* (Nashville: Abingdon, 1995), 10.

THE LATE 1990S

In the late 1990s, when the SAHS began, we were on the other side of the historical and literary turns in modern biblical studies and immersed in the postmodern turn.[6] The literary turn, and the postmodern turn with its wild pluralism, brought trenchant critiques to bear on historical criticism. However, to a large extent they left the foundation of human autonomy firmly in place, so that historical criticism remained the default mode of interpretation. Nevertheless, the loosening of the regnant paradigm in biblical studies for over a hundred years – historical criticism of one form or another – did provide the space for the exploration of fresh approaches and for reconceiving biblical interpretation so that it invited us to the feast of Scripture. Indeed, our second consultation on *The Crisis in Biblical Interpretation* attended to the issue of whether or not biblical studies was amidst a crisis.

Brevard Childs's canonical criticism and the work of scholars like Francis Watson attempt to overcome the gap between *theology and biblical studies*, producing a body of very helpful work.[7] However, the canonical approach associated with Childs is deeply influenced by Karl Barth and shared his suspicion of philosophy. Comparably, Watson appeals for a regional theological hermeneutic in biblical studies. While doing my PhD, I had written a paper on the influences upon Childs's canonical hermeneutic. My sense that it was deeply influenced by Karl Barth was confirmed during a memorable evening at our third SAHS consultation at Selwyn College in Cambridge, where Childs shared with us the story of his journey as a Christian scholar.[8] I still regret that we did not record that wonderful evening. Having done his doctorate under historical critics, Childs then spent time studying under Barth in Basel, and he evocatively described the OT scholars sitting with their Hebrew Bibles open in front of them listening to Barth lecture, having no idea what exactly he was doing with Scripture. As I understand it, once Childs grasped the profundity of Barth's work he spent the rest of his life attempting to redo biblical studies along Barthian lines, and the results were exhilarating.

---

6. See Craig G. Bartholomew, *Introducing Biblical Hermeneutics: A Comprehensive Framework for Hearing God in Scripture* (Grand Rapids: Baker Academic, 2015).

7. Brevard S. Childs, "Interpretation in Faith: The Theological Responsibility of an Old Testament Commentary," *Interpretation* 18 (1964): 432–49; Francis Watson, *Text, Church, and World: Biblical Interpretation in Theological Perspective* (Grand Rapids: Eerdmans, 1994); *Text and Truth: Redefining Biblical Theology* (Grand Rapids: Eerdmans, 1997); "The Old Testament as Christian Scripture: A Response to Professor Seitz," *Scottish Journal of Theology* 52 (1999): 227–32.

8. See Daniel R. Driver, *Brevard Childs, Biblical Theologian*, FzAT 2, 46 (Tübingen: Mohr Siebeck, 2010); Christopher R. Seitz and Kent H. Richards, eds., *The Bible as Christian Scripture: The Work of Brevard S. Childs* (Atlanta: SBL, 2013).

One could choose far worse influences than Karl Barth! Trained as a Reformed evangelical, I learnt that Barth was a liberal – but we never actually read him. Later in life I did so, and discovered just what a fertile theological exegete Barth is. For example, he devotes some one hundred pages to small print commentary on Genesis 1:1–4a, and his theological exegesis is profound.[9] Barth almost single-handedly brought the liberal edifice down – contrary to what I had been taught – and revived a genuinely theological reading of the Bible, to which the SAHS is deeply indebted.

Nevertheless, in Barth, and I also think in Childs, we find an unresolved tension between the neutrality of historical criticism and a theological reading of the so-called final form of the biblical text.[10] If I recall correctly, Childs argued that at its best philosophy could be *bent towards* biblical interpretation. In my view deeper work needed to be done to overcome the gap between ecclesial reception of the Bible as God's Word and rigorous, academic biblical scholarship.

PHILOSOPHICAL HERMENEUTICS

Meir Sternberg points out that biblical interpretation is at the intersection of the humanities.[11] This insight alerts us to the fact that even though opening up the dialogue between biblical studies and theology is helpful and important, it is nowhere near as radical – getting down to the roots – an approach as is required to renew biblical interpretation. The very foundations need reconsideration, including issues such as our views of history, of language and literature, of how understanding takes place, of the kerygmatic nature of Scripture, of the role of listening in analysis, etc. Where might we find resources for such depth reassessment?

The emerging discipline of philosophical hermeneutics attended to precisely these sorts of issues. For example, Hans-Georg Gadamer (1900–2002), the father of modern philosophical hermeneutics, in his magisterial *Truth and Method*[12] alerts us to the limits of a "right method" approach to interpretation. He emphasizes these limits so much so that some have suggested his book should

9. See Craig G. Bartholomew, "Calvin, Barth, and Theological Interpretation," in *Calvin, Barth, and Reformed Theology*, ed. Neil B. MacDonald and Carl Trueman (Milton Keynes: Paternoster, 2008), 163–77.

10. See Karl Möller, "Renewing Historical Criticism," in *Renewing Biblical Interpretation*, SAH Series 1, ed. Craig Bartholomew, Colin Greene, and Karl Möller (Grand Rapids: Zondervan, 2000), 145–71.

11. Meir Sternberg, *The Poetics of Biblical Narrative: Ideological Literature and the Drama of Reading* (Bloomington, IN: Indiana University Press, 1987), 21–22.

12. H.-G. Gadamer, *Truth and Method* (New York: Seabury, 1975).

be entitled *Truth or Method* or *Truth Against Method.* However, Gadamer does not reject method but resituates it within a dialogue[13] between reader and text. The opening section of *Truth and Method* explains how we engage with an artwork, dialoguing back and forth until a fusion of horizons takes place.

Philosophical hermeneutics can be traced back to Edmund Husserl's phenomenology, which was taken in a hermeneutic direction by his pupil Martin Heidegger. However, Gadamer, Paul Ricoeur, and others such as Karl Apel did the heavy lifting in developing philosophical hermeneutics as a discipline in its own right. Our hunch in the SAHS was that philosophical hermeneutics at least raised the questions that needed to be attended to for any renewal of biblical interpretation to occur.

We were never suggesting that theology was unimportant, but we needed Christian perspectives from multiple disciplines on the issues being attended to by philosophical hermeneutics. Fortunately, courtesy of Alvin Plantinga, Nicholas Wolterstorff, C. Stephen Evans, and William Alston, who were all participants in the SAHS alongside many others, we were in the midst of an astonishing revival of Christian philosophy with rich resources to draw upon. The Reformed epistemology of Plantinga and Wolterstorff functions mainly in the analytic philosophical tradition, whereas philosophical hermeneutics is continental. Nevertheless, the range of the work of the Reformed epistemologists and other Christian philosophers along with their fertile participation in our Seminars contributed invaluable resources for the sort of work we were trying to do.

Following many scholars (Meir Sternberg, N. T. Wright, Anthony Thiselton, etc.), we identified three major strands in Scripture and their interrelationship as requiring attention, namely the historical, the theological or kerygmatic, and the literary. However, we recognised that there are deeper philosophical and religious foundations underlying these. In my "Introduction" to *Renewing Biblical Interpretation* I depicted the shape of the volume along the following lines:

* * *

The interplay between philosophy and the three main strands, history, literature, and theology, can be illustrated as follows:

---

13. When Gadamer retired, he spent several years at McMaster University in Hamilton, Ontario, Canada. Years later I met his student chauffeur, and he told me that when Gadamer returned home in the evening he would invariably read Plato in the Greek. Dialogue is Plato's method, and it is not hard to see the influence of this on Gadamer.

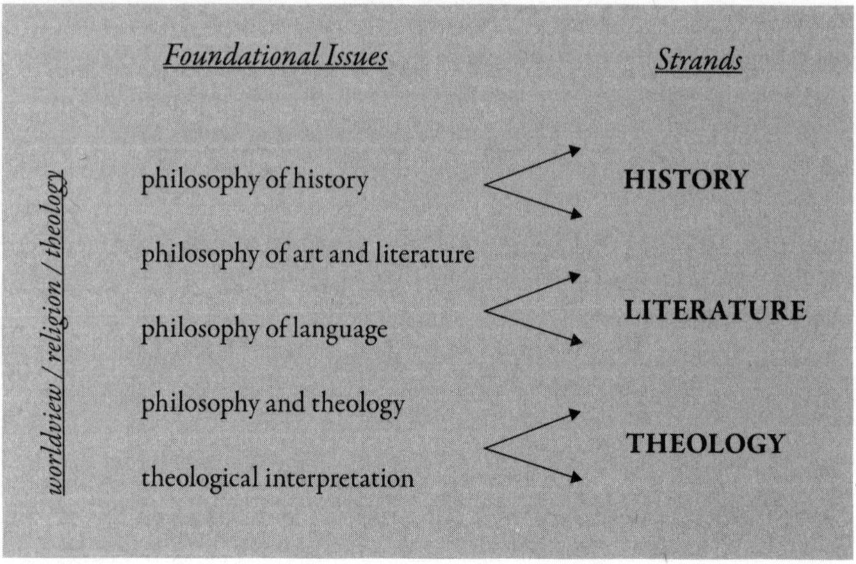

* * *

Our sense of the importance of deep philosophical issues was already present at our first consultation held in Cheltenham in 1998 on speech-act theory (SAT) and biblical interpretation. It was attended inter alia by Anthony Thiselton, Nicholas Wolterstorff, and Kevin Vanhoozer, all experts on speech-act theory and Christian thought. By this time I was on the staff of Cheltenham and Gloucester College of Higher Education, soon to become the University of Gloucestershire. Gordon Wenham had built up Old Testament studies there over most of his career and we – Gordon McConville was a senior part of the team – were attracting PhD students from around the world. However, our expertise in philosophy of language was limited, and I still remember purchasing copies of J. L. Austin's *How to Do Things With Words*[14] at Blackwells in Oxford for our group as we sought to get up to speed on SAT in preparation for the event! The vocabulary of performatives and of *locution*, *illocution*, and *perlocution* was relatively new to us.

At this consultation we were not agreed whether speech-act theory had the resources to take biblical interpretation forward, but it became clear that any attempt to renew biblical interpretation in the academy would require a process with multiple consultations to address the key areas we thought required

14. J. L. Austin, *How to Do Things with Words* (Oxford: Oxford University Press, 1962, 1975).

attention. The papers from this event were never published, but we concluded with a session on what topics needed addressing if biblical studies was to be renewed. We mapped out an eight year agenda for renewing biblical interpretation to address the following topics:

The crisis in biblical interpretation	1999
Philosophy and theology of language and biblical interpretation	2000
The use of the Bible ethically and politically	2001
History and the Bible	2002
Biblical theology and biblical interpretation	2003
Reading a book of the Bible in relation to key hermeneutical issues	2004
Reading the Bible canonically	2005
The Bible and the university: the view both ways	2006

Our 1998 consultation on SAT was thus followed by eight international consultations held at venues around the world systematically addressing these topics, with a specially invited group of some fifteen to twenty of the top scholars in each area as well as a constant core of participants. A volume in The Scripture and Hermeneutics Series (Paternoster and Zondervan) was published each year for eight years, following each consultation.

Our September 1999 consultation at Selwyn College, Cambridge, at which we were privileged to have Brevard Childs and Walter Brueggemann present, was called *The Crisis in Biblical Interpretation.* At this very stimulating event, it became clear that not all of us thought that biblical interpretation was in a crisis. Most did, but others were reluctant to emphasize this. We were all agreed, though, that biblical interpretation needed renewal, hence the title of the first volume was *Renewing Biblical Interpretation.*

Our consultations were rich events indeed, in which so many scholars gave so generously of their time and a cohort of doctoral students increasingly formed part of our community. I remember with gratitude, for example, my repeated visits to Oliver O'Donovan at Christ Church, Oxford, in preparation for our consultation on reading the Bible ethically and politically, published as *A Royal Priesthood.* Memorably, on one visit Oliver had been listening to his favourite composer, Bach. He provided me with a wonderful trinitarian analysis of the music, and followed up with an email of recommendations for listening to Bach. Oliver went on to respond to every chapter in *A Royal Priesthood.*

I also had the privilege of getting to know Brevard Childs during these years. He was humble and courteous, and it was great to meet such a prestigious scholar who wanted to discuss where the best preaching was to be found. He was a great support, and we will not forget the evening he related his academic journey as a Christian scholar to us. Nicholas Wolterstorff also attended many of our consultations, and with his brilliant mind he was indispensable for catalyzing our discussions early on, which was absolutely vital for a forty-eight-hour event. The late Mary Hesse, professor of philosophy of science at the University of Cambridge, participated at several of our consultations, and as a sign of the interdisciplinary nature of what we were doing I still remember her and the South African philosopher Elaine Botha going back home to try and work out what a "chiasm" was. They found a medieval definition! At our consultation in Rome, we were graced by the presence of Jean Vanier. We met amidst the searing July heat of Rome in a room without air conditioning, but, as one participant rightly observed, after Jean had spoken we felt calm and cool. Needless to say, recent revelations about abuse by Jean have been devastating to many of us.[15]

By the time we met in Rome we were blessed with a vibrant Catholic involvement in the SAHS, which has continued to this day. With the help of our Catholic participants, we invited the then Cardinal Ratzinger to our Rome consultation; somewhere I have his gracious handwritten letter of decline. When we met in Rome, he was Pope Benedict XVI! Cardinal Marc Ouellet from Canada also attended our consultation in Rome. Since 2010 he has been the prefect of the Congregation for Bishops and the president of the Pontifical Commission for Latin America.

Five elements were indispensable in making the SAHS possible. *Firstly*, my doctoral supervisor and then colleague Gordon Wenham, who had developed Cheltenham from virtually nothing into a major global centre for biblical studies over the course of his career. Without his seminal work, none of our work would ever have been possible. *Secondly*, our partner and main funder the British and Foreign Bible Society, which welcomed my proposal for the SAHS. Colin Greene, the Society's head of Theology and Public Policy, and I worked closely together throughout the process. Along the way, the Bible Society provided me with a full-time administrator in the person of Rosemary Hales, whose commitment to the SAHS was exemplary. *Thirdly*, the Religion and Theology Department at the University of Gloucestershire was an enormous help. Dame Janet Trotter, vice chancellor of the University of Gloucestershire, supported and often attended our consultations. Stanley Rudman and then Fred Hughes as head of the Department were active in their support of the project. After Religion and Theology fell upon hard times at the University of Gloucestershire, I moved to Redeemer University in Canada and took the SAHS and Rosemary

15. For example, see https://www.larche.org/documents/10181/2539004/Inquiry-Summary_Report-Final-2020_02_22-EN.pdf/6f25e92c-35fe-44e8-a80b-dd79ede4746b.

Hales with me. Redeemer graciously provided a home for the SAHS in its final years. *Fourthly*, Anthony Thiselton was a constant presence at our Seminars, both metaphorically and literally. No one has done more to entrench a profound knowledge of hermeneutics within biblical studies, and our work would have been impossible without his. Wonderfully, Anthony came on board in the process as co-series editor. *After Pentecost* was dedicated to him in recognition of his remarkable contribution to biblical hermeneutics. *Fifthly*, we are grateful for our publishers Paternoster and Zondervan. When we conceived the Series, Pieter Kwant was in charge of Paternoster, which took the Series on. Pieter then brought Zondervan in as our American publisher. All eight volumes remain in print with Zondervan, and Katya Covrett of Zondervan recently reminded me of those heady days when each year there would be a huge pile – a veritable Tower of Babel – of our latest volume at the Zondervan booth during the SBL Annual Meeting.

THE ETHOS OF THE SAHS

One of the best compliments paid to the SAHS was by my friend David Beldman when he said that one needs to taste the SAHS to understand it. From the start we worked to develop a distinctive ethos for the SAHS, which I described as follows:

> The Seminar is thus *academic*. It recognizes the fundamental importance of opening the Book at all levels in our cultures, but the Seminar itself is an academic initiative, aimed first at biblical interpretation in the academy.
>
> The Seminar is *interdisciplinary*. Meir Sternberg rightly notes that biblical studies is at the intersection of the humanities, and the Seminar is based on the understanding that at this intersection interdisciplinary insight is required if biblical studies is to be saved from some of its isolation and fragmentation, and for new ways forward to be forged. It has been a delight at our consultations to find philosophers rubbing shoulders with educationalists and theologians, and missiologists working with literary scholars to renew biblical interpretation.
>
> The Seminar is *Christian*. Modernity has marginalized faith in the great public areas of culture but this is a travesty of a Christian perspective in which faith relates to the whole of life. The Seminar is ecumenical and has a wide range of Christian perspectives represented within it. However, it is a rule of the Seminar that faith is not to be excluded from the consultative process that

> forms the heart of the Seminar. We have been asked about Jewish and other faiths being involved, and we are keen that such dialogue should emerge.[16] However, we have judged it important to keep the Seminar's Christian character intact at this stage so that the interdisciplinary and faith dynamics have time to be nurtured.
>
> The Seminar is *communal*. The modern academy is deeply individualistic. But we recognize that a renewal of biblical interpretation will require communal work. And a great aspect of the Seminar is the emerging sense of community among Christian scholars of diverse disciplines.[17]

The SAHS's insistence that Christian faith not be left at the door but be fully engaged in the most rigorous biblical interpretation should be noted. Amidst the global resurgence of religion that came to the fore after the SAHS began and the cracks appearing in the Enlightenment project, the role of religion in biblical studies remains controversial. John Barton's inaugural volume at Oxford was wary of the calls for a religious hermeneutic in biblical studies,[18] and more recently he insists that theology should be bracketed out of biblical criticism.[19] From the outset we have argued *the reverse*; if the Christian faith is true, then all its resources need to be leveraged in the search for truthful interpretation of the Bible. This does not deny space for other approaches to biblical interpretation. Academic biblical studies, in my view, requires a *genuine* pluralism in which different approaches are allowed to come to fruition so that open dialogue can take place.

Once the series of eight consultations were concluded, the SAHS continued to meet each year around the SBL Annual Meeting, often against many odds. I remain profoundly grateful to those who hung in with me during several lean years – you know who you are. The SAHS has since published two additional volumes, *Hearing the Old Testament: Listening for God's Address* and *A Manifesto for Theological Interpretation*.[20] Further publications are planned. More recently

16. In 2018 the SAHS engaged in a joint session with the Jewish Theology session at the SBL Annual Meeting in a dialogue with Jeremiah Unterman and his excellent book *Justice for All: How the Hebrew Bible Revolutionized Ethics* (Lincoln, NE: University of Nebraska Press, 2017). At the conclusion of this event, Jerry received a standing ovation. In 2021 the SAHS hosted an extraordinarily rich online event with Leon Kass on the occasion of the publication of his new commentary on Exodus.

17. Craig Bartholomew, "Introduction," in *Renewing Biblical Interpretation*, SAH Series 1, ed. Craig Bartholomew, Colin Greene, and Karl Möller (Grand Rapids: Zondervan, 2000), xxvi.

18. John Barton, *The Future of Old Testament Study* (Oxford: Clarendon, 1993).

19. John Barton, *The Nature of Biblical Criticism* (Louisville: Westminster John Knox, 2007).

20. Craig G. Bartholomew and David J. H. Beldman, eds., *Hearing the Old Testament: Listening for God's Address* (Grand Rapids: Eerdmans, 2012); Craig G. Bartholomew and Heath A. Thomas, eds., *A Manifesto for Theological Interpretation* (Grand Rapids: Baker Academic, 2016).

we have partnered with the Institute for Biblical Research (IBR), and the SAHS has developed into four flourishing Seminars, namely the SAHS itself, Scripture and Doctrine, Scripture and Church, and most recently Scripture and the University. The communal side of our work is embodied in our Annual Meal each year on the Saturday night of the SBL Annual Meeting – in my opinion, one of the best things we do. At our 2019 meal we were privileged to host Edith Eger, Holocaust survivor and author of *The Choice*,[21] as our guest speaker. It was a sheer delight to have her and friends with us for that evening.

THE ACHIEVEMENTS AND RECEPTION HISTORY OF THE SAHS

The eight volumes of the SAH Series have the strengths as well as some of the weaknesses of multiauthor volumes. By their nature they are not fully coherent, systematic treatises, as one would expect from a single author. Some are more obviously coherent than others. *A Royal Priesthood*, for example, has a long introduction to Oliver O'Donovan's work up to 2000,[22] and his generosity as a dialogue partner at the consultation event and as a respondent to each chapter in writing after the event makes the volume unique and wonderfully rich and stimulating.

We prepared well for each year, sending out a context-setting paper well ahead of time. Essays were submitted and distributed beforehand in a bound hard copy, and then revised for publication after the event. A core of participants were present throughout the process so that a rich sense of community, dialogue, and continuity developed. The volumes contain rich materials, much of which still needs to be received. Our hope is that not only will this volume function as a useful textbook for courses in biblical hermeneutics, but that it will also push readers back into the eight-volume Series which remains available through Zondervan. In what follows I seek to whet the appetite of readers for that Series.

Renewing Biblical Interpretation approaches the crisis in biblical interpretation from multiple angles, with most essays seeking not only to analyze the crisis but to propose fruitful ways out of it. This makes the essays and the responses wonderfully rich. For example, I wrote an essay on the philosophical and theological foundations of modern historical criticism, and Al Wolters provided a constructive proposal for a multilayered approach to interpretation.

21. Edith Eger, *The Choice: Even in Hell Hope Can Flower* (London: Penguin, 2017).

22. In 2019 at the SBL Annual Meeting, the SAHS hosted a Seminar on his more recent trilogy "Ethics as Theology."

My essay seeks to lay bare the philosophical foundations of historical criticism as it developed – foundations that since Wellhausen are little known or critically examined. I further developed this work in my *Introducing Biblical Hermeneutics*,[23] and especially in my recent *God Who Acts in History: The Significance of Sinai*.[24] This work is also foundational for my current work on a four-volume project titled Old Testament Origins and the Question of God (SPCK; Baker Academic). Wolters's proposal for a nuanced, multidimensional reading of the Bible as a response to the biblical interpretation crisis was well received and, for example, was required reading for all participants at a consultation of practical theologians held in the UK.

In a fascinating essay Christopher Seitz excavates the *theological* background for the current "crisis," in contrast to my focus on its philosophical context.[25] Seitz makes the valid point that a general hermeneutic too easily ignores central theological issues such as the relationship between the OT and the NT. He attends to the book of Daniel and the shift in the framework of interpretation from Edward Pusey to Charles Gore, culminating in Childs's work which, he argues, appropriates the insights of historical criticism while retaining the theological witness of Daniel. An element in Seitz's argument, which was and is central to the SAHS's mission, is that none of us thought the answer to the current challenges was to retreat behind modern biblical interpretation into pre-"critical"[26] exegesis. We all acknowledged the great achievements and progress of modern interpretation and sought a *postcritical* solution.

Walter Sundberg[27] – with a response by John Riches – agrees that we are amidst a crisis. Sundberg explores the political context of academic biblical interpretation and its *social implications* for the church as a faith community. He fingers – indeed, embodies in his essay – the enduring tension between critical interpretation and faith as central to the crisis. Sundberg's solution is for us to teach biblical criticism comprehensively: its history, its effects, and its presuppositions. As he asserts, we need to be conscious of the price tag that accompanies it.

23. Craig G. Bartholomew, *Introducing Biblical Hermeneutics* (Grand Rapids: Baker Academic, 2015).

24. Craig G. Bartholomew, *God Who Acts in History: The Significance of Sinai* (Grand Rapids: Eerdmans, 2020).

25. Amidst Seitz's many books, see *Prophecy and Hermeneutics: Towards a New Introduction to the Prophets*, Studies in Theological Interpretation [This series emerged out of the work of the SAHS, but never developed fully as we hoped it might.] (Grand Rapids: Baker Academic, 2007); *The Character of Christian Scripture: The Significance of a Two-Testament Bible*, Studies in Theological Interpretation (Grand Rapids: Baker Academic, 2011); *The Elder Testament: Canon, Theology, Trinity* (Waco, TX: Baylor University Press, 2018); *Convergences: Canon and Catholicity* (Waco, TX: Baylor University Press, 2020).

26. I say pre-"critical" because it is a myth of much modernity that all that preceded it was uncritical.

27. See the important book by Roy A. Harrisville and Walter Sundberg, *The Bible in Modern Culture: From Baruch Spinoza to Brevard Childs*, 2nd ed. (Grand Rapids: Eerdmans, 2002).

Neil MacDonald, with a strong response from Mary Hesse, argues that developments in analytical philosophy of language can help us retrieve typological interpretation of the Bible. He attends in particular to the relationship between Adam and Christ. With a focus on Amos, Karl Möller closely attends to the different views of historical criticism and pleads for retaining an historical emphasis in biblical studies, with a renewal of historical criticism such that it is genuinely open to transcendence. By the time the SAHS began, N. T. Wright's epochal series, Christian Origins and the Question of God, was underway, and Thorsten Moritz reflects on Wright's first volume, *The New Testament and the People of God*. On all accounts, the "historical" in historical criticism needs close attention, and Colin Greene opens up this topic through attention to modern developments in Christology. He finds rich dialogue partners in Wolfhart Pannenberg and Jürgen Moltmann for finding a way forward in our approach to history and Christology and thereby to a renewal of biblical interpretation.

If you refer back to my diagram on p. 8, you will see that I identify "literature" as an important part of a biblical hermeneutic. In this respect Stephen Wright's and Trevor Hart's essays provide vital input. Amidst a plethora of literary approaches, with "literary" often falsely set against "historical" – cf. Meir Sternberg's seminal work – Wright finds resources in C. S. Lewis's *An Experiment in Criticism* for developing a rich approach to the literary dimension of the Bible, and extends this into preaching.[28] Allied to this, Hart explores the indispensable role of imagination in biblical interpretation, with a response by Nicholas Wolterstorff. One of our best literary scholars, David Lyle Jeffrey, regularly participated in the SAHS. Under his leadership in the latter stages of the SAHS, Baylor University became a partner and hosted our final consultation on the Bible and the university. The then president of Baylor, Robert Sloan, attended our consultation on *Reading Luke* in Oxford. In *"Behind" the Text* you will, for example, find an excellent chapter by David on literature and history and the Bible.[29]

Much of postmodernism emerged out of literary theory, and Brian Ingraffia, author of the important *Postmodern Theory and Biblical Theology*, attends in his chapter to postmodern readings of the Bible and in particular to postmodern identification of *ontotheology* – rational construction of belief in God – as the bogeyman that must be deconstructed. Ingraffia argues that such an approach uncritically misses the difference between ontotheology and biblical theology.

---

28. Cf. Charles Scobie's chapter on "Biblical Theology and Preaching" in *Out of Egypt: Biblical Theology and Biblical Interpretation*, SAH Series 5, ed. Craig Bartholomew et al. (Grand Rapids: Zondervan, 2004), 448–65.

29. See also Stephen Chapman's essay on imagination and biblical interpretation in *Out of Egypt*.

One of my regrets is that the great Lesslie Newbigin (1909–98) died shortly before the SAHS got going. I met him a few times before his death, and he was supportive of the SAHS and keen to be involved in the project. Returning to the UK from India when he retired, Newbigin unequivocally alerted us to the West as the great mission field of our day. Newbigin was himself deeply concerned to see a renewal of biblical interpretation and approached George Caird at Oxford to help in this regard. Wonderfully, Lesslie's close friend, Dan Beeby – himself an extraordinary figure – was able to attend the SAHS and addressed the topic of missional interpretation, arguing not only that biblical interpretation is in a serious crisis, but that we need to prioritize a missional hermeneutic as a way forward. Through the seminal work of scholars like the South African missiologist David Bosch (1929–92) and Newbigin, a missional hermeneutic was emerging, and Beeby's emphasis is picked up in later volumes in essays by Michael Goheen, who did his PhD on Newbigin's missional ecclesiology, and Chris Wright.[30]

Returning to this first volume, I am struck afresh by the calibre and fecundity of the scholars who assembled for this consultation. Indeed, the volume concludes with a courteous and provocative reflection on our consultation by Walter Brueggemann, who attends to positive aspects of postmodernism, to "wounded" rereading of the Bible, and to the vital role of praxis in interpretation.

It is hard, to allude to Neuhaus's previous comment about Oden's *Requiem*, to deny that *Renewing Biblical Interpretation* – and indeed the eight-volume SAH Series – offers a feast. "Here are arguments you can sink your teeth into, conceptual flights of intoxicating complexity, and truths to die for." Brueggemann rightly noted in his Retrospect that "all of us would agree that our rereading is under the aegis of the gospel and a sense of the whole in the single narrative of the gospel."[31] Childs reminds us that the gospel is an explosion of good news, and here you will find a diversity of Christian scholars embracing that news and seeking to read the Bible in the light of it so that we keep reemerging into it.

Ours was and is a generous orthodoxy, seeking to bring Christian scholars

30. See Michael W. Goheen, "A Critical Examination of David Bosch's Missional Reading of Luke," in *Reading Luke: Interpretation, Reflection, Formation*, SAH Series 7, ed. Craig G. Bartholomew, Joel B. Green, and Anthony C. Thiselton (Grand Rapids: Zondervan, 2005), 229–64; Michael W. Goheen, *A Light to the Nations: The Missional Church and the Biblical Story* (Grand Rapids: Baker Academic, 2011); Michael W. Goheen, ed., *Reading the Bible Missionally* (Grand Rapids: Eerdmans, 2016), which includes chapters by Richard Bauckham, Craig Bartholomew, N. T. Wright, Joel Green, and Dean Flemming, amongst others; and Michael W. Goheen and Christopher J. H. Wright, "Theological Interpretation and a Missional Hermeneutic," in *A Manifesto for Theological Interpretation*, ed. Craig G. Bartholomew and Heath A. Thomas (Grand Rapids: Baker, 2016), 171–96.

31. Walter Brueggemann, "A First Retrospect on the Consultation," in Bartholomew, Greene, and Möller, *Renewing Biblical Interpretation*, 343.

together to reflect hard on how to reconceive our approach to the Bible *coram Deo*, so that we might hear God's address today. However, it is a seriously academic, interdisciplinary, and demanding feast. Rarely are biblical scholars trained amidst this kind of dialogue and input. Brueggemann anticipates emphases such as postcolonialism and wounded readings that have moved front and centre today. I will get to these later, and the reader is referred to the essays in Part III. Nevertheless, the major issues raised and addressed in this volume remain, and in the spirit of Stephen Wright's chapter and Lewis's *An Experiment in Criticism*, there remains a need for these essays to be read, received, and developed further today.

Janet Martin Soskice attended our Cambridge consultation, and Fergus Kerr our *After Pentecost* one, but I was unable to persuade Kerr to submit his paper for publication since he felt there were unresolved issues in it. However, initially, our Catholic participation was small. In time I met Peter Williamson, who introduced me to Mary Healy and Scott Hahn, and from then on Catholics became an integral and much welcome part of the SAHS. Nuria Calduch-Benages of the Gregorian in Rome, has, for example, a chapter on the Italian OT theology of Marco Nobile in *Out of Egypt*.

In an introductory essay of this nature, I cannot engage with each volume as I have just done with *Renewing Biblical Interpretation*. The introduction to and overview of the eight volumes in Part II will give you a taste of the feast that awaits. For several years I used *After Pentecost* as one of the textbooks in my philosophy of language course at Redeemer University. The issue of language is utterly central to postmodernism and has recently flared up in all sorts of new ways, not least ethically. The distinguished and delightful Christian philosopher Bill Alston, much missed, attended our event on history, contributed a great chapter, and expressed admiration for the ways in which Kevin Vanhoozer had appropriated his work on speech-act theory in *After Pentecost* and brought it to bear on biblical hermeneutics. I continue to think that Wolterstorff's piece profiled in this volume is vitally important. I have already referred to the richness of *A Royal Priesthood: The Use of the Bible Ethically and Politically*, which engaged with and received generous responses by Oliver O'Donovan, and I will restrain myself from further comments on it here.

The SAHS took place amidst a truly phenomenal renaissance of Christian philosophy, and Alvin Plantinga attended our conference on *history and biblical interpretation – Behind the Text?* – held at Gordon College in the USA. Indeed Wolterstorff, Plantinga, Peter van Inwagen, Alston, and C. Stephen Evans were all present! Eleonore Stump attended our later event in Rome. Plantinga has made forays into biblical interpretation at several points in his illustrious career, and his penetrating and transformative insights still need to be appropriated by biblical scholars. At this event we hosted a dialogue between Plantinga, Robert Gordon (then Regius Professor of Hebrew at Cambridge University), and me. Leading scholars from Baylor University had by then become involved, and the volume published afterwards includes chapters by C. Stephen Evans and David Lyle Jeffrey, as well as Murray Rae, Iain Provan, and others.

Any renewal of biblical interpretation must wrestle with the unity and diversity of Scripture. Biblical theology is that discipline which seeks to articulate the unity of the Bible according to its own categories, and thus, not surprisingly, our fifth consultation at St Andrews focused on this area. There is a wonderful mix in this volume of Catholic and Protestant authors, and of theologians (e.g., John Webster, Trevor Hart) and biblical scholars (e.g. Richard Bauckham, James Dunn, Francis Martin). Two major biblical theologians present were Charles Scobie of Canada and William Dumbrell of Australia. By this time Mike Goheen and I had a draft available of our *The Drama of Scripture: Finding Our Place in the Biblical Story.*[32] Mike had spent time as a visiting scholar at the University of Gloucestershire, and our consultation hosted a panel responding to the draft manuscript. *Drama* is a narrative biblical theology drawing on both Newbigin's exhortation to indwell the biblical story as the true story of the world and N. T. Wright's fertile proposal that we think of the Bible as a drama in – in our view – six acts. Jim Kinney of Baker Academic and I met around the time of the inception of the SAHS, and he attended each of our consultations. Jim agreed to publish *Drama*, and it has turned out to be a surprise bestseller, now available in some twelve languages. In the USA, Faith Alive got permission to publish the shorter SPCK edition as *The True Story of the Whole World*, and this has been so well received that Brazos recently (2020) published it in a second edition. At the KLC we are aware that we need a glut of such resources for all ages for the church if we are to retrieve Scripture as a whole, and we are working in this direction.

Hermeneutics has been criticized as an unnecessary detour from the more important task of reading the Bible for the church. We never viewed things this way, and, as is apparent from what I said earlier, our work sought again and again to land in the Bible. To make our concern with actual biblical interpretation unequivocal, we focused our sixth consultation on one book of the Bible, namely

32. Craig G. Bartholomew and Michael W. Goheen, *The Drama of Scripture: Finding Our Place in the Biblical Story*, 1st ed. (Grand Rapids: Baker Academic, 2004). SPCK in London, UK, published a shorter version under the same title. Craig Bartholomew and Paige P. Vanosky recently published *The 30-Minute Bible* (Downers Grove: InterVarsity Press, 2021), which makes this approach to the Bible available at a very accessible level.

Luke. Our consultation on *Reading Luke* brought together in Oxford many of the major Lukan scholars of the day, including Joel Green, David Wenham, David Moessner, I. Howard Marshall, John Nolland, Max Turner, and Francois Bovon. Charles Scobie attended to the journey motif in Luke, Robby Holt and I to prayer in/and Luke, and Heidi and Mikeal Parsons to Luke in Italian Renaissance and Baroque paintings! Anthony Thiselton wrote an invaluable introduction and preview for the volume, and Joel Green an afterword.

Our seventh consultation on *Canon and Biblical Interpretation* was held in Rome, amidst all the signs of the catholic church that you witness there. Gerald Collins, Jean Vanier, Frances Young, Eleonore Stump, Cardinal Ouellett, and many others were participants. Sr. Nuria Calduch-Benages was a great help to Rosemary Hales in organizing this event. As I mentioned earlier, it was stiflingly hot there when we met in a room without air conditioning! A high point was having Jean Vanier present. He addressed us on the Samaritan woman, and then Frances Young reflected on Vanier's hermeneutic. Jean enabled us to feed *lectio divina* – devotional reading of the Bible – into our discussions, a topic I also addressed in a short paper at the event.[33]

As an explosion of good news, the gospel illuminates all areas of life. Thus, it was important for us to conclude the series of eight international consultations with one on *The Bible and the University*, hosted by Baylor University and edited by David Lyle Jeffrey and C. Stephen Evans.[34] This rich volume was appropriately dedicated to Rosemary Hales for her sterling work as our administrator.

As I described earlier, the SAHS has continued to meet annually and publish new material since this decade of intense work. Most recently we are delighted to have entered into an arrangement with Zondervan Academic to publish one multivolume book per year from our work, and we are excited about this possibility to take our communal work forward in all sorts of creative ways. This volume is the first in that new Series.

It is, of course, hard to assess the reception and influence of the SAHS, its work, and the Series. It gets referred to all over the place, and I have alluded to some of the ways in which it has been received. Kevin Vanhoozer republished his essay in *After Pentecost* in his *First Theology: God, Scripture and Hermeneutics* (IVP Academic 2002). Murray Rae developed his work from *"Behind" the Text* into his monograph *History and Hermeneutics* (T&T Clark, 2005). Rae notes that his project began with our invitation to him to participate in our

---

33. See Bartholomew, *Introducing Biblical Hermeneutics*, for an attempt to integrate lectio into biblical hermeneutics.

34. See Bartholomew, *Introducing Biblical Hermeneutics*, for a chapter on Scripture and the university, a rare emphasis in books on biblical hermeneutics.

consultation on history and biblical interpretation in 2002 at Gordon College. My *Introducing Biblical Hermeneutics: A Comprehensive Framework for Hearing God in Scripture* appeared in 2015 (Baker Academic), building on the work of the SAHS over the years. Christopher Tomlins makes surprising and substantial use of *Reading Luke* in his *In the Case of Nat Turner: A Speculative History* (Princeton UP, 2020). While I was at the University of Gloucestershire, one certainly had a front row seat to how PhDs under our supervision changed as hermeneutical issues came to play a far more substantial role in dissertations. Many of our PhD students attended the SAHS consultations, some writing on areas integrally related to the concerns of the SAHS.[35] These are just a few of the ways in which the work of the SAHS has developed and been received. In my view, the feast in the eight volumes remain to be more fully received and developed, and one aim of this volume is to reignite interest in both the Series as a whole and the ongoing work of the KLC Scripture Collective.

LOOKING FORWARD

2022 is the twenty-fifth anniversary of the inception of the SAHS. As we look back, we also need to look forward. Our journey was never a quick fix, but part of that long obedience in the same direction which, according to Nietzsche, always produces great things. The topics addressed in the eight-volume SAH Series remain as relevant as ever, but times have also changed, and our list of topics was far from exhaustive.

During the decade of the SAH Series, Philip Jenkins was publishing a series of important books on global Christianity and its renaissance in the majority world.[36] The extraordinary renaissance of religion – what Mark Lilla calls the postponement of the twilight of the idols – accompanied by a hardening of secularism in the West means that the SAHS now needs to attend far more consciously to global Christianity. Our work needs to be proactively brought into dialogue with the new centres of Christianity, especially in Africa and Asia, from whom we have so much to learn.[37] Hence our emphasis on this in Part III.

With the hard secularism in the West and the manifestation of identity politics – for better and for worse – a plethora of new ethical challenges have

35. E.g., Ryan O'Dowd, William Olhausen, Aubrey Spears, etc.

36. Philip Jenkins, *The Next Christendom: The Coming of Global Christianity*, 3rd. ed. (Oxford: Oxford University Press, 2011).

37. Cf. Philip Jenkins, *The New Faces of Christianity: Believing the Bible in the Global South* (New York: Oxford University Press, 2006).

come to the fore. Thus, far more work needs to be done on reading the Bible ethically in relation to current issues, as John Wyatt indicates in his essay in Part III. Theology has always been part of the SAHS, as is apparent from all I have shared, but the SAHS's philosophical orientation means that the relationship between doctrine and biblical interpretation needs much greater attention, as is evident in the emergence of our Scripture and Doctrine Seminar. At our seminars, there was a congenial tension between the Barthians and those of us committed to philosophical hermeneutics. However, the relationship between theology and philosophy needs fresh attention, and I review this conversation in my essay in Part III.

A truly astonishing phenomenon of our time is the emergence of French Catholic phenomenology, with its range across theology and philosophy and its unashamed drawing on the Bible in the process. Much of this fertile development seems to have been missed by biblical scholars, and we are glad to include several essays in Part III introducing this development and one of its best practitioners, namely Jean-Louis Chrétien.

Within the West, the modern university has been the intellectual bastion of the privatization of religion and secularization. Thus, it was important that the final volume of the SAH Series attend to Scripture and the university. Even within the plethora of Christian colleges and universities with which North America is blessed, it is unusual to find sophisticated understandings of how Scripture functions normatively among the disciplines. In recent years, the psychologist Dr Eric Johnson and I led a series of consultations on Transdisciplinarity, an attempt to develop a new model in this respect, since we believe that the common model of integration appears to be failing. This work has now become our latest Seminar, Scripture and the University. David Beldman provides a fresh essay in Part III on the relationship between the Bible and scholarship.

I began this essay with evocative quotes from Bernanos and Chrétien, which alert us to the rich telos of biblical engagement. In Rome we reflected on Jean Vanier's lectio-type reading of Scripture, and I gave a short paper arguing for the integration of lectio with academic interpretation, a position I have developed further in my *Introducing Biblical Hermeneutics*. In my view, this remains a topic that requires far more rigorous attention, attention which would likely lead us to new models of the commentary, placing the most rigorous academic work within the context of listening for God's address. I believe that the primary place for the reception of the Bible is in the church. Academic work makes a huge contribution, if done well, but it is a secondary activity. Thus, I was keen for us to develop a Seminar in practical theology that would attend closely to the

Bible and the church, and I am delighted that this has become our Scripture and Church Seminar.

In Part III of this volume, you will find a series of short, programmatic essays looking forward as we continue on the road of seeking to renew biblical interpretation in and for our day.

NEW GENERATIONS

The SAHS has developed into a rich community, including new and emerging generations of scholars. Nowhere is this community more evident than in our Annual Meal. While we continue to do our work, we wish to hand the baton on to new generations in cooperation with our brothers and sisters around the world. The West shows many signs of being in a crisis and perhaps in decline, but there is a Christian renaissance in the majority world. The need for work on the Bible that enables us to hear God's address is urgent and requires a community of scholars working together – not least with our brothers and sisters in the majority world – to forge a new paradigm in biblical studies so that our most rigorous work contributes to resting on that breast from which all light comes forth. We invite you, the reader, to join us on this journey.

The SAHS has moved around as I moved from the UK to Canada and then back again. From 1 January 2021 the Kirby Laing Centre for Public Theology in Cambridge came into existence as an independent charity, with our lovely offices at Margaret Beaufort Institute in Cambridge. Our four Seminars now have a fixed home and operate through the KLC under the name of our Scripture Collective; Rev Dr Michael Wagenman was recently appointed as its director. Each seminar is being encouraged to develop a community at the heart of its work, and we are hoping that each Seminar will host meetings during the year, climaxing each year at the SBL/AAR Annual Meetings. We are truly delighted about our publishing partnership with Zondervan Academic, and we already have this volume and two others in the pipeline scheduled for publication by November each year in time for the SBL/AAR gatherings.

Opening the Book anew for each generation is an immense responsibility. I mentioned Lesslie Newbigin earlier. Having spent most of his working life in India, Lesslie retired and returned to the UK where he began, or *so it seemed to us*, the most fertile years of his ministry. He alerted us that modern, Western culture was the greatest missional challenge of our day, and he was convinced that a depth missional encounter between the gospel and Western culture would only be possible if "a coherent and intellectually tenable doctrine of Scriptural authority" was recovered.[38] When it came to the Bible, Newbigin thought that both liberals and conservatives had succumbed to the metanarrative of modernity. He approached George Caird at Oxford for help in a recovery of the Bible. Caird replied, "You are asking for a total revolution in the way biblical scholars see their job."[39] My sense is that both Newbigin and Caird were right. A paradigm shift is required. Above all, God addresses us in and through the Bible, and we need not refuse – indeed we should welcome – that address in our lives and in our scholarship. Our hope and prayer is that the ongoing work of our Scripture Collective will contribute to that end.

Veni Creator Spiritus.

---

38. Lesslie Newbigin, "The Bible and Our Contemporary Mission," *The Clergy Review* 69/1 (1984): 9–17, 7, https://newbiginresources.org/1984-the-bible-and-our-contemporary-mission/. I am indebted here to Michael Goheen. Among his other works see *The Church and Its Vocation: Lesslie Newbigin's Missionary Ecclesiology* (Grand Rapids: Baker Academic, 2018).

39. Lesslie Newbigin, *Unfinished Agenda: An Autobiography*, 2nd ed. (Edinburgh: St Andrews, 1993), 249.

PART II

Retrospect

CHAPTER 2

A Portal into the Eight-Volume Scripture and Hermeneutics Series

Craig G. Bartholomew

with David J. H. Beldman
and William Olhausen

INTRODUCTION

Undoubtedly the very word "hermeneutics," let alone "*philosophical* hermeneutics,"[1] is enough to put some people off. Indeed, when in the late twentieth century hermeneutics came to the fore in theology and biblical studies, a joke was that Herman Neutics was a German theologian! However, if you can get past the name "hermeneutics" to what it is about, then you will begin to see why it is so important. Hermeneutics deals with *how we go about understanding something*, and clearly we want to understand the Bible. Hermeneutics can help us with this!

1. Philosophical hermeneutics is complex, and if you have not done any work in (continental) philosophy you will find it dense and difficult. To enter this terrain you need a guide, and in biblical studies and theology we have one of the best, Anthony C. Thiselton. Among his many books see *New Horizons in Hermeneutics: Theory and Practice of Transforming Biblical Reading* (Grand Rapids: Zondervan, 1992); *Hermeneutics: An Introduction* (Grand Rapids: Eerdmans, 2009); *Why Hermeneutics? An Appeal Culminating in Ricoeur* (Eugene, OR: Cascade, 2019). See also Craig G. Bartholomew, *Introducing Biblical Hermeneutics: A Comprehensive Framework for Hearing God in Scripture* (Grand Rapids: Baker Academic, 2015).

Many of us see the need for hermeneutics but find the literature difficult and complex. Take our eight-volume Scripture and Hermeneutics Series, for example. It is chock-full of high-level scholarship. The aim of this section is to provide an accessible introduction to the Series and briefly review the eight volumes. In the *Harry Potter* novels you often get from one place to another through a portal. For those who want to get into hermeneutics but are feeling hesitant, our hope is that this essay will be a portal enabling you to get excited about hermeneutics and to participate in the feast that is present in our eight volumes.

UNDERSTANDING AND THE LIMITS OF THE RIGHT METHOD

The father of modern philosophical hermeneutics, Hans-Georg Gadamer (1900–2002), in Part 1 of his hugely influential book *Truth and Method*,[2] discusses how we understand an artwork. Imagine yourself sitting in a gallery before a great, original artwork. How *do* you go about understanding it? In posing this question, Gadamer was alerting us to the fact that understanding is about far more than simply getting *the method* right. This has been the mistake of far too much modern thought. Method is indeed invaluable. There is much to be gained from knowing about the time in which the artwork was produced, from knowing the medium in which the artist works, from analysing the artist's use of pigments, and understanding the style of the work. However, you could do all these things and still not encounter the artwork's powerful communication. Gadamer did not deny the role of method, but he resituated it within dialogue. You pose your questions to the artwork, and you see how it "responds." To and fro the dialogue goes until your "horizon" fuses with that of the artwork in the act of understanding.

As Gadamer saw it, the mistake of much modern thought was to assert that if we only get the method right, then we will arrive at the truth. In biblical studies this modern emphasis has been embraced by both conservatives and liberals. For example, when Craig and William read theology at Oxford University, they were inducted into the following methods of analysing the Old Testament: source criticism, form criticism, tradition-historical criticism, and redaction criticism. Students were then tested on their ability to apply these methods correctly to the Old Testament. Comparably, conservative Christians emphasised the grammatico-historical *method* of interpretation.[3] Ironically, both camps bought into modernity's privileging of method, albeit in very different ways.

2. Hans-Georg Gadamer, *Truth and Method*, 2nd ed. (London: Sheed and Ward, 1975, 1989).

3. See, for example, Louis Berkhof, *Principles of Biblical Interpretation* (Grand Rapids: Baker, 1950).

Why is this emphasis on right method problematic? Because it ties into the autonomy of human reason that is central to modernity, thereby giving the false impression that a neutral, God's-eye view of the Bible is possible and fails to take account of the fact – which hermeneutics points out unequivocally – that the reader of the Bible is as much embedded in history as the biblical text. Modernity creates the myth that we are neutral, scientific, and have the right method and that the challenge to biblical interpretation arises from the Bible coming to us from alien, far-removed, unscientific cultures. Once we see that we are as embedded in history, with all our own predispositions, as the Bible, then we begin to see that understanding the Bible is more complex than simply applying the right method. A major focus of hermeneutics is the interpretation of texts, and thus hermeneutics is almost immediately relevant to biblical interpretation.

In *Renewing Biblical Interpretation* there is an essay by Al Wolters specifically addressing method in biblical studies. We now introduce this seminal essay.

Al Wolters, "Confessional Criticism and the Night Visions of Zechariah" (SAH Series, volume 1)

Renewing Biblical Interpretation, the inaugural volume of the Scripture and Hermeneutics Series, deals with foundational matters in biblical interpretation. Gadamer's epochal *Truth and Method* problematizes the view that if we just get the method right, true interpretation will follow. This is, however, not to denigrate method but to recontextualize it. Al Wolters's essay "Confessional Criticism and the Night Visions of Zechariah" is an excellent contribution to the volume in this respect. The value of the essay is in Wolters's thoughtful exposition of nine levels of biblical interpretation and their intricate interrelationship. Wolters helpfully and briefly introduces the nine levels (from textual criticism to "confessional criticism") and makes a compelling case for how these levels build upon each other logically and conceptually in a "bottom-up" relationship. The genius of the essay is that although these levels seem to move from more to less objective, the reality is that the seemingly more subjective levels (e.g., redemptive-historical analysis and confessional criticism) often do and indeed should influence decisions made at the lower levels in what Wolters calls top-down relationships among the levels. Pushing back deliberately against modern biblical studies, which insists on a separation between faith and academic study, Wolters's essay is, in his own words, "essentially a plea for *integrality* in biblical studies, an integrality which reflects the fundamental religious nature of both the Bible and its interpreters." Wolters illustrates his points with countless examples from the night visions of Zechariah (1:7–6:8). In the introduction to his essay "A Critical Examination of David Bosch's Missional Reading of Luke" in *Reading Luke: Interpretation, Reflection, Formation*, Michael Goheen engages with Wolters's essay, registering his appreciation for it and expanding on Wolters's eighth level (redemptive-historical analysis) so as to integrate the vital notion of the mission of God. Leveraging Christopher Wright's essay "Mission as a Matrix for Hermeneutics and Biblical Theology" in *Out of Egypt: Biblical Theology and Biblical Interpretation*, Goheen insists that "redemptive-historical interpretation is not only messianic, but missional" (p. 230), which is a helpful clarification.

THE EXHILARATION OF BIBLICAL HERMENEUTICS

Biblical hermeneutics *is* exhilarating. The Bible is the field in which is hid the pearl of great price, and learning how to dig in it – not a bad metaphor for biblical hermeneutics – opens up the possibility of repeated encounter with the trinitarian God who has come to us in Jesus. In Part 1 of this book, Craig quotes Thomas Oden's evocative comment about the difference between the Christian tradition and modern theological studies. Right at the heart of the feast Oden refers to is the Bible with its authoritative testimony to God. As God's Word, there is a great deal at stake in how we *understand* the Bible. Biblical hermeneutics at its best helps us *to understand how we understand*, so that we can approach the Bible in a way that most likely grants us access to the great messianic feast. This, after all, is why most of us get into biblical studies. We want more, far more, of Jesus and the trinitarian God. Alas, modern biblical interpretation is littered with people who started off with this passion but have ended up either jaded and confused or dogmatically certain about their confusion!

The second consultation of the Scripture and Hermeneutics Seminar was titled "The Crisis of Biblical Interpretation." For each consultation Craig sent out a document preparing participants for the event. In the one for this event he wrote:

> It is widely recognised that at the turn of the millennium biblical interpretation is in a state of flux. Biblical studies is increasingly characterised by fragmentation and pluralism and there is no sign of an emerging consensus about the way forward. Once dominant historical criticism is now radically questioned by many, and a smorgasbord of alternative methodologies is being applied to the Bible. Very different responses are being made to this situation:
>
> > Some are trying to reform historical criticism and get it back on track. This is the equivalent in biblical studies of J. Habermas and C. Norris's desire in philosophy to get modernity back on track.
> >
> > Some welcome a methodological pluralism in which all methods are equal on the hermeneutic smorgasbord. This view celebrates the pluralism of postmodernity.
> >
> > Others are proposing that we develop a comprehensive theological hermeneutic for biblical interpretation. This response is connected with the current reassessment of a religious hermeneutic.
>
> From a theological perspective this is an intriguing situation. . . . There is an urgent need to understand the turmoil in biblical interpretation and to critically engage the current situation so that constructive ways forward can be found. . . . The Seminar is based on the understanding that starting points differ, and that provided these are developed with critical rigour, this is not a bad thing. Indeed, thorough critical analysis involves allowing different starting points to come to fruition so that different academic approaches can be fully compared. The Seminar is focused on the theological interpretation of the Bible *as* Scripture, and seeks to re-engage this discussion in the current context. . . . The combination of faith seeking understanding, with critical rigour, in an interdisciplinary context, focused on renewing biblical interpretation constitute the key and unique elements of the response that the Seminar is making to the current situation in biblical interpretation.

Our second international consultation involved thirty-eight interdisciplinary Christian scholars and took place in Cambridge in September 1999. It focused on analysing the present crisis in biblical hermeneutics. There was Catholic, Orthodox, Anglican, and (a variety of) Protestant representation at this consultation, and disciplines represented included systematic theology (Janet Martin Soskice, Trevor Hart), practical theology, church history (Walter Sundberg), philosophy and history of science (Mary Hesse), missiology, Old and

New Testament studies (Walter Brueggemann, Brevard Childs, Christopher Seitz, Rex Mason), education, philosophy (Nicholas Wolterstorff), and literary studies (Brian Ingraffia).

Not all who participated in this consultation agreed that biblical studies is in a crisis. Certainly Thomas Oden, mentioned earlier, believes there is a problem. In Craig's view a crisis remains; but whatever your view is, there is surely much to be gained in reflecting on how to renew biblical interpretation – note the title of SAH Series, volume 1 – so that it ushers us again and again into the presence of the living God, serves the church, and contributes to the flourishing of the world. Our contention is that biblical hermeneutics is an indispensable partner in such a project, and, as such, is exhilarating.

BIBLICAL HERMENEUTICS IS COMPLEX: ENTER PHILOSOPHY

However, biblical hermeneutics *is* complex. Meir Sternberg notes that biblical hermeneutics takes place at the intersection of the humanities, resulting in myriad disciplines impinging on biblical interpretation. Take Old Testament Israel, for example. Israel was an ancient Near Eastern nation, a *society* in a covenant relationship with YHWH. Sociology is the discipline that studies how societies work, and thus it is no surprise that good sociological analysis, both ancient and modern, has much to offer to biblical studies. However, some influential sociology is rooted in Marxism, and clearly one should not quickly leverage this to understand the Old Testament. This does not deny for a moment that sociology contains rich insights, but we must insist that the process of appropriating these insights for Christian interpretation of the Bible is complex. We find a different approach to sociology in the work of the Jewish sociologist Philip Rieff, who insists that culture making always involves the translation of sacred order into social order. Such an approach resonates deeply with the Bible.

We referred previously to the roots of sociology. The Canadian philosopher Charles Taylor makes the point that in any discipline you can ask deeper and deeper questions. Eventually you hit bedrock and, says Taylor, that is philosophy! Taylor is alerting us to the fact that the foundations of any and every discipline are philosophical. True, "philosophy" easily scares people off, and one or two classes in philosophy do not always help. Let us explain what we think philosophy is, and this should help you to see why it is important for biblical hermeneutics.[4] Philosophy attends to the (God-given) structures of reality and has three main divisions:

Ontology or Metaphysics investigates the nature of reality.
Epistemology explores how we go about knowing something so that we can trust the results.
Anthropology explores what it means to be human.

If you stop and think about these three foundational areas, you will see that they shape all academic disciplines in one way or another. Take Marxist sociology, for example. Clearly it works with a very specific view of what it means to be human, and this profoundly shapes the scholarship it produces. And, of course, the Marxist view of what it means to be human is one among many. For example, a Christian view of humans as made in the image of God will yield a significantly different sociology to that of Marxism.

Because biblical interpretation operates at the intersection of the humanities it will inevitably use insights from other disciplines, but in the process care needs to be taken lest alien ideologies are unconsciously imported. One major way we take such care is by being alert to the philosophical foundations of disciplines.

While we find Taylor's approach just described very helpful, in our view there is an even deeper level to foundational or philosophical bedrock in a discipline, and that is religious presuppositions. Look again at the three major areas of philosophy we just listed and ask yourself, "Does Christian faith and belief influence how one thinks about these three areas?" Of course, it does. And if we seek the sort of integrality that Wolters pleads for in his chapter profiled earlier, then we will want to make sure that from the foundations up our biblical interpretation is integrally Christian.

This means that we need not just philosophy but *Christian philosophy*. In recent decades we have seen an extraordinary renaissance of Christian philosophy, and many of the luminaries in this movement participated in the SAHS. Alvin Plantinga is one of the greatest (Christian) philosophers of our day. His major work is on epistemology, and he has very helpfully developed it in relation

4. If you recognize the need to secure a basic understanding of philosophy, Craig recommends Richard Tarnas, *The Passion of the Western Mind: Understanding the Ideas That Shaped Our World View* (New York: Ballantine, 1991). See also Tarnas's accompanying videos on YouTube. You might also find helpful Craig G. Bartholomew and Michael W. Goheen, *Christian Philosophy: A Systematic and Narrative Introduction* (Grand Rapids: Baker Academic, 2013).

to biblical interpretation. At our consultation at Gordon College on history and biblical hermeneutics, Robert Gordon and Craig responded to Plantinga's work and then he responded to them. We now introduce this seminal chapter by Plantinga.

Alvin Plantinga, "Two (or More) Kinds of Scripture Scholarship" (SAH Series, volume 4)

The fourth volume of the SAH Series, *"Behind" the Text: History and Biblical Interpretation*, centres around history and the historical dimension of biblical interpretation. Among the many excellent essays in this volume, Alvin Plantinga's essay penetrates to critically foundational matters, as anyone who knows Plantinga's work might expect. The "two kinds" of Bible scholarship Plantinga addresses are essentially (1) so-called "objective," "scientific" scholarship (what Plantinga refers to as "historical biblical criticism" or HBC) and (2) confessional scholarship that brings faith to bear on the scholarly endeavour (Plantinga's "traditional Christian biblical scholarship"). The genius of the essay is how Plantinga on the one hand shatters the myth of objectivity in the former and on the other hand provides a robust case for the warrant of Christian faith in the latter. The essay covers a lot of ground and the weeds of the argument can seem a bit complicated at times, but there is a reason that Al Wolters has said in conversation that this essay is essential reading for every aspiring biblical scholar of faith. The bias against faith in biblical scholarship was a staple of modern biblical scholarship, and it still exists today – Plantinga offers a sound and thorough defence for the role of faith in biblical scholarship that is rare (and yet so vital) today. The original volume includes two essays (authored by Craig Bartholomew and Robert Gordon) that respond to Plantinga's essay and Plantinga's own reflections on these responses.

FAITH AND BIBLICAL HERMENEUTICS: ENTER THEOLOGY

In any course taught, paper written, or research project executed, some epistemology will be involved. If, as we asserted earlier, epistemology is how to go about knowing something so that you can trust the results of the knowing process, then this is simply unavoidable. Alas, epistemology may often be unconscious, but it will always be present. A major trend in modernity was to argue that if we want true knowledge then we need to set aside faith from the start. One could argue towards faith but never presuppose it. As you saw from the introductory essay to this volume, from the start the SAHS took a diametrically opposite position – namely, that we wanted faith fully engaged in and at the heart of our reflections on biblical hermeneutics. This was the one major rule of the SAHS.

In the preparatory paper for our second consultation on "The Crisis in Biblical Hermeneutics" Craig wrote, "The Seminar embodies an approach of faith seeking understanding, in which faith is not excluded from the investigative process but operates with critical rigour. It is particularly with Christian faith seeking understanding that the Seminar is concerned with at this stage, although it is hoped that as the Seminar develops dialogue with scholars of other faiths and starting points can be initiated."

We embodied the rule of having our faith fully engaged in the way we designed our consultations. All our hard, rigorous work was done in the context of simple liturgy, and on occasions we celebrated the Eucharist together. At our consultation in Rome Jean Vanier powerfully embodied *lectio divina*, and Craig gave a short, unpublished paper on *lectio divina* and academic biblical interpretation. At our Oxford consultation on *Reading Luke*, the issue of prayer and biblical interpretation was specifically addressed by Craig and Robby Holt in their chapter "Prayer in/and the Drama of Redemption in Luke: Prayer and Exegetical Performance" (SAH Series, volume 6). Our practice of doing our work *coram Deo* – before the face of God – was not just window dressing. Our desire was for our faith and Christian beliefs to penetrate into and shape our reflections.

Not surprisingly, therefore, the issue of theology and biblical hermeneutics is a central theme in the eight-volume Series. "Theology" is, however, a word used in significantly different ways. It can refer to basic Christian beliefs as, for example, encapsulated in the Apostles' Creed. Alternatively, it can refer to sophisticated systematic theology and to many levels in between. Whereas philosophy reflects on the structure of the world, theology, in one way or another, reflects on the Bible and the Christian tradition in order to set out what Christians believe today. This is clearly important for biblical hermeneutics. Calvin, for example, wrote his *Institutes* in order to help believers read the Bible better.

The relationship between theology and philosophy remains a controversial issue, and different views are expressed about this in the eight volumes.[5] It remains a crucial issue to resolve for biblical hermeneutics. Craig addressed this issue directly in the opening chapter of *Renewing Biblical Interpretation*, introduced next.

Craig G. Bartholomew, "Uncharted Waters: Philosophy, Theology and the Crisis in Biblical Interpretation" (SAH Series, volume 1)

Do we need a general (philosophical) or special (theological) hermeneutic for reading and understanding Scripture as God's Word? This seminal question is only just below the surface of the various discussions about Christian theological interpretation of the Bible over the last several decades (and beyond) and naturally appeared in the Scripture and Hermeneutics Seminar consultations (and in the Series' volumes). It seems appropriate, therefore, that the very first essay in the very first volume of the SAH Series (a volume that maps out the initial ten years of the SAHS project) aims to chart the often-unfamiliar waters of the relationship between philosophy and theology in the interpretation of Scripture. And there are few scholars so adept at navigating and charting these waters as Craig Bartholomew, the founder and long-time director of the SAHS. The context of the essay is the crisis in biblical interpretation, a crisis that Bartholomew maintains is at least philosophical and one which we ignore at our peril. The essay demonstrates, as one example, that historical criticism (and every other approach to biblical interpretation) is shaped by philosophical convictions (much to the contrary of claims of "objectivity"). An honest foregrounding of the philosophical substructure of approaches to biblical interpretation will permit the real discussion of how we might appropriately interpret the Bible. In the end, the essay argues for an integrative model of biblical interpretation that takes seriously both philosophy and theology in the process of listening to Scripture. This water-charting essay is not only a significantly seminal one for the whole SAHS project but also for the project of renewing biblical interpretation today in the academy and beyond.

---

5. See Craig's essay in Part III.

ART AND BIBLICAL HERMENEUTICS

It is a truism, but one worth repeating, that we do not and should not read the Bible alone but in the context of the one, holy, catholic, and apostolic church. There is rich history to the interpretation of the Bible, and we have much to learn from it. Not surprisingly, therefore, the development of what is known as *reception history* in hermeneutics has received growing attention in biblical studies over recent decades.

The Bible relates to all of life, and in its history it is received as such. Thus, reception history of the Bible extends way beyond commentaries, important as they are, to things like sermons, poetry, literature, music, culture, and art. Recently the reception of the Bible in art is receiving particular attention.[6] Some of the prominent players in this development participated in the SAHS. In *Reading Luke*, Heidi J. Hornik and Mikael C. Parsons contribute a chapter titled "Illuminating Luke: The Third Gospel in Italian and Baroque Painting."

However, the SAHS's engagement with art extended further. For the early volumes of the Series Craig worked with two distinguished South Africans, the sculptor Gert Swart and the artist Zak Benjamin, to produce images for the covers. These images – see below – often involved reworkings of classic paintings. Craig would brief Gert on the contents of a volume and then Gert and Zak

6. See, for example, Heidi J. Hornik, Ian Boxall, and Bobby Dykema, eds., *The Art of Biblical Interpretation: Visual Portrayals of Scriptural Narratives*, Bible and Its Reception 3 (Atlanta: SBL Press, 2021).

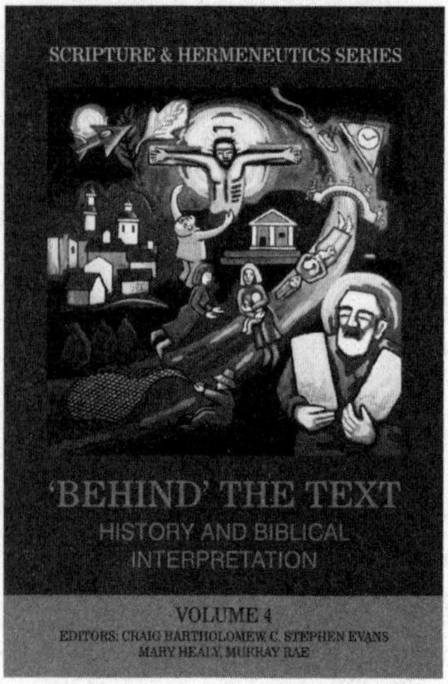

would come up with ideas for an image, after which Zak would paint it. On occasion, such as with our consultation in Cheltenham on *A Royal Priesthood? The Use of the Bible Ethically and Politically: A Dialogue with Oliver O'Donovan*, Craig used Zak's reworking of Goya's evocative *The Third of May 1808* to introduce the proceedings.

Recently the KLC has developed a close relationship with Deus ex Musica, based in Boston. One of this group's chief goals is to explore the relationship between Scripture and music.[7] In all these ways the SAHS has been sensitive to the potentially rich relationship between the arts and the Bible.

LANGUAGE, LITERATURE, AND BIBLICAL HERMENEUTICS

The Bible is a book, a long sprawling one, consisting of a library of sixty-six individual books and two Testaments in different languages. As such, it is made up of words, sentences, sections, and stretches of discourse – in a word, of language. This is obvious, but its implication has too often been missed. Language is like what Augustine says of time; we all know what it is until we stop and ask, "What is language?" We are born into language; it surrounds us even before birth when we are in the wombs of our mothers, and so we easily take it for granted like the air we breathe.

7. Deus ex Musica, https://www.deus-ex-musica.com/.

However, language is complex, and when we ask questions like "How does language work?" we soon discover that there is a very long debate about such issues and serious disagreements among scholars. The hugely influential Greek philosophers Plato (*Cratylus*) and Aristotle (*On Interpretation*) differed on how language worked, and debates have continued before and since then. When J. L. Austin (1911–60) was a professor at Oxford University, a common view was that only statements or propositions made sense. Austin drove a bus through this view, and in his book *How to Do Things with Words*[8] he argued persuasively that there are many, many other things that we do with words apart from making statements. He coined the word "performatives" for all these other things; with words we perform myriad actions like warning, encouraging, praising, distracting, rebuking, pronouncing, etc. Not surprisingly, his philosophy of language became known as speech-act theory.

Austin identified three main aspects of a speech act:

Locution: the basic meaning of the sentence
Illocution: the force of the speech act, which identifies the action being performed
Perlocution: the effect of the speech act

In our opinion, the distinction between locutions and illocutions is a crucial insight. Let us give you an example. Take a sentence like, "There is a snake in the garden." We all understand the meaning of the words and the sentence (locution). But what is unclear is the sentence's illocutionary force. It could be:

- a warning that danger lurks
- an encouragement for a lover of snakes to have a look
- an alert, if "snake" is a metaphor for a vicious person in your garden that you want to avoid

And so on. Context alone will determine which illocutionary force is at work in any particular speech act. Clearly, however, if we are to understand the statement then we need more than the locution; we need to be attentive to its illocutionary force.

Anthony Thiselton in particular, but also many others, have done seminal work in showing again and again just how fruitful speech-act theory is for

8. J. L. Austin, *How to Do Things with Words* (Oxford: Oxford University Press, 1962, 1975).

biblical interpretation.[9] Our very first SAHS consultation attended to speech-act theory and biblical interpretation, although the results were not published. Craig well remembers going off to Oxford to purchase copies of Austin's *How to Do Things with Words* for himself and his colleagues at the University of Gloucestershire in preparation for the event. His department was a powerhouse of biblical interpretation, but they were unfamiliar with Austin's approach and his threefold distinction just described!

Our third consultation, held at Redeemer University in Ontario, Canada, attended to the theme of "Language and Biblical Interpretation." Nicholas Wolterstorff gave a paper on speech-act theory, responded to by Mary Hesse, introduced next.

Nicholas Wolterstorff, "The Promise of Speech-Act Theory for Biblical Interpretation" (SAH Series, volume 2)

Along with two other contributors to the Scripture and Hermeneutics Series, Alvin Plantinga and William P. Alston, Nicholas Wolterstorff is a leading voice for a Reformed Christian approach to and through philosophy. In this essay he brings his analytic skills to bear on two closely related topics that are central to how Christians read the Bible: firstly, he provides a critical engagement with the implicit philosophy of language characteristic of the modern hermeneutic tradition as received and exemplified by Hans-Georg Gadamer. Secondly, Wolterstorff discusses how we might better understand what Christians mean by a "doctrine of Scripture." Drawing on speech-act theory, he takes us from what he sees as the central aim of hermeneutics, authorial-discourse interpretation, to divine discourse interpretation; that is, reading the human written texts of Scripture to hear the actual words of God. Readers unfamiliar with Wolterstorff's work have here an excellent example of his scholarship: closely argued and very clearly written. They will also have an outstanding introduction to his important 1995 book based on a series of lectures delivered at Oxford University, *Divine Discourse: Philosophical Reflections on the Claim That God Speaks*.

9. See, for example, Anthony C. Thiselton, *Promise and Prayer: The Biblical Writings in the Light of Speech-Act Theory* (Eugene, OR: Cascade, 2020).

"How to Be a Postmodernist and Remain a Christian: A Response to Nicholas Wolterstorff" (SAH Series, volume 2)

Mary Hesse

Many of the essays in the eight SAH volumes were accompanied by a shorter "response." Professor Mary Hesse, the late Cambridge philosopher of science, was present at our consultation in Canada. Hesse provided a short but illuminating response to Wolterstorff's essay. She makes the case for a more sympathetic "postmodern" approach to biblical interpretation. Grounding her argument in the seminal developments in the philosophy of science, she argues for the irreducibly metaphorical character of language and theory. Taken together with Wolterstorff's essay, this exchange captures something of the debates and questions that have raged around biblical and theological hermeneutics since the late 1960s.

Biblical scholars *should* be attuned to the importance of how language works. Craig wrote the following in a report on the publication resulting from our consultation on language and biblical interpretation, namely *After Pentecost: Language and Biblical Interpretation* (SAH Series, volume 2).

> In the 60s we became aware, courtesy of James Barr, that linguistics was important for biblical interpretation and that word studies could not continue as usual! In the 70s the literary turn alerted us to the radical implications of the nature of the Bible as literature. In the 80s and 90s language has been at the heart of postmodernism, and this has faced biblical interpretation with a range of challenges. The SAH Seminar was aware from the outset that any renewal of biblical interpretation would have to attend to the issue of language. In this rich and creative volume the importance of linguistic issues for biblical interpretation is analysed, the challenge of postmodernism is explored, and some of the most creative recent developments are assessed and updated, most notably by Nick Wolterstorff (response by Mary Hesse), Anthony Thiselton and Kevin Vanhoozer. . . . The thorny issue of gender language and the Bible is examined (David Lyle Jeffrey . . .), the Bible as literature is revisited (Stephen Wright, Brian Ingraffia), there is a major chapter on translation of the Bible

(Ray van Leeuwen), and the relevance of a theology of language to biblical interpretation is opened up. These issues are brought repeatedly to bear on actual exegesis, most notably on Deuteronomy (Gordon McConville), Amos (Karl Möller), and parts of the Gospels.

If there was one development that should have alerted biblical scholars to the importance of language, it was the emergence of *postmodernism* in the 1980s and the wild pluralism of methods it led to for reading the Bible. Absolutely central to postmodernism is language and how it works. Jacques Derrida's hugely influential deconstruction of texts, for example, is based on a – misguided in our view – very particular understanding of how language works.

It is interesting to look back and see what Craig set out as the aims for our consultation on language and biblical interpretation:

The aims of the consultation are:

1. to foreground the interrelationship between philosophy of language and biblical interpretation
2. to reflect on ways in which views of language have influenced biblical interpretation historically
3. to examine the ways in which philosophy of language is central to postmodernity (Habermas, Ricoeur, Derrida, Levinas) and postmodern readings of the Bible
4. to further our earlier (1998 consultation) examination of speech-act theory and biblical interpretation, with particular respect to Anthony Thiselton's, Kevin Vanhoozer's and Nicholas Wolterstorff's advocacy of its use in biblical interpretation. Speech-act theory is central to the current debate about postmodernism and biblical hermeneutics, and Thiselton, Vanhoozer and Wolterstorff have all proposed diverse ways ahead building on speech-act theory
5. to examine metaphorical understandings of language (Hesse, Lakoff and Johnson, Ricoeur, Derrida) and their implications for biblical hermeneutics, and to compare this with the approach of speech-act theory
6. to evaluate postmodern understandings of language (Derrida, Habermas, Ricoeur, Levinas) and what they yield in biblical interpretation
7. to examine a rhetorical hermeneutic and the possibilities of a communicative biblical hermeneutic as a unifying focus for interpretation of the Bible as Scripture.

Anthony Thiselton has done an enormous amount of work on speech-act theory, its developments since Austin, and its implications for biblical interpretation. He has also written extensively on postmodernism and biblical interpretation. His chapter in *After Pentecost* is now introduced.

Anthony Thiselton, "'Behind' and 'In Front of' the Text: Language, Reference and Indeterminacy" (SAH Series, volume 2)

In the English-speaking world, Anthony Thiselton is one of the foremost scholars in biblical hermeneutics. Alongside his outstanding commentary on 1 Corinthians in the *NIGTC* commentary series, his books include *New Horizons in Biblical Hermeneutics, The Hermeneutics of Doctrine*, and, more recently, *Hermeneutics: An Introduction*. Thiselton has not only been a good friend and Series editor for the Scripture and Hermeneutics Seminar, but he has also contributed several important essays. This one comes from volume 2 of the Series, focusing on the place of language in biblical interpretation. Thiselton draws on his detailed understanding of language and the hermeneutic tradition to provide a nuanced and informed response to certain elements in postmodern philosophy and literary theory.

Language and language use, Thiselton argues, are much more complex in their dependence on human agency and the extralinguistic world than some theorists allow or realize. Biblical texts are not only capable of revealing things that are true, but they also resist simply being used and abused by the consumerist tendencies of postmodern readers. This essay is characteristic of Thiselton's approach: informed deeply by a knowledge of the literature in hermeneutics and philosophy; a sensitivity to those aspects of philosophical hermeneutics that have informed biblical interpretation; and courteous in his engagement with other scholars – even when he disagrees with them. Students of biblical and theological hermeneutics will not only enjoy this essay as an important contribution to the central questions of biblical hermeneutics, but will also have a resource from which further explorations can be pursued.

The title *After Pentecost: Language and Biblical Interpretation* calls for some comment. It alludes to George Steiner's book *After Babel: Aspects of Language*

and Translation.[10] Steiner also wrote a very important book called *Real Presences* in which he argues that we need a "grammar of creation" in order to respond to the challenges of postmodernism.[11] The title *Real Presences* alludes to the Eucharist, and in response to Derrida Steiner argues that deconstruction confronts us with a choice: either nihilism or "In the beginning was the Word," a quote from John 1:1. Steiner's work thus foregrounds the theological issues in our views of language and interpretation.

Babel is the great symbol of miscommunication among languages. Derrida's philosophy of language is Babelian in its assertion that all language is slippery and vulnerable to endless deconstruction. Pentecost, as is far too seldom noted by commentators, reverses Babel, and on that great birth day of the church the good news of Jesus is told truly and accurately in the variety of languages present in Jerusalem on that feast day. "After Pentecost" thus evokes the point that the real possibility of miscommunication does not have the final word; language is a good gift from God and when used properly is a wonderful vehicle for telling the truth about God and the world. All of this is evoked in Zak Benjamin's painting for the cover of SAH Series, volume 2, reproduced above, serving as a reminder that faith and theology are important ingredients in language and biblical hermeneutics.

As with most aspects of hermeneutics, views of language are always already involved in our biblical interpretation, albeit often unconsciously. The problem with a lack of awareness is that we are destined to appropriate outdated views of language which obscure rather than clarify our understanding of the Bible. Awareness of language and how it works have a major contribution to make towards biblical interpretation as part of the messianic feast.

Perhaps nowhere is this more clearly the case than in *the Bible as Literature*. One of the amazing things that humans do with words is to write and create literature. Fiction is literature, but not all literature is fictional. *Historical* narrative, of which we have a great deal in the Bible, is also literature, as are poetry and the wisdom writings.

---

10. George Steiner, *After Babel: Aspects of Language and Translation*, 3rd ed. (Oxford: Oxford University Press, 1998).

11. George Steiner, *Real Presences* (Chicago: University of Chicago Press, 1989).

Up until the 1970s historical concerns dominated mainstream biblical studies, as is made clear by the name of the method used to interpret the Bible: *historical criticism*. Both liberals and conservatives tended to ignore the literary nature of the Bible. Conservatives often approached the Bible looking for its propositions, and in some systematic theologies it was argued, for example, that theologians simply collect the facts in the Bible and assemble them in systematic categories.

In the 1970s there was a major (re)discovery of the literary nature of the Bible, primarily due to Jewish literary scholars. Of particular note in this respect are scholars like Robert Alter and Meir Sternberg. Literary analysis has revealed that there is a sophisticated poetics – use of literary devices – in the Bible and that we access the message of the Bible through attending closely to the poetics of the books.

In a variety of ways the literary turn challenged many of the tenets of historical criticism. For example, what was seen as a "doublet" – a similar story occurring twice – and thus evidence of a different source was now explored as a possible example of intentional "repetition," a major trope in literature. Whereas historical criticism tended to carve up books into sources and then focus upon them, the literary turn brought sections, books as a whole, and collections of books into view and yielded remarkably fresh and insightful readings.

The SAHS did not host a separate consultation on the Bible as literature. Perhaps this is something that we still need to do. However, there are a number of important and rich chapters in the first two volumes that do attend to this issue – chapters by Stephen Wright, Brian Ingraffia, Trevor Hart, Ingraffia and Todd Pickett, and Ian Paul.

Before the implications of the rediscovery of the Bible as literature for historical criticism could be worked through – and there are radical implications – postmodernism was upon us with its bewildering variety of the readings of the Bible. Drawing largely from complex and often deliberately abstruse French philosophy, a smorgasbord of readings of the Bible emerged. Postmodernism did challenge the hegemony of historical criticism, but it was largely deconstructive rather than constructive. Consequently, even though postmodernism has waned, historical criticism remains the default mode of much mainstream biblical interpretation.

ETHICS AND BIBLICAL HERMENEUTICS

The Pentateuch is known by Jews as the Torah. "Torah" is often translated as "law," but a better translation is "instruction." From the opening chapters of the

Bible to the end we see that God is concerned to instruct us about how to live according to the grain of his creation. Thus, we can glorify him and flourish as human beings, contributing to the flourishing of the whole creation. Seen in this light, ethics is good news!

Much of the Bible's ethical teaching is clear, and one does not need a course in biblical hermeneutics to understand it. We know from the Ten Commandments, for example, that murder is clearly wrong and that God does not look kindly on adultery. Just as God is faithful in relationship, so too he expects husbands and wives to behave similarly. Likewise we know that false testimony – the ninth commandment – is forbidden. Not only are these teachings clear, but it is relatively easy to apply them today. Take false testimony, for example. In our view, false testimony under the name of the "Big Lie" endlessly perpetuated by Donald Trump and his allies, claiming that he in fact did not lose the 2020 U.S. presidential election, is an egregious violation of the ninth commandment and has brought American democracy under threat. Little wonder that the Ten Commandments forbid falsehood. Application of this commandment is straightforward, and one wonders why more American pastors don't do so when so much is at stake.

However, we live in cultures that are significantly different to those in which the Bible came into existence, and the application of the ethical teaching of the Bible to the many, often complex ethical issues that we face is by no means straightforward. Oliver O'Donovan evokes this challenge in his *The Desire of the Nations*,[12] when he observes that while a pastor may move from the Bible to how to deal with Iraq "today" in thirty minutes, for the scholar this move may entail a lifetime's work.

Let us offer further examples. None of the cultures in which the Bible came into existence was a democracy, and thus political ethics/theology requires a detailed understanding not only of politics in the Bible but also of how politics has developed over centuries in order to make the move from the Bible to contemporary politics and back again. We may think that applying the Bible to home life and marriage is relatively simple, and in many cases it may well be. However, as historians have shown, our modern understandings of domesticity and the nuclear family are significantly different from the family and the home in biblical times. Thirdly, large chunks of the Pentateuch are what scholars call law codes. However, they are an example of customary rather than our modern

12. Oliver O'Donovan, *The Desire of the Nations: Rediscovering the Roots of Political Theology* (Cambridge: Cambridge University Press, 2008).

statutory type of law, and it is vital to know the difference if you are working on biblical and contemporary law. These examples confirm that, again and again, when it comes to ethics the move from the Bible to contemporary issues is complex, and we require hermeneutical insight into how to make such moves.

As if this were not complex enough, nowadays it is not uncommon to hear people acknowledge the ethical instruction of the Bible but reject it as oppressive and coercive – what has become known as ideological critique of the Bible. For all these reasons, it was imperative that the SAHS devote one of its consultations to the Bible and ethics. Oliver O'Donovan is one of the premier theological ethicists of our day; his work is characterised by close attention to the Bible, and with his generous cooperation we focused this consultation on a dialogue with his work. In the preparatory paper for this consultation Craig wrote as follows:

> The focus of the fourth consultation to be held in Cheltenham in June 2001 will be *the use of the Bible ethically*. Prof. Oliver O'Donovan's creative work in this area will be used as a focus and springboard for the discussion. Prof. O'Donovan has agreed to be involved in the consultation and thus, in dialogue with O'Donovan's use of the Bible and with particular reference to the use of the Bible in political ethics, the consultation will examine:
>
> > reasons why the Bible is neglected ethically today, including ideological and socio-critical critique of the Bible
> >
> > ways in which the Bible has been/is used ethically
> >
> > key hermeneutical issues in the use of the Bible, such as how the Bible might function in a Christian ethic for today and the relationship between the Old Testament and New Testament
> >
> > the use of specific biblical themes and texts ethically, such as election, kingdom, Deuteronomy, and the Psalms
> >
> > historical, philosophical, and theological constituents of a biblical, Christian ethic
> >
> > the use of the Bible politically with practical reference to charitable choice in the USA and human rights in Europe.

The result was a wonderfully fertile dialogue with O'Donovan, and in the published volume he generously responded to each essay. Walter Moberly, a prominent British Old Testament scholar, was one of the participants, and you can read more about his chapter and the volume in the following block.

Walter Moberly, "The Use of Scripture in *The Desire of the Nations*" and O'Donovan's Response (SAH Series, volume 3)

A Royal Priesthood? The Use of the Bible Ethically and Politically: A Dialogue with Oliver O'Donovan (2002) is an exceptional book, largely due to O'Donovan's generosity as a dialogue partner. The volume contains not only an introduction to theological ethics and O'Donovan's work (by Craig Bartholomew) as well as chapters of engagement with his work by leading scholars, but also fourteen acute and creative responses by O'Donovan to individual chapters. Since 2002 O'Donovan has continued to produce a series of major works. Of particular note is his "Ethics as Theology" trilogy, namely *Self, World, and Time* (2013), *Finding and Seeking* (2014), and *Entering into Rest* (2017). In 2019 at the SBL Annual Meeting in San Diego, the Scripture and Hermeneutics Seminar hosted an event engaging with this trilogy.

How to read the Bible for ethics remains of vital importance today, with a tsunami of issues bearing down upon us (see the essays on ethics in Part III). As a major Old Testament scholar, Walter Moberly has also made important contributions to theological interpretation. In his chapter "The Use of Scripture in *The Desire of the Nations*," he drills down on O'Donovan's use of Scripture, focusing on where the history of Israel is to be found, O'Donovan's substantial use of the Psalms but limited attention to the Pentateuch, and O'Donovan's understanding of the relationship between the Old Testament and the New. Equally interesting, of course, is O'Donovan's pithy and stimulating response.

HISTORY AND BIBLICAL HERMENEUTICS

Historical concerns dominated much of twentieth-century biblical interpretation among both liberals and conservatives. Again and again historical criticism called into question the story the Bible tells, and again and again conservatives responded by defending the historicity of the Bible. As we noted earlier, both the rediscovery of the Bible as literature and postmodernism challenged the hegemony of historical criticism in major ways. Thus, it was inevitable that the SAHS would host a consultation on history and biblical interpretation.

In order to grasp why it was so important for the SAHS to attend to history, you need to revisit our section on "Understanding and the Limits of the Right Method." One issue is the reliability of the historical narratives of the Bible, but there is more. Once you see that hermeneutics alerts us to the fact that the reader/s of the Bible is as much embedded in history as is the Bible, care must be taken lest you soon find yourself on the slippery slope to relativism. If all readings of the Bible along with the Bible itself emerge in and from history, and if history is simply flux and change as some postmoderns argue, then it is difficult to see how we might ever be able to arrive at a right, true reading of the Bible. Of course, the elephant in the room is how we understand "history" – a complex issue.

The volume resulting from our consultation on history and the Bible is titled *"Behind" the Text: History and Biblical Interpretation*. "'Behind' the Text" is a metaphor that comes from the work of one of the major philosophers of hermeneutics, namely Paul Ricoeur. In his insightful work on texts and literature, Ricoeur distinguishes between that which lies *behind the text*, that which is *in the text*, and the world opened up *in front of the text*. "'Behind' the text" is about that to which the text refers, and was thus an appropriate metaphor for our volume.

In the preparatory document for our consultation, Craig wrote the following:

> Modern biblical interpretation has been inextricably interwoven with issues of "history" – a reality that is evident from the shorthand reference to modern method in biblical study as *historical criticism*. However, the name "historical criticism" easily obscures the complex and manifold ways in which history impinges upon biblical interpretation. Consider the following aspects of history and biblical interpretation:
>
> - To start with it is by no means clear that there is one such entity as historical criticism – within modern biblical interpretation that goes by this name there is considerable variety. How did historical criticism develop, and what is the extent of its diversity? Despite the diversity, are there sufficient common traits to indicate a family resemblance?
> - What is the status of "history" *in* the biblical narratives? Of course, this question has distinctive challenges in the Old Testament and the New and in the

different parts of the Testaments. Recent decades have seen the emergence of very radical views of Old Testament history, and within some versions of canonical interpretation historical issues are sometimes regarded as of little importance. By comparison projects like that of Tom Wright stress that history is fundamentally important for the New Testament and Christian faith.

- How significant a role have (and do) philosophies of history played in biblical interpretation? For example, was the epochal work of scholars like de Wette, Strauss and Wellhausen, etc., shaped in any significant way by particular philosophies of history? And what does this mean for biblical interpretation?
- To what extent are the philosophies of history undergirding historical criticism part of the project of modernity, and has postmodernism subverted them?
- How is history to be conceived of theologically, and does this have implications for biblical interpretation and especially for theological interpretation of the Bible as Scripture? In his outstanding *The Interpretation of the New Testament 1861–1961*, Stephen Neill made the point in conclusion that New Testament study urgently needed a theology of history. Not that this would solve all the problems of New Testament study, but that it would provide the ring within which solutions would be found! Is this true for contemporary biblical interpretation? What would such a theology of history look like? If we oppose the common division between theology and biblical interpretation, how should a theology of history affect biblical hermeneutics?

Hopefully this gives you some idea of the range of issues we want to address in Boston. . . . For the time being here are some recommended readings for the consultation. [The chapter by Plantinga is essential reading for the consultation as we will have a unique opportunity to interact with him at the consultation.][13]

Browse through the contents of *"Behind" the Text* on the KLC's website (https://kirbylaingcentre.co.uk/scripture-collective/the-scripture-and-hermeneutics-seminar/) and you will see the wealth of expertise that our consultation assembled to address these issues. A rich feast, indeed. By this time the SAHS contained a vibrant contingent of Catholic scholars, and next we introduce Mary Healy's contribution.

13. Alvin Plantinga, "Two (or More) Kinds of Scripture Scholarship," in *Warranted Christian Belief* (New York: Oxford University Press, 2000), 374–421.

Mary E. Healy, "Behind, in Front of . . . or Through the Text? The Christological Analogy and the Lost World of Biblical Truth" (SAH Series, volume 4)

Mary Healy's essay comes from the 2002 consultation of the Scripture and Hermeneutics Seminar held in Boston, USA, at which the Seminar focused its attention on how our understanding of history, the world behind the text, affects and interfaces with biblical interpretation. Healy's argument proceeds in four steps. She begins by identifying the Kantian legacy in biblical studies through considering the approach of New Testament scholar Rudolf Bultmann. Secondly, she explores how more recent hermeneutical theory elucidates the ways in which narrative mediates historical events. Interestingly, the big epistemological questions raised by our considerations of history rest in large part on philosophical questions about language and its use. Thirdly, Healy considers the particular case of biblical narrative and its claims to mediate both history and God's agency in and through history. Finally, she suggests that the christological analogy represents the best hermeneutical key for the "communicative aims of biblical narrative." In explaining the christological analogy, Healy takes seriously the doctrine of inspiration. The Bible is a human artefact, but is still an artefact that claims to have been inspired by the Spirit of God. Consequently, in order to interpret the Bible faithfully the reader must take seriously the divine as well as human character of the text. We are reminded that the Second Vatican Council affirmed the Chalcedonian understanding of the Bible as both human and divine and therefore its close relationship to and with the Word made flesh. Healy's essay is paradigmatic of the values of the Seminar: faith-filled, philosophically aware, and writing for the edification of the church. We might also add that Healy's essay engages attentively with other essays in the volume, which speaks of her commitment to scholarship practised in community.

BIBLICAL THEOLOGY AND BIBLICAL HERMENEUTICS

A major issue that has developed in biblical studies is the question of the unity and diversity of the Bible. A legacy of historical criticism has been to endlessly fragment the Bible with such a strong emphasis on diversity that it has become harder and harder to see the Bible as a unity. However, for those of us who affirm the Bible as God's Word its unity is clearly a major concern.

Enter biblical theology. Biblical theology is not theology that is biblical, although we certainly want this, but is a subdiscipline of biblical studies that *seeks to articulate the unity of the Bible using categories drawn from the Bible itself.* Our volume on biblical theology is entitled *Out of Egypt: Biblical Theology and Biblical Interpretation.* "Out of Egypt" alludes to Matthew's typological use of Hosea to show how Jesus fulfils the Old Testament (Matthew 2:15). Typology – the recurrence of patterns from the Old Testament in the New – is one of the ways in which we can access the unity of the Bible, and thus "Out of Egypt" was an appropriate title for the book.

Although biblical theology as a discipline is a modern development, it has a long history of precursors. In the first chapter of *Out of Egypt*, Gerald Bray attends to the church fathers and biblical theology. Francis Martin then introduces us to recent developments in Catholic biblical theology and Sr. Nuria Calduch-Benarges of the Pontifical Gregorian University in Rome introduces us to Marco Nobile's Italian Old Testament theology. When our consultation convened at St Andrews, Charles Scobie's large *The Ways of Our God: An Approach to Biblical Theology* had recently been published.[14] Scobie was in attendance, and Karl Möller contributed an evaluation of Scobie's biblical theology. Scobie himself contributed a chapter on biblical theology and preaching. Because we met at St Andrews, several of its faculty participated – as well as an array of PhD students sitting in – and the volume includes chapters by John Webster, Richard Bauckham, and Trevor Hart. Bauckham attends to monotheism as a great theme in the Bible and Stephen Barton to the unity of humankind.

Already at our second consultation the late Dan Beeby had flagged the importance of mission for biblical hermeneutics (see his essay in *Renewing Biblical Interpretation*). This theme was taken up by Chris Wright at St Andrews. We now introduce Chris's seminal essay.

Christopher J. H. Wright, "Mission as a Matrix for Hermeneutics and Biblical Theology" (SAH Series, volume 5)

The concept of "mission" (and its adjectival form "missional") has become mainstream in some Christian spaces. It has certainly exponentially

14. Charles Scobie, *The Ways of Our God: An Approach to Biblical Theology* (Grand Rapids: Eerdmans, 2003).

grown in popularity since the publication of the fifth volume in the SAH Series, in which Christopher Wright's essay first appeared in 2004. Few individuals have done more than Christopher Wright in the intervening decades to bring into focus the centrality of mission (the *missio Dei*) in the biblical story and to advocate for a "missional" approach to reading Scripture. Too often the church's notion of mission is derived from a few choice texts, mostly from the New Testament. Wright demonstrates the radically missional nature of the whole of Scripture – it's all about God's mission and God's invitation to humans to participate in it. The unity of Scripture (which is the heart of biblical theology) is bound up in the *missio Dei*. Wright's essay is not only seminal in recovering the centrality of mission in the Bible (it was published just two years before Wright's magnus opus *The Mission of God: Unlocking the Bible's Grand Narrative* [IVP, 2006] came out), but it is just as relevant and timely as it was when it was first published. For those who have read his larger work, this essay will be a helpful refresher; for those who have not, it will provide an excellent entry to the main contours of Wright's thinking on mission. Essentially, the essay argues persuasively that mission is at the heart of the biblical story and proposes a missional hermeneutic for reading the Bible. Having published widely on the Bible over the last few decades (including several biblical commentaries), Wright has been able to show the abundant fruit of such a missional hermeneutic for the Bible.

At our Oxford consultation the following year on *Reading Luke*, Michael Goheen made a further contribution in this area with his chapter "A Critical Examination of David Bosch's Missional Reading of Luke."

At this consultation Craig and Mike presented on story and biblical theology, and it should be mentioned that Mike and Craig also presented a draft of their forthcoming *The Drama of Scripture: Finding Our Place in the Biblical Story*.[15] Mike had come as a visiting scholar to the University of Gloucestershire, and during that time they had completed the draft. *Drama* has gone on to become a bestseller, and is now in some twelve languages and in multiple English versions. Recently Craig and Paige Vanosky published *The 30-Minute Bible:*

15. Craig G. Bartholomew and Michael W. Goheen, *The Drama of Scripture: Finding Our Place in the Biblical Story* (Grand Rapids: Baker Academic, 2004; 2nd ed., 2014).

God's Word for Everyone,[16] an attempt to make this kind of approach to the Bible as accessible as possible.

In recent years academic biblical theology has fallen on hard times, and certainly in the UK it is rare to find courses devoted to this topic. *Out of Egypt* remains a major resource for the renewal of biblical theology, with many areas waiting to be further developed.

READING LUKE

A criticism sometimes made of biblical hermeneutics is that it amounts to an endless detour rather than getting on with reading the Bible for the church. This is not our view, but we were concerned throughout the process of our nine, international Seminars to land our reflections in actual biblical exegesis. The concern for actual interpretation will be evident to you as you browse through the content of the volumes on our KLC website. Furthermore, we devoted one consultation to this very topic with a focus on Luke's Gospel at our Oxford event. This consultation attracted many of the major Lukan scholars of our day, and begins with a marvellous introductory essay by Anthony Thiselton.

Joel Green, who has written extensively on Luke and Acts, was present, and an introduction to his contribution follows.

Joel B. Green, "Learning Theological Interpretation from Luke" (SAH Series, volume 6)

Biblical hermeneutics rightly understood is not an unnecessary detour away from exegesis but a means to rich and more profound exegesis so that we might hear what God is saying to us today. The organizers of the SAHS thus considered it essential that one of our eight international consultations should focus exclusively on a part of the Bible. Our choice was the Gospel of Luke, and our consultation assembled many of the current leading authorities on Luke. Consequently, in *Reading Luke* an extraordinarily rich collection of essays is brought together under the subtitle *Interpretation, Reflection, Formation*. Anthony Thiselton

16. Craig G. Bartholomew and Paige P. Vanosky, *The 30-Minute Bible: God's Word for Everyone* (Downers Grove: IVP, 2020).

provides a wonderful introductory essay, reviewing the reception history of Luke through the lens of hermeneutics and overviewing the essays in the volume. This essay in itself is worth its weight in gold, bringing the vast array of Thiselton's scholarship to bear on the topic. Joel Green is the author of one of the most significant recent commentaries on Luke (*The Gospel of Luke*, NICNT [Grand Rapids: Eerdmans, 1997]), and this essay provides insight into the hermeneutical framework that has enabled him to do such fertile exegesis. Green's thesis is that "in his narrative representation of history, Luke engages in interpretation of Israel's Scriptures in order to reform the theological imagination of his Model Readers" (*Reading Luke*, p. 56). Key elements in Green's case are the Bible as *Scripture* along with the role of imagination, narrative, and the Model Reader. Luke works with history in order to do theology. Green thus concludes, "Theological interpretation has much to learn from the narrative approach Luke has exhibited, not least about the role of scriptural reading as a community-forming activity – a reading, then, that would accord privilege to our locating ourselves within the great story of God and his people as this is articulated in Luke-Acts, rather than to a particular exegetical technique or method" (*Reading Luke*, p. 74).

CANON AND BIBLICAL HERMENEUTICS

Christians speak of the Bible as the canon of Holy Scripture. "Canon" refers to the list of authoritative books that constitute the Bible. Clearly the canonicity of the Bible has implications for biblical hermeneutics, to put it mildly. Indeed, over a lifetime of rich scholarship Brevard Childs – who attended our second consultation – produced a significant corpus of works arguing for a canonical hermeneutic for the Bible which acknowledged the contribution of historical criticism but went beyond it in reading the Bible for its authoritative witness to the trinitarian God. Canonicity has not, however, been without its controversies,[17] and thus our eighth consultation, which met at the Pontifical

17. See, for example, Lee Martin MacDonald and James A. Sanders, eds., *The Canon Debate* (Peabody, MA: Hendrickson, 2002); Craig G. Bartholomew, "Canon," in Bartholomew, *Introducing Biblical Hermeneutics*, 251–78.

Gregorian University in Rome, was devoted to the topic of canon and biblical interpretation.

In spite of the heat during our time in Rome, we continually saw signs of the one, holy, catholic, and apostolic church around us. As mentioned in Part I, we had even unsuccessfully lobbied Cardinal Ratzinger, who would become Pope Benedict XVI, to attend. Nevertheless, since we were in Rome a number of major Catholic scholars participated, not all of whom are published in the seventh SAH Series volume, *Canon and Biblical Interpretation.*

Canon and Biblical Interpretation includes a republished essay by Brevard Childs, a chapter by Christopher Seitz – himself a regular participant in the SAHS – an important chapter on canon and liturgical hermeneutics by Scott Hahn, and multiple chapters relating canon to actual interpretation of the Bible. An introduction to Scott Hahn's essay follows.

Scott W. Hahn, "Canon, Cult and Covenant: The Promise of Liturgical Hermeneutics" (SAH Series, volume 7)

How does liturgy (worship) help us to elucidate the ways in which we understand and interpret the canon of Scripture? In answering this question, Scott Hahn exemplifies what he consistently does so well: setting the canon of Scripture in dialogue with the beliefs and practices of the church. Drawing on the seminal thinking of the then Cardinal Joseph Ratzinger, among others, Hahn suggests that a "liturgical hermeneutic" will enable us to hold together the worlds "behind," "in," and "in front" of the text. Hahn argues that Scripture is often inspired by, and reflected in, the worship practices of Israel and the church. However, this cultus-based origin does not negate or eclipse the historical events to which they bear witness in their ritual celebration. He affirms the need for historical and literary scholarship to grasp a properly biblical theology around the big themes of creation, exodus, and the Davidic kingdom. He argues that all these themes together give cohesion to the Old and New Testaments. According to Hahn, because a liturgical hermeneutic is also a canonical hermeneutic it will honour the economy of God, the typological themes that are reiterated through Scripture, and the mystagogical wonders expressed most profoundly in the Eucharist.

THE BIBLE AND THE UNIVERSITY

To this day, most academic biblical interpretation takes place in universities. This is not without its challenges. The modern university is the powerhouse of knowledge in the modern world, and, as we have noted earlier, modernity has far too often been opposed to religion playing a major role in scholarship and is antithetical to the authority of the Bible as Scripture. In a fascinating book, *The Invention of Hebrew*, Seth Sanders argues that modernity muted the Bible. Sanders's case is persuasive, and, of course, the aim of the SAHS has been precisely the reverse, namely to allow the Bible to speak so that we hear it in its full acoustics. Not surprisingly, therefore, the final volume in our eight-volume Series is *The Bible and the University*. By this time Baylor University, who hosted this consultation, had become our American partner and Craig had moved to Redeemer University in Canada.

Again, the list of contributors is impressive, with chapters by David Lyle Jeffrey, C. Stephen Evans, William Abraham, Dallas Willard, and many others. Amongst others, the volume contains chapters on the Bible and law, the educated imagination, and American literature. An introduction to Dallas Willard's chapter follows.

Dallas Willard, "The Bible, the University, and the God Who Hides" (SAH Series, volume 8)

David Lyle Jeffrey and C. Stephen Evans (Baylor University) were regular participants in the SAHS, and the former president of Baylor, Robert Sloan, also participated in our Oxford consultation. Baylor came on board as a partner institution during the process of our Seminars, and the final consultation – on the Bible and the university – was hosted by Baylor. The resultant volume, *The Bible and the University* (2007), is full of good things.

Dallas Willard is most well-known for his writings on Christian spirituality, but he was also a significant philosopher with a particular emphasis on phenomenology (Edmund Husserl). In this chapter he attends to the importance of the university as one of the "standing sources" that humans depend on for knowledge in order to know how to live. Alas, the Bible as a source of knowledge has been dismissed by the modern university. Willard traces how this has come about, attends to why the Bible remains of vital importance for the university, and provides guidance for how Christian scholars might operate in this context.

AFTER BAYLOR

After the completion of our nine international consultations and the publication of the eight-volume Series, the SAHS continued to meet each year around the SBL Annual Meeting, as noted in the introductory essay to this volume. Two further volumes were published by the SAHS, namely *Hearing the Old Testament: Listening for God's Address*, edited by Craig and David,[18] and *A Manifesto for Theological Interpretation*, edited by Craig and Heath Thomas.[19] Both of these books are important. Introductions to the Old Testament do many good things, but few focus on how to listen to the different parts of the Old Testament so as to hear God's address. This, by comparison, is the specific focus of *Hearing the Old Testament*. Amidst postmodernism a minority renaissance of interest in theological interpretation of the Bible emerged, and Craig was one of the editors for the award-winning *Dictionary for Theological Interpretation of the Bible*.[20] Theological interpretation has been a big tent encompassing a variety of approaches. However, it related closely to the concerns of the SAHS, and *A Manifesto* was our attempt to encapsulate and promote healthy, theological biblical interpretation. The actual manifesto is available for download on the KLC website: https://kirbylaingcentre.co.uk/wp-content/uploads/2021/09/BartholomewThomas_ManifestoInterpretation_Ch1Manifesto.pdf.

TODAY

At the end of Craig's introductory essay to this volume in Part I, he suggests, with Lesslie Newbigin, that we need a paradigm shift in biblical studies if all the rigour of our work is to serve the church and contribute towards the flourishing

18. Craig G. Bartholomew and David J. H. Beldman, eds., *Hearing the Old Testament: Listening for God's Address* (Grand Rapids: Eerdmans, 2012).

19. Craig G. Bartholomew and Heath A. Thomas, eds., *A Manifesto for Theological Interpretation* (Grand Rapids: Baker Academic, 2016).

20. Kevin J. Vanhoozer et al., eds., *Dictionary for Theological Interpretation of the Bible* (Grand Rapids: Baker Academic, 2005).

of the world. The SAHS was established twenty-five years ago to try to facilitate a renewal of biblical interpretation in the service of the church and the world. That challenge remains even as fresh questions and opportunities for biblical hermeneutics have emerged, many of which are addressed in the Part III essays of this volume.

Reviewing the eight volumes, it is hard not to feel that in them the SAHS has served up a feast – a rigorously academic one, but nevertheless a feast. In the marketing information for this volume, Zondervan Academic – not us! – writes the following about the SAHS:

> For twenty-five years, the Scripture and Hermeneutics Seminar has produced a steady stream of influential, global, diverse, ecumenical, and world-class research and publications that have impacted a generation of scholars now in mid-career, teaching or ministering at various universities, seminaries, divinity schools, or churches around the globe. The volumes of the Seminar have resourced countless classrooms and have been cited thousands of times in scholarly research and in the pulpits and Bible studies worldwide. Tightly organized, carefully arranged and cross-referenced, this volume:
>
> 1. Highlights the work of a significant movement in biblical interpretation in the academy
> 2. Charts a path of biblical interpretation from the past to the future
> 3. Helps readers understand the philosophical and theological commitments that undergird biblical interpretation
> 4. Helps readers construct a theological hermeneutics that yields a deeper, richer reading of Scripture
> 5. Introduces readers to stories of the Seminar from scholars and ministers impacted by it.
>
> This celebratory volume not only gives a unique perspective on the architecture of biblical interpretation in the first quarter of the twenty-first century, but it is offered in hope of preparing fertile soil for the next generation of women and men to cultivate biblical interpretation for years to come.

Reading this certainly gave us pause for thought. We have been so immersed in the process of the SAHS that it is often hard to get a healthy perspective on it. We do think that the work of the SAHS is important. As such, the volumes published need to be received again and again, even as the SAHS, now part of our four-seminar Scripture Collective in the KLC, continues its work.

We will never facilitate a profound renewal of biblical interpretation as long as we drink the Kool-Aid of Western individualism. The KLC is deeply committed, by contrast, to research in the context of intellectual community rooted in deep spirituality. As you will see from the Part III essays, we now see far more clearly that such a community must include majority world scholars, the context in which there is a remarkable renewal of Christianity even as a hard secularism takes root in the West. Amongst other things, this book is an invitation for like-minded scholars to join us in carrying this vision forward. There is much at stake.

PART III

Thinking Together

Retrospect and Prospect

Since we completed the eight-volume SAH Series, neither biblical studies nor associated disciplines have stood still. In Part III you will find ten specially commissioned essays not only looking back at the work the SAHS has done but primarily attending to creative, contemporary trends and looking forward to work that needs to be done. Our hope is that these short, programmatic essays will be informative and of use to students, professors, and pastors, as well as signposts to where future research needs to be done. An area that we think biblical interpreters need to become aware of is French Catholic phenomenology. Amongst this "school" Jean-Louis Chrétien's work is notable for its engagement with the Bible. We are thus delighted to include a translation into English of Chrétien's essay "Martha and Mary, Hospitality's Twins," in which he discusses the Mary-Martha story from Luke 10:38–42. We are grateful to Andrew Sackin-Poll for accepting the commission to do this translation for us.

Philosophy, Theology, and Hermeneutics

CHAPTER 3

Theology, Philosophy, and Biblical Interpretation

Craig G. Bartholomew

INTRODUCTION: THEOLOGICAL INTERPRETATION AND HERMENEUTICS

Tertullian's provocative question, "What has Jerusalem to do with Athens?" continues to haunt biblical interpretation *in all sorts of ways* and needs to be resolved if we are to facilitate its renewal, which is the ambitious aim of the KLC Scripture Collective. If Jerusalem stands for the Bible and theology, and Athens for philosophy, Tertullian's rhetorical question means that the Bible and theology have no need of philosophy and it is best for them to stay away from it.

"In all sorts of ways" is in italics because it is not just the relationship between biblical studies and Athens (philosophy) that needs attention, but also the relationship between biblical studies and Jerusalem (theology). A chasm has opened up between much of biblical studies and theology, but in recent decades, under the name of "theological interpretation," there have been major efforts to bridge this chasm. I think here of the rich work of Brevard Childs, Francis Watson, Christopher Seitz, N. T. Wright, Kevin Vanhoozer, Dan Treier, the Scripture and Hermeneutics Seminar, and many others.

The candle of the so-called "theological interpretation" of the Bible shone brightly for a while, with new commentary series and multiple books being published. One hopes this will continue, but one is also aware that theological interpretation is a large tent with many different approaches housed within it. A major area where proponents of theological interpretation have differed is on *the role of philosophy* (Athens) and, more particularly, of philosophical hermeneutics.

Few proponents of theological interpretation would pose the question as strongly as Tertullian, but this issue continues to divide its adherents, who are part of a movement – of which one can legitimately see the SAHS as a part – which seeks to renew biblical interpretation so that the Bible is read for the church. In many ways Karl Barth – along with Dietrich Bonhoeffer and then Brevard Childs and the so-called Yale school – is the father of the recent renaissance in theological interpretation. Barth's contribution was truly Herculean, and his work remains a fertile source for rich, theological interpretation, awaiting discovery by new generations of biblical scholars.[1] However, Barth, as is well known, was extremely wary of philosophy and eschewed the possibility of a Christian worldview or Christian philosophy.[2] For Barth, theology was *the* Christian science and thus the queen of the sciences. At our SAHS consultation in Cambridge when Brevard Childs was with us, he argued, if I recall correctly, that at best philosophy can be bent towards biblical interpretation. This left philosophy and other disciplines unaffected by God's revelation in Christ, and also meant that historical criticism continued to be acknowledged by Barth and Childs as a neutral, necessary enterprise, except that we needed to go beyond it to attend to the testimony of the Bible to the trinitarian God.

Hermeneutics is, of course, a development in modern *philosophy*. Hermeneutics has a very long history, but, in my view, the father of modern philosophical hermeneutics is Hans-Georg Gadamer (1900–2002). Gadamer's major work in this regard was his *Truth and Method*.[3] In much modern thought *method* has been privileged as the royal route to truth. Get the method right, apply it correctly, and you will arrive at a true understanding. Within biblical studies many of us were trained in this paradigm, whether in the mainstream or in conservative circles. When I read theology at Oxford we were inducted into source criticism, form criticism, tradition criticism, and redaction criticism; taught how to apply these methods to the OT in particular; and then tested on our ability to do so. Within conservative circles students were inducted into the grammatical-historical method, taught how to apply it, and then tested on their ability to do so. Both approaches, whatever their respective merits, assume the modern faith in correct method.

---

1. Barth's *Church Dogmatics* has a good biblical index in the final volume, and my practice is to consult the index when working on the Bible to see if Barth wrote on the passage/s I am working on.

2. See Michael W. Goheen and Craig G. Bartholomew, *Living at the Crossroads: An Introduction to Christian Worldview* (Grand Rapids: Baker Academic, 2008), 20–21.

3. Hans-Georg Gadamer, *Truth and Method*, rev. 2nd ed. (London: Bloomsbury Academic, 2004).

Gadamer launched a head-on challenge to this trust in method. He was not opposed to method, but resituated it within the larger context of *dialogue*. In Part 1 of *Truth and Method*, he asks us to reflect on how we come to understand an artwork. Of course, analysis of the medium, the form, and the historical background all have their place, but we can do all these things without encountering the work. Rather, we begin where we are and open up a dialogue with the work. On the basis of our situatedness in history we pose our questions and listen to the work in response, and so the dialogue goes back and forth until a fusion of our horizon and that of the artwork takes place in an event of understanding. Far from prejudgments needing to be bracketed out of the process of understanding, they are the basis upon which we move forward to understanding.

Utterly central to hermeneutics is the historical turn and the consequent recognition that the reader is *as* embedded in history as the text is. Ask a class why it is hard to understand the Bible, and again and again the obstacles will all be located in the biblical text having come into existence in ancient cultures far removed from our own. What is so often missed is that we are *as* embedded in history and particular cultures as the Bible is. This is *the* major insight of hermeneutics, and it foregrounds, as we will see, a host of major issues to attend to.

In my opinion it is clear that biblical interpretation needs both theology and philosophy, as I will argue shortly. After we have attended to theology and philosophy, we will turn to recent developments in these two disciplines that may be fertile nodes for biblical interpretation to engage with them. In the conclusion we will foreground the elephant in the room: how does theology relate to philosophy?

BIBLICAL INTERPRETATION AND THEOLOGY

Liberals and non-Christians are not the only people who have eschewed any role for theology in biblical studies. One of my great heroes in biblical studies is F. F. Bruce. As I have gotten older I have come to appreciate his rigorous work more and more, but I am told that when asked he replied that theology has almost nothing to contribute to biblical exegesis. Within evangelicalism, along with other traditions of biblical interpretation, there is thus a reluctance to concede any role to theology.

What are we to make of this? Well, we need to think hard about it. We can begin by asking, "What is theology?" There are many levels of theology, ranging from the short confessional credos we find in the Bible itself, to creeds like the

Apostles' and Nicene Creeds, to church confessions, and ultimately to rigorous systematic theology. Historically, the church has found it essential to summarize what it believes in short, pithy statements like the Apostles' Creed. Such creeds enable Christians to affirm their core beliefs as well as protect the church from error. For Christians who believe in "one, holy, catholic and apostolic church" it is hard to see how we can confess this on Sunday but see it as irrelevant to our biblical studies on Monday to Friday. Indeed, we will only do this if we buy into the modern view of religion as a private affair needing to be kept separate from the public spheres of life, including academic biblical studies. Once we take seriously the basic Christian confession that "Jesus is Lord" (1 Cor 12:3) over all of life, then it becomes impossible to maintain such a bifurcation.

But, even conceding this, why might the biblical scholar need the creeds? Is not the Bible the final authority for faith and life? Indeed, it is. Amidst orthodox Christianity it is never asserted that the church imposed canonicity on the Bible; rather, the church recognised the books of the Bible as canonical and inspired, and thus as authoritative for her life and belief. However, this is no free pass for Western-style individualism in biblical interpretation in which each reader is free to become his or her own "pope." The Bible is received and read as God's Word written in the context of that one, holy, catholic, and apostolic church.

Furthermore, we need to reflect on the nature of the book God has given us. We may wish that God had rather given us something like the Westminster Standards or the Augsburg Confession, but he did not. God has given us a library of at least sixty-six books that embody a range of genres and came into existence over hundreds of years in cultures that are often very different from our own. This is the glory of the Bible, but it also means that such a sprawling, capacious literature needs summaries of its core beliefs like the creeds to keep us on track even as we receive it and indwell it as the true story of the world. At a basic level, for example, if we find ourselves interpreting the Bible in a way that contradicts the creeds, this should serve as a red flag that we are likely going astray in our interpretation.

Insofar as the creeds provide us with a pithy summary of the overarching message of the Bible, they are also indispensable in enabling us to read parts of the Bible in relation to the whole. Take the first article of the Apostles' Creed, for example: "I believe in God the Father Almighty, creator of heaven and earth." "Heaven and earth," echoing Genesis 1:1, is a merism for the totality, for everything. An exegete who takes this seriously would be wary of the view, now not uncommon among readers of Genesis 1, that God may have created the world from pre-existent matter (cf. John 1:3). Similarly, an exegete fully aware of the Apostles' Creed would never make the mistake of not asking how the second article of the Creed, "and in Jesus Christ . . . ," relates to the first. The Creed pushes us to think about the relationship between redemption and creation and resists the perennial evangelical temptation of reducing soteriology to individual salvation apart from God's purposes for his entire creation. Close attention to this relationship would have saved generations of evangelicals from the sacred-secular dualism, a capitulation to modernity's privatization of religion and a reading of the Bible that has been catastrophic for their public witness.

So much for the creeds, but what about *systematic theology*? In my view, what systematic theology does – or should do – is to reflect on the Bible above all else, but also on the Christian tradition. In the light of both, it seeks to articulate the core beliefs of Christians in detail and in relation to the questions of our day. Hence the typical attention of theologians to the great loci of Christian belief, such as the doctrine of the church, the doctrine of God, the doctrine of the person and work of Christ, etc. Alas, just as biblical studies has become detached from theology, so too much theology has become detached from the Bible.

Although I defend a form of prooftexting when it takes account of both the context of the verse it refers to and the context of the whole Bible, the use of the Bible in theology is far more complex than simply assembling the facts we find in the Bible under the right headings. Just think, for example, of the different ways in which "faith" is used in the Bible, and you will soon see that developing a doctrine of faith is complex and involves sophisticated interpretation and development and a deep knowledge of the Christian tradition. If this were not hard enough, when one considers the fragmentation of mainstream biblical studies the reluctance of some theologians to engage directly with the Bible becomes somewhat understandable. However, in my opinion this is still not acceptable. In Bruce Ashford's and my *The Doctrine of Creation*, we sought to engage deeply with the Bible, and it reminded me just what hard work this is.[4]

Assuming that we are thinking of good, healthy systematic theology that is deeply engaged with the Bible, how might this relate to biblical interpretation? As it turns out, this is very similar to the relation of the creeds to biblical interpretation. What theologians do is akin to what academics of all disciplines do. They abstract a small part of reality from the whole in which we encounter it, and then analyze that part in detail. This often results in remarkably fruitful discoveries, but a test of good academic work is that it deepens our understanding of the whole in which the part is embedded. If you think of "the church," for example, it is clearly a major theme in the NT and has important roots in the OT. However, it has also developed in practice throughout church history in a

4. Bruce R. Ashford and Craig G. Bartholomew, *The Doctrine of Creation: A Constructive Kuyperian Approach* (Downers Grove: IVP Academic, 2021).

whole variety of ways and has been reflected upon again and again in the tradition. A theologian will focus on the church in the Bible, in the tradition, and in relation to questions today, attempting to set out a systematic, logical account of the doctrine of the church for today.

Clearly, there is a real sense in which such work moves *from* the Bible *to* theology. However, there is far more to it than that, and here is where John Calvin comes to our aid. Calvin's *Institutes* is renowned as a work of theology. However, he states clearly that one reason he wrote the *Institutes* was in order to help Christians read the Bible better! In my opinion, this is the gift of really good theology. Having abstracted a particular theme – such as the church – from its setting in the Bible and the tradition, theology's close attention to this theme enables us to better read the Bible in relation to the church and other issues today.

Theology is a great and indispensable gift to the church. It can never replace or supersede the Bible, but it can and should inform biblical interpretation and be a vital dialogue partner with it. Indeed, if we can renew the use of the Bible in theology, and theology in biblical studies, then the stage would be set for rich engagement between the two disciplines.

PHILOSOPHY AND BIBLICAL INTERPRETATION

Can one avoid philosophy in biblical interpretation? The academic formation of a biblical scholar takes years and includes extensive language study, and thus it is not surprising that biblical scholars may be reluctant to add to the requirements for doing their job well. However, like it or not, philosophy is unavoidable in biblical studies. Let me provide a few examples. As readers will be aware, the extent to which the historical narratives of the Bible are in fact historical is contested. Enter into this debate, and you will soon find yourself immersed in questions like: What is history? What is historiography?, etc. In other words, you will find yourself amidst the traditional hunting grounds of *philosophy of history*. The Bible is also a written text. Examine it in detail, and sooner or later you will be wrestling with how language works. In other words, go deep enough and you will have backed yourself into *philosophy of language*. The Bible is, for example, chock-full of *metaphor*, which is currently an extensive area of study in philosophy of language. At a certain point one of James Barr's penetrating critiques of much biblical study was that it did not take into account how language works; i.e., it was out of touch with developments in philosophy of language and linguistics and thus fell into avoidable errors. From the 1970s onwards, we witnessed a very creative recovery of the Bible as literature. Explore this in detail, and you will find yourself amidst *philosophy of literature*. And we could continue with other examples.

It seems undeniable to me that philosophy is always already present in biblical studies. The only question, then, is the extent to which scholars are conscious of this reality and are intentional about it. For Christian exegetes, the major question that emerges is *whether or not the Christian perspective or worldview affects our understanding of history, language, textuality, etc.* To phrase the question in another way, is it enough to be conscious of the role of philosophy in biblical interpretation, or do we need insight from Christian philosophy when it comes to our view of history and language, etc.?

Where postmodernism with its wild pluralism has been helpful is in unequivocally alerting us to the fact that there is no one agreed view of history or historiography, there is no one agreed view of how language works, there is no one agreed view of authorial intention, there is no one agreed view of textuality and how texts work, etc.; these are all issues that impinge on biblical studies. If biblical scholars are not to work with particular views unconsciously shaping their scholarship, then they will need to choose among the views on offer. Again, the question emerges for the believing scholar: Does my faith affect the view of history or language I appropriate?

If faith relates to all of life, then it surely does. Again, at its best, postmodernism has inadvertently pushed this issue to the surface. In his extraordinary work *Real Presences*, the Jewish scholar George Steiner argues that when it comes to how language works, Jacques Derrida's deconstruction confronts us with either "In the beginning was the Word" or nihilism. Steiner argues that rigorous engagement with the great classics of literature, including the Bible, *requires a grammar of creation* which insures the reality of the real presences we encounter in literature and the Bible. All of this means, in my view, that Christian philosophical insight will potentially be invaluable to the biblical scholar. Wonderfully, we are heirs to a remarkable renaissance of Christian philosophy in recent decades, led by luminaries such as Alvin Plantinga, Nicholas Wolterstorff, C. Stephen Evans, William Alston, Eleonore Stump, etc. A vast body of work has emerged, and some of these philosophers have reflected directly on how their work relates to biblical studies.

Of course, just as we find different emphases among theologians, so too we find different emphases among Christian philosophers. Indeed, it is sometimes joked that there are as many different definitions of philosophy as there are philosophers! In my view, the reason for this is that one's view of philosophy is deeply rooted in one's worldview. This is unavoidable. Thus, just as there are different worldviews, so there are many different definitions of philosophy and diverse philosophical methods. My working *definition of philosophy* is that it seeks to examine the structures of creation and to systematically and logically describe what is subject to those structures.[5] Whereas theology focuses on the Bible and the Christian tradition in particular, Christian philosophy, in the light of faith, focuses on the nature of reality *as creation* seeking to gain insight into how our world works. The major areas of philosophy are ontology (the nature of reality), epistemology (how we go about knowing something so that we can trust the results of the knowing process), and anthropology (our view of the human person). Clearly there is overlap between theology and philosophy, but the focus of their attention is significantly different.

Recent decades have not only witnessed a remarkable renaissance of Christian philosophy but also the emergence of identifiable groups amongst the reengagement with philosophy – and theology – from a Christian perspective. The biblical scholar or student does well to be aware of these groups so that he or she can discern where best to dig in so as to gain the most help for his or her work. In the remainder of this chapter, I will set out some of the main groups that have emerged, indicate which one/s I think are most fertile for biblical interpretation, and end by recommending some initial reading for biblical scholars who wish to enhance their knowledge in this area.

ANALYTIC THEOLOGY

Since we began the Scripture and Hermeneutics Seminar things have not stood still in the relationship between theology and philosophy. One of the newest kids on the block, as it were, is analytic theology (AT). "Analytic" is a reminder that a basic division in philosophy is that between continental and analytic philosophy, with the latter focused primarily on logic. In my limited exposure to analytic theology, it has seemed like a furtherance of classical theism or perfect being theology, defined by Katherin Rogers as making two assumptions when it comes to God: God is the most perfect being, and human reason is able to and should use philosophy to explain God as the most perfect being.[6] Tom McCall in his *An Invitation to Analytic Christian Theology* notes the concern of some theologians that "analytic theologians bypass and effectively ignore God's own revelation as it occurs ultimately in the incarnation of the Holy Son and reliably

5. Drawing on L. Kalsbeek, *Contours of Christian Philosophy* (Toronto: Wedge, 1975).

6. Katherin A. Rogers, *Perfect Being Theology*, Reason and Religion (Edinburgh: Edinburgh University Press, 2000), vii.

in the Bible as Holy Scripture."[7] I admit I share this concern, and thus am grateful that McCall's second chapter is on AT and the Bible.

McCall explores the relationship that both natural theology and perfect being theology have with AT. He rightly notes that theologians take different views on both these topics, but denies that AT is essentially connected to either one. For example, he asks "what is the relation of analytic theology to natural theology? The answer, frankly, is that there isn't much of one, and there isn't necessarily one at all."[8] He argues that one can make a good case for revealed theology and perfect being theology being *compatible*, but "perfect being theology is in no way essential to the ambitions, style or approach of analytic theology."[9]

This is all very helpful and clarifying, but it still leaves one wondering what exactly AT is. McCall defines AT as follows: "Still, perhaps we can safely say that what is common across the range of uses is this: *analytic theology* signifies a commitment to employ the conceptual tools of analytic philosophy where those tools might be helpful in the work of constructive Christian theology."[10] The problem I see here is that this is such a thin definition that it is hard to think of any serious theologian who would not see him or herself included in it. Perhaps a way forward is to inquire further after the nature of *analytic philosophy*. Peter Angeles defines analytic philosophy as,

> A twentieth-century philosophic movement particularly strong in England and the United States that concentrates on language and the attempt to analyze statements (or concepts, or linguistic expressions or logical forms) in order to find those with the best and most concise logical form which fits the facts or meanings to be presented. Central to analytic philosophy is the forming of definitions – linguistic or nonlinguistic, real or contextual. (Contextual definitions primarily refer here to those that define the specific use of symbols whereby one set of symbols may be substituted for another.)[11]

Angeles goes on to mention Bertrand Russell, G. E. Moore, the early Ludwig Wittgenstein, and Rudolph Carnap as examples of analytic philosophers. Of course, analytic philosophy has not stood still since 1981 when Angeles published his dictionary, but the names he supplies should give us pause. These philosophers are all strong proponents of human autonomy and the sufficiency

---

7. Thomas H. McCall, *An Invitation to Analytic Christian Theology* (Downers Grove: IVP Academic, 2015), 38.

8. McCall, *An Invitation*, 40–41.

9. McCall, *An Invitation*, 52.

10. McCall, *An Invitation*, 16 (emphasis original).

11. Peter A. Angeles, *Dictionary of Philosophy* (New York: Harper and Row, 1981), 10.

of neutral, objective reason and logic to enable us to arrive at the truth about the world, and a danger of AT is that it unwittingly imports this disposition into theology. None of the aforementioned figures would see insights from the Bible as essential to truly understanding the world. Now, it is true that Christian philosophers such as Plantinga and Wolterstorff have effectively challenged the classic foundationalism of such analytic philosophers and argued that core Christian beliefs can quite justifiably be assumed as properly basic. In the process they have developed a Christian way of doing analytic philosophy which has turned out to be very fruitful. However, it is not at all clear that this is where AT situates itself.

Logic is part of rationality, and, in my view, Alasdair MacIntyre has rightly argued that all rationality operates within a tradition. The only question is, which one? My concern with AT remains the same as my concern with perfect being theology, namely that one can do theology with philosophical concepts apart from, albeit alongside, the Bible. Perfect being theology historically developed its concepts from Greek philosophy rather than from the Bible, which is one reason, I suspect, why biblical scholars find it hard to relate to. When it comes to perfect being theology, the best one can argue is, as McCall observes, "Minimally, it seems safe to conclude that a strong case can be made for the *compatibility* of perfect being theology and revealed theology."[12] Perfect being theology may be compatible with revealed theology, but it does not emerge out of the Scriptures. In my view, this is inadequate. When it comes to theology we should look for a style deeply engaged with Scripture and clearly emerging out of and returning to the Bible. There are welcome signs of such work emerging, and it will provide a basis for dialogue between biblical scholars and analytic theologians.

RADICAL ORTHODOXY

Radical orthodoxy's (RO) light shone brightly at the end of the twentieth and the start of the twenty-first century through the work of theologians such as John Milbank, Catherine Pickstock, Graham Ward, and others. Central to RO is a diagnosis of the malaise of modernity and the need for a theological remedy. "Today the logic of secularism is imploding. Speaking with a microphoned and digitally simulated voice, it proclaims – uneasily, or else increasingly unashamedly – its own lack of values and lack of meaning. In its cyberspaces and theme-parks it promotes a materialism which is soulless, aggressive, nonchalant and nihilistic."[13]

12. McCall, *An Invitation*, 50 (emphasis added).

13. John Milbank, Catherine Pickstock, and Graham Ward, eds., *Radical Orthodoxy: A New Theology* (New York: Routledge, 1999), 1.

Christians should challenge modernity through the Christian story. "The central theological framework of radical orthodoxy is 'participation' as developed by Plato and reworked by Christianity, because any alternative configuration perforce reserves a territory independent of God. The latter can lead only to nihilism (though in different guises). Participation, however, refuses any reserve of created territory, while allowing finite things their own integrity."[14] Reason is thus "rational" only if it operates within the contours of Christian theology.

RO illuminated the theological sky brightly for a while, but its light has dimmed with time. In my view, there are major theological insights in it that we need to retain and develop. However, RO tends to ignore the Reformation with its epochal retrieval of the Bible, and RO's failure to engage with Scripture is notable and unhelpful for biblical scholars.

CANONICAL THEISM

William Abraham is one of our best contemporary theologians. He recently completed a four-volume series on *Divine Agency and Divine Action* with Oxford University Press, and it is full of important and stimulating insights that biblical scholars will want to be aware of. Amongst many other things, he defends a robust theology of divine action, revisits the biblical theology movement, and in the final volume has a great chapter on epistemology and the book of Exodus.

As a Methodist, Abraham is much concerned with the renewal of the church today. In recent years he has advocated what he calls "canonical theism" as a way forward for the church and theology.[15] He defines canonical theism as "the version of theism adopted publicly, intentionally, and explicitly by the church as it was initially driven to articulate, celebrate, and live out its fundamental convictions on the other side of conversion and the gospel. I refer to this theism as 'canonical theism' because it is indeed canonical; it was the theism, the beliefs about God, listed and officially adopted by the church prior to the schism between East and West."[16] In *Canonical Theism* Abraham sets out thirty theses that explain the contours of this movement.[17]

Central to canonical theism is a reconception of the relationship between Scripture and tradition. Thesis XVII asserts:

---

14. Milbank, Pickstock, and Ward, eds., *Radical Orthodoxy*, 3.

15. William J. Abraham, Jason E. Vickers, and Natalie B. Van Kirk, eds., *Canonical Theism: A Proposal for Theology and the Church* (Grand Rapids: Eerdmans, 2008). See also William J. Abraham, *Crossing the Threshold of Divine Revelation* (Grand Rapids: Eerdmans, 2006).

16. Abraham, *Crossing*, xii.

17. Abraham in Abraham, Vickers, and Van Kirk, eds., *Canonical Theism*, 1–6.

> Canonical theism's vision of canon differs from the standard Western vision of canon in two ways. First, it extends canon beyond the canon of scripture or the Bible. Here it draws on the original meaning of canon as a "list." Second, it eschews conceiving canon as an epistemic criterion, relocating canon within the church rather than within the field of epistemology and philosophy. In canonical theism canon is construed fundamentally as a means of grace, a way through which the Holy Spirit reaches and restores the image of God in human agents.[18]

Abraham's work is unerringly stimulating. His view of the Bible as canon and epistemology has proved controversial, and Abraham rejects any attempt to "canonize" a particular epistemology. The restructuring of the relationship between Scripture and tradition proposed by canonical theism also needs careful evaluation. For our purposes it remains to be seen if canonical theism will yield rich and fertile biblical interpretation.

READING THE BIBLE FOR PHILOSOPHY

We are familiar with reading the Bible for theology, but may not have come across reading the Bible for philosophy! A decade ago the Jewish scholar Yoram Hazony blazed a trail in this direction with his *The Philosophy of Hebrew Scripture* (2012).[19] More recently Dru Johnson has followed suit in the Christian tradition with his *Biblical Philosophy: A Hebraic Approach to the Old and New Testaments* (2021).[20] Both of these works are wonderfully creative, and the authors are to be credited with taking seriously what the Bible teaches and how this relates to philosophy.

If I have a concern about this approach, which is still in its early stages, it is whether or not one can approach the Bible as a philosophy book. Of course, much depends on how one defines philosophy! In my opinion, the Bible functions more at a pretheoretical level to orient us to the world, so that it yields more of a *worldview* than a philosophy per se. This worldview can be developed to yield philosophy, but I am hesitant about the move directly from the Bible to philosophy. Having said this, the yields are significant, and

---

18. Abraham in Abraham, Vickers, and Van Kirk, eds., *Canonical Theism*, 4. For Abraham on canon see William J. Abraham, *Canon and Criterion in Christian Theology* (Oxford: Clarendon, 1998).

19. Yoram Hazony, *The Philosophy of Hebrew Scripture* (Cambridge: Cambridge University Press, 2012).

20. Dru Johnson, *Biblical Philosophy: A Hebraic Approach to the Old and New Testaments* (Cambridge: Cambridge University Press, 2021).

interpreters of the Bible will need to assess the extent to which this move from the Bible to philosophy casts its light back on the Bible so that it enhances biblical interpretation.

FRENCH CATHOLIC PHENOMENOLOGY

The Catholic tradition has a long history of rigorous work in philosophy. The great example of classic theism or perfect being theology, referred to earlier, is that of Thomas Aquinas. My concern with this tradition, still mined by many Catholics and evangelicals today, is the role of so-called unaided human reason in this enterprise. However, in the last century Catholics have produced a range of rich work on philosophy and theology, not least amidst what is known as the Catholic *Ressourcement* movement. This movement began in Europe in the 1920s and positioned itself more loosely in relation to Thomism than traditional Catholic theology, thereby opening up avenues for fresh engagement in theology and thus with Scripture.[21]

In my opinion the most exciting philosophy today is French Catholic phenomenology. Whereas Catholic – and many Protestant – philosophers have previously approached the portals of theology but not entered, some of the major philosophers in this "school" move far more freely between philosophy and theology, and in some cases attend closely to the Bible. Jean-Louis Chrétien is my favourite among these philosophers. For example, in his *The Ark of Speech*,[22] which covers the philosophy of language, "Ark" stands for Noah's ark, a metaphor for a positive, Christian view of language as the means by which we recognise and preserve the alterity of the other. Chrétien has also written specifically on the Bible in his *Under the Gaze of the Bible*.[23] His wonderfully creative *Spacious Joy: An Essay in Phenomenology and Literature* contains an extended discussion of Psalm 119.[24] Here are poignant examples of the use of the Bible in philosophy, which reflect back on how *we* read the Bible and how we might do so with other disciplines and the public domains of life in mind.

This movement is, in our opinion, so fertile for biblical interpretation that

21. See Gabriel Flynn and Paul D. Murray, eds., *Ressourcement: A Movement for Renewal in Twentieth-Century Catholic Theology* (Oxford: Oxford University Press, 2012).

22. Jean-Louis Chrétien, *The Ark of Speech*, trans. Andrew Brown (New York: Routledge, 2004).

23. Jean-Louis Chrétien, *Under the Gaze of the Bible*, trans. John Marson Dunaway, Perspectives in Continental Philosophy (New York: Fordham University Press, 2015).

24. Jean-Louis Chrétien, *Spacious Joy: An Essay in Phenomenology and Literature*, trans. Anne A. Davenport (New York: Rowman and Littlefield, 2019). Note that following the Vulgate Chrétien refers to Ps. 119 as 118.

we have included an essay on it by Amber Bowen and Aaron Simmons later in this book, as well as a new translation of Chrétien's essay on the Mary-Martha story in Luke's Gospel.

THE KUYPERIAN TRADITION

The Kuyperian tradition, emerging from the work of Dutch Calvinists such as Abraham Kuyper, Herman Bavinck, and their colleagues and followers, has been exceptionally productive in the area of philosophy. Within the more continental style it has yielded the Reformational philosophy of Herman Dooyeweerd, Dirk Vollenhoven, and their students and followers, as well as the work of Cornelius Van Til. Within the analytic style of philosophy it has exploded and generated the renaissance in Christian philosophy I referred to earlier. Alvin Plantinga and Nicholas Wolterstorff have been central to this renaissance, and both have their roots in Kuyperian soil. They lead the way in an identification and reexamination of the epistemology that has governed academic work for centuries, namely that of classic foundationalism, and have shown it to be badly lacking in terms of any good reasons for embracing it. By comparison, both men have proposed in different ways an approach to epistemology in which Christians are entirely justified or warranted, as Plantinga would put it, in bringing their core beliefs and faith with them into the heart of their academic work without waiting for such beliefs to first be "proved" on the basis of an alternative epistemology.

Both Plantinga and Wolterstorff have explicitly addressed biblical interpretation,[25] and you will find Plantinga's explosive and rich essay on two or more types of biblical interpretation in *"Behind" the Text*. In my opinion, the invitation Plantinga's essay offers waits to be received by biblical scholars. In my forthcoming series, Old Testament Origins and the Question of God, I attempt to respond to Plantinga's invitation in relation to the field of OT studies.

Philosophical hermeneutics is, I believe, of vital importance for biblical interpretation. In different ways Anthony Thiselton, along with myself and many others, has particularly sought to show this again and again. However, in my view, Gadamer's theory with his *two* horizons, for all its very real fecundity, will not suffice for Christian biblical interpretation. What we need is a philosophical hermeneutics shaped by *three* horizons, not only that of the reader and

25. N. T. Wright's wonderfully creative work on the NT is also connected to Kuyperian soil, as the dedication to Brian Walsh of *The New Testament and the People of God* makes clear. Walsh formerly taught worldview at the Institute for Christian Studies, founded in the Kuyperian tradition, in Toronto.

the text but that of God and his revelation of himself in Christ. In my view, the Kuyperian tradition is best poised to produce such work, which with theological interpretation would be an enormous gift to biblical scholars today.

CONCLUSION

It is clear that in my view Jerusalem has everything to do with Athens, and that a renewal of biblical interpretation in our day will need both theology and philosophy. The discussions I covered are complex and wide-ranging. A renewal of biblical interpretation therefore needs a community – and it is a goal of the KLC and our Seminars, including the SAHS, to practise Christian scholarship in community rooted in deep spirituality.

In the examples of recent theological and philosophical developments I gave, the unaddressed elephant in the room is the question of *the relationship between theology and philosophy*. Readers will find this issue addressed in detail in my essay "Uncharted Waters"[26] as well as elsewhere in my writings.[27] In brief, I think both theology and philosophy can and should emerge out of a Christian worldview, are foundational for Christian scholarship including biblical interpretation, and need each other as they develop. One might call this an *Augustinian model*, since one finds philosophy and theology mixed together in Augustine's writings. In my opinion the Kuyperian tradition, as I just discussed, is best poised to deliver such a model. As is apparent from what I wrote in "Uncharted Waters," scholars are by no means agreed on this issue, and it is one that cries out for close attention today. In fact, it would certainly be a worthy topic for a PhD. Clarity in this area would be of immense help to any renewal of biblical interpretation.

For those readers who recognise the need to engage in philosophy and theology for their interpretation of the Bible, what are resources that will get you going on the journey?

For a relatively painless – indeed fun – immersion in the history of philosophy, I recommend to my students Richard Tarnas's outstanding and accessible *The Passion of the Western Mind: Understanding the Ideas That Have Shaped Our World View* (London: Pimlico, 1991). For a Christian approach to philosophy

---

26. Craig G. Bartholomew, "Uncharted Waters: Theology, Philosophy and the Crisis of Biblical Interpretation," in *Renewing Biblical Interpretation*, SAH Series 1, ed. Craig Bartholomew, Colin Greene, and Karl Möller (Grand Rapids: Zondervan, 2000).

27. See, e.g., Craig G. Bartholomew, *Introducing Biblical Hermeneutics: A Comprehensive Framework of Hearing God in Scripture* (Grand Rapids: Baker Academic, 2015), and especially my tree of knowledge model on p. 597.

there are several good volumes available such as C. Stephen Evans, *A History of Western Philosophy: From the Pre-Socratics to Postmodernism* (Downers Grove, IL: IVP Academic, 2018). A further example is my and Michael Goheen's *Christian Philosophy: A Systematic and Narrative Introduction* (Grand Rapids: Baker Academic, 2013). References in this volume will take you deep into the literature of Christian philosophy.

For theology, there is a lot of good work emerging. Within the Kuyperian tradition the renaissance of the work of Herman Bavinck in recent years is notable. His multivolume *Reformed Dogmatics* and other works are a great place within which to immerse oneself.[28]

Of course, I should not fail to mention this volume, the eight-volume Scripture and Hermeneutics Series, and the two additional volumes published by the SAHS, namely Craig G. Bartholomew and David J. Beldman, eds., *Hearing the Old Testament: Listening for God's Address* (Grand Rapids: Eerdmans, 2012); and Craig G. Bartholomew and Heath A. Thomas, eds., *A Manifesto for Theological Interpretation* (Grand Rapids: Baker Academic, 2016).

Biblical interpretation is a privilege, a gift, and a feast. The argument of this paper is that attention to philosophy and theology considerably enhances that feast when it is done well.

28. Bavinck's multivolume *Reformed Dogmatics* is available in a one-volume abridged version, Herman Bavinck, *Reformed Dogmatics: Abridged in One Volume* (Grand Rapids: Baker Academic, 2011).

CHAPTER 4

Phenomenology, Hermeneutics, and Christian Scholarship

Amber L. Bowen and J. Aaron Simmons

INTRODUCTION

One of the challenges for Christian scholars receiving much of their training in seminary contexts is that there are broad philosophical assumptions that often operate behind the scenes in undiagnosed ways. As such, the idea of doing the work required to become better acquainted with different philosophical approaches can seem more like a distraction than a helpful way forward. It is an intellectual version of being several miles down a hiking trail and realizing that it was not the trail you had planned to take. Since it is late in the day, or late in your studies, it seems to make more sense just to keep going in the direction you are headed than to turn around. Indeed, not having enough time or energy to start down the other path is a very real problem, both for those who spend lots of time in the mountains and for those who spend lots of time in libraries. However, as David Foster Wallace and Martin Heidegger both remind us, what we tend to take for granted is usually what becomes most problematic in our thinking.[1] The "obvious" ends up becoming the unquestioned, which then slips into a domain of the unquestionable that closes us off to following truth

1. See David Foster Wallace, *This Is Water* (New York, New York: Little, Brown, and Co., 2009); Martin Heidegger, *Being and Time*, trans. Joan Stambaugh, rev. Dennis J. Schmidt (Albany and New York: State University of New York Press, 2010).

wherever it might lead.[2] In order to resist such intellectual complacency, it is important to take stock of some of the general philosophical frameworks that can open up new spaces for how to revitalize what might otherwise threaten to become stagnant.

One particular philosophical approach that we take to be especially fecund for Christian scholarship in general and biblical hermeneutics in particular, is phenomenology – especially the *new* phenomenology of those thinkers associated with the "theological turn" in France. Phenomenology is perhaps most generally defined as a philosophical approach that seeks to offer accurate descriptions of human experience in ways that are attentive to the dynamics of first-person perspectives. In this way, phenomenology shifts away from a broadly metaphysical or ontological approach that seeks to understand reality from an objective "God's eye" perspective, and instead turns toward the lived experience of what is given to consciousness. Such a shift of perspective, approach, and methodology should not be interpreted as a rejection of the metaphysical and ontological priorities that are often prominently on display in Christian scholarship, but simply as a reminder that there is nothing obvious about how we proceed. Phenomenology presents an opportunity to reflect on the ways that our perspectives are already nested in interpretive frameworks that reveal and conceal a host of things that we should take more seriously. Accordingly, phenomenology often goes hand in hand with trends in philosophical hermeneutics that serve to emphasize the embodied perspective of human knowing.

Phenomenology and hermeneutics both stress the epistemological stakes of metaphysical speculation, specifically the risk of reducing the world to abstractions and totalizing frames that miss its inner life and our immersion in it. At their most basic, they encourage humility as a prerequisite for reflective inquiry. Christian scholarship, we believe, should be especially adept at embracing such humility given the way that it takes as its foundation a recognition of creaturely status, finitude, and embodiment as the context in which all Christian theory and practice would occur.

In this chapter, we hope to lower the bar of access to phenomenology in order to demonstrate the ways in which such work stands as a compelling archive upon which those working in Christian theology and biblical studies should more commonly draw. Hence, we will begin by offering a general introduction to phenomenology as a philosophical tradition and distinguish it from metaphysical/ontological conceptions. Then we will move on to several specific areas of Christian scholarship and offer suggestions for ways in which phenomenology

2. See Plato's *Euthyphro* 14c, in Plato, *Complete Works*, ed. John M. Cooper (Indianapolis and Cambridge: Hackett, 1997).

can speak into their current debates in helpful ways and open new directions for them moving forward. We hope to show that phenomenology is a good tool to add to your backpack regardless of what trail you are on.

PHENOMENOLOGY: A PRIMER

It might seem a fairly easy task to give a basic synopsis of phenomenology, but things are complicated by the fact that such an account is not simply a matter of historical analysis. Instead, phenomenology is a living tradition. Although it is widely agreed that classical phenomenology began with the work of Edmund Husserl (1859–1938) – specifically in his *Logical Investigations* of 1900–1901 – it quickly began to change as Husserl's work was appropriated by such diverse thinkers as Martin Heidegger, Maurice Merleau-Ponty, Edith Stein, and Max Scheler, among others. As a result, there is no easily articulated phenomenological "faith statement." Instead, if Whitehead was right to say that all philosophy is simply a series of footnotes to Plato, we might be right to say that phenomenology is not only a series of footnotes to Husserl, but a series of Husserlian methodological *heresies*.[3] Because the temptation to overstate the coherence of phenomenology continues to press upon anyone seeking to summarize its main tenets and commitments, Dermot Moran is entirely right to remind us that "it is important not to exaggerate . . . the extent to which phenomenology coheres into an agreed *method*, or accepts one theoretical outlook, or one set of philosophical theses about consciousness, knowledge, and the world."[4]

Nonetheless, even if definitional precision is slippery and suggestions of phenomenological orthodoxy are largely overblown, that doesn't mean that we should throw our hands up and declare phenomenology to be an incoherent mess. We think that by considering just a few recent attempts to articulate phenomenology's basic commitments we can begin to see some ways of pulling various threads together. For example, Robert Sokolowski suggests that "Phenomenology is the study of human experience and of the ways things present themselves to us in and through such experience."[5] In this way, he stresses the importance of *experiencing*, rather than that which is *experienced* – as metaphysical or ontological approaches might do. Alternatively, David Cerbone

---

3. See J. Aaron Simmons and Bruce Ellis Benson, *The New Phenomenology: A Philosophical Introduction* (London: Bloomsbury, 2013).

4. Dermot Moran, *Introduction to Phenomenology* (New York and London: Routledge, 2000), 3 (emphasis original).

5. Robert Sokolowski, *Introduction to Phenomenology* (Cambridge: Cambridge University Press, 2000), 2.

claims that "Phenomenology can be characterized as the study of intentionality."[6] Intentionality is simply the idea that consciousness is always *consciousness-of* something. In other words, there is no Cartesian *cogito* that can stand alone without a *cogitatum*. Phenomenology disavows brute awareness. You can only be aware *of* something. The same is true for thinking and even imagining or desiring. By defining phenomenology as the study of intentionality, Cerbone is not rejecting the centrality of experience but highlighting the sort of experience that characterizes conscious perception as always reflecting an essential connection between the act of thinking and what is thought. Sokolowski and Cerbone, thereby, are stressing two dimensions of the fact that phenomenology is not interested in causal theories about the world but instead is concerned with conscious experience of the world.

Unlike the metaphysics of representation, according to which the mind is an "inner" chapter full of representative images that (hopefully) correspond to the "real" things in the "outside" world, phenomenology breaks down the inner/outer division, demonstrating how the subject (me) and the object (the phenomenon that gives itself to me, or that "appears") are always in immediate relation to one another in conscious experience. Consciousness, therefore, is not conscious "of" internal mental representations, but "of" the "things themselves." As such, phenomenology subverts the purported binary between subject and object and between appearance and reality. It thereby sidesteps the epistemic skepticism (and even solipsism) that modernity's metaphysics of representation inevitably creates and provides a way of knowing and relating to the world in light of which we can live with humble confidence.

It is with this in mind that we can understand Husserl's early suggestion of the phenomenological motto as "back to the things themselves."[7] Rather than being stuck with a phenomenal representation of an unknowable noumenal object, or always only able to relate to a mental image rather than the object itself, phenomenology is invested in experience such that experience is

---

6. David Cerbone, *Understanding Phenomenology* (New York: Routledge, 2014), 4.

7. There are a variety of ways that one might make sense of this movement. For example, Wittgenstein's notion of going "back to the rough ground" seems to hit on similar notions of the primacy of givenness. There has been significant work done bringing Wittgenstein into conversation with philosophy of religion. See, for example, Robert L. Arrington and Mark Addis, eds., *Wittgenstein and Philosophy of Religion* (New York and London: Routledge, 2001); Brian R. Clack, *An Introduction to Wittgenstein's Philosophy of Religion* (Edinburgh: Edinburgh University Press, 1999); and Thomas D. Carroll, *Wittgenstein Within the Philosophy of Religion* (London: Palgrave, 2014). See also Bruce Ashford, "Wittgenstein's Theologians: A Survey of Ludwig Wittgenstein's Impact on Theology," *Journal of the Evangelical Theological Society* 50, no. 2 (June 2007): 357–75. Although Wittgenstein was not a phenomenologist, it is valuable to appreciate the similarities that might emerge when seeing possible points of resonance between his much more linguistic framework and Husserl's notion of the "things themselves." Both are devoted to the value of experience as the context for philosophical (and theological) inquiry.

experience of the things themselves as they present themselves to consciousness. Yet, the experience of *what* is experienced – or the object toward which intentional consciousness is oriented – must always "appear" or be "given." To that end, Moran claims that "Phenomenology . . . emphasises the attempt to get to the truth of matters, to describe *phenomena*, in the broadest sense as whatever appears in the manner in which it appears, that is as it manifests itself to consciousness, to the experiencer."[8]

Notice that Moran's focus is on the way that description requires attending not only to the experience, or what is experienced, but *how* it is experienced: the mode in which it appears. Taken together, these aspects serve to form a "world" of meaning such that experience is not only descriptive but is normatively situated as significant in various ways. Dan Zahavi stresses this aspect when he writes that "Phenomenology should . . . be understood as a philosophical analysis of the different types of world-disclosure."[9] Simply put, the "world" reveals itself to our consciousness only insofar as we perceive phenomena as meaningful, intelligible, and shared.

In all of these definitional statements, we find each thinker stressing different aspects which they take to be foundational to phenomenology. Nonetheless, what underlies all of the phenomenological variants and brings together experience, intentionality, appearance, and meaning is a commitment to giving accurate accounts of human experience in ways that are attentive to the dynamics of first-person perspectives. Our addition of the specifically first-person perspective to the definitions already offered is consistent with all the other accounts because, as Shaun Gallagher explains, "The *first-person point of view* means that the phenomenologist, the investigatory of consciousness, studies his or her own experience from the point of view of living through that experience."[10] However, it is important to note here that this stress on first-person perspectives does not reduce phenomenology to introspective psychology. Rather, by attending to such perspectives we begin to realize that all experience is only possible *as someone's*. Yet phenomenology seeks to eschew any problematic subjectivism and instead stresses that phenomenological accounts of first-person viewpoints are, themselves, not radically individualistic. Instead, such accounts provide the primary mode of objective description of the act of experiencing as a lived phenomenon. In fact, while phenomenology is distinct from all naturalistic and causal narratives, Husserl still claims that it is a "rigorous science" in that it is not interested

8. Moran, *Introduction to Phenomenology*, 4 (emphasis original).

9. Dan Zahavi, "Introduction," in *The Oxford Handbook of Contemporary Phenomenology*, ed. Dan Zahavi (Oxford: Oxford University Press, 2012), 3.

10. Shaun Gallagher, *Phenomenology* (New York: Palgrave Macmillan, 2012), 7 (emphasis original).

in *my* experience because it is mine, but because of the way experience is, in each case, objectively singularized.

By highlighting the idea that experience occurs in contexts such that phenomena appear as meaningful and our descriptions of such experience can be understood by others, we can easily see how phenomenology would open onto hermeneutics. We don't simply perceive X, but we perceive X *as-something.* As Gallagher explains, phenomenology "begins with the fact that we, as agents who must act, and as thinkers who try to get a grasp on what we are doing, are always *already situated* in the world."[11] Being situated is a matter of both existential and epistemic relevance. We are situated insofar as we inherit the world as already meaningful. We do not start with inquiry in order to figure out how to live. Instead, inquiry is an option only for those already living. Yet the conditionality of life itself motivates an appreciation of the perspectival limitations of embodied finitude. We are unable to get outside of existence to figure out what is true about existing. Instead, only as invested participants are we ever able to ask questions about what it means to participate.

With these basic contours in place, let's offer a typical Husserlian example of how this all might work. Consider the tree outside the window of the room in which we are currently writing this sentence:

> It is quite large, with green leaves and branches spreading in all directions. The tree slightly leans forward toward where the sun is located in the afternoons. On the ground around the tree is a ring of flint rocks (all about the size of a shoebox), and inside the ring is light tan mulch that serves to accentuate the whiteness of the rocks.

We can begin to see how phenomenology is distinguished from metaphysical or ontological approaches, on the one hand, and scientific or naturalistic approaches, on the other hand. Although all these approaches might also start from the description of the tree, they quickly move in different directions relative to their particular orientation and concerns. The botanist might see the tree as a particular species that is native to this area and of not much interest. The ecologist might see the tree as a guard against climate change and soil erosion. The apologist might see the tree as an example of biological complexity operating internal to design arguments. The sociologist might see the tree as a site for communal gathering. The artist might see it as a subject of her next painting.

The list could go on and on. But for the phenomenologist the tree itself is, to

11. Gallagher, *Phenomenology*, 1 (emphasis original).

some degree, incidental. The phenomenologist attempts to "bracket" all theoretical frameworks regarding the tree's existence in order to speak to the experience as experienced regardless of whether the experiencer is a botanist, ecologist, apologist, sociologist, or artist. This "bracketing" is what Husserl calls the phenomenological reduction or *epoché*. This might seem odd, and it is reasonable to protest that only if the tree exists is it possible to experience it. In response to such an objection, Husserl discusses the "modes" of presentation. Think of it this way: I can perceive the tree in the mode of direct presentation (by looking at it out the window), in the mode of remembrance (by thinking about the tree I looked at yesterday), or in the mode of desire (by wishing for the tree and the shade it provides when I am especially hot while mowing the lawn). Other options abound. The point is that in all these cases the object of my intentional consciousness is the tree itself – not a mental representation of the tree. Yet I can also shift my consciousness from the tree to my thinking about the tree, and in so doing my intentional object is not the tree, but my own thought. Nonetheless, Husserl contends that the "principle of all principles" in phenomenology is that we allow evidence to be given from itself. What is given to consciousness is relevant from the start *as evidence*. We do not need a sociological or scientific theory for evidence to operate. Givenness, itself, is evidential.

Once we perform the reduction, we then begin to notice that I don't actually "see" the tree in totality, but only from a particular perspective or "adumbration." I then "fill in" the rest of the object so that I do not take myself to be seeing only a two-dimensional slice, but the full tree. So experience is, in this way, constructive such that our consciousness fills in the gaps left by perception. Moreover, I realize that the tree is not simply presented by itself, but is actually framed by a variety of other phenomena that serve to allow it to signify as such. The kid's fort behind the tree, the fence behind the fort, the sky showing through the leaves, the distance between me and the tree, etc., all of this forms the "environment" in which the tree is able to be experienced in the way that it is. I can easily turn my attention from the tree to the fort or the fence, but in my doing so the tree then recedes into the environing background.

Husserl suggests that everything that appears or is given to consciousness is presented against a "horizon" that situates it as the thing that it appears to be. Such horizons might be spatial, temporal, or cultural. Regardless, you can see how the phenomenologist is not engaging in debates about the existence of the tree (think apologetics) or the causal relationships that the tree has with other objects (think scientific inquiry). Instead, phenomenology seeks to take seriously what it means to find oneself confronted in very concrete ways by specific phenomena. Attending to such confrontation invites a greater awareness of the implications of embodiment (as Merleau-Ponty shows), of history (as Heidegger explains), and of linguistic as well as sociocultural framing (as Paul Ricoeur details).[12]

This general example of the sort of phenomenological process found in classical phenomenology gets radicalized and deepened by new phenomenologists such as Michel Henry, Emmanuel Levinas, Jacques Derrida, Jean-Luc Marion, Jean-Louis Chrétien, and Jean-Yves Lacoste. Although wrongly accused of smuggling in revealed theology to phenomenological philosophy,[13] they all realize that phenomenology's commitment to the principle of all principles requires that we expand our conception of what counts as "appearance." Namely, sometimes we find ourselves confronted by that which does not "appear" in any straightforward way. For example, Henry details the way that "Life" functions as the backdrop for all manifestation.[14] Alternatively, Levinas discusses the ethical depth that shows up in the "face" of the other person which serves to "overflow comprehension."[15] Marion describes the way that the glory of the Eucharist is not simply there in the bread and wine, and yet it is nonetheless given for the religious person engaging in the liturgy.[16] Similarly, Derrida talks about the way that phenomena such as gifts and justice all fall away from our grasp when we attempt to locate them concretely in experience.[17] Chrétien suggests that the call to selfhood is something that can't ever be located objectively but only ever resounds in the response to the call.[18] And Lacoste considers how the experience of liturgy allows us to experience "place" in ways that are not defined by the horizon of the "world."[19] In all these cases, new phenomenologists move beyond a concern for the experience of specific phenomena and begin to think through the conditions of phenomenality itself.

---

12. See Maurice Merleau-Ponty, *Phenomenology of Perception*, trans. Donald A. Landes (New York and London: Routledge, 2014); Heidegger, *Being and Time*; Paul Ricoeur, *The Conflict of Interpretations*, ed. Don Ihde (Evanston, IL: Northwestern University Press, 1974).

13. See Dominique Janicaud et al., "The Theological Turn of French Phenomenology," trans. Bernard G. Prusak, in *Phenomenology and the "Theological Turn": The French Debate* (New York: Fordham University Press, 2000).

14. Michel Henry, *The Essence of Manifestation*, trans. Gerard Etzkorn (The Hague: Martinus Nijhoff, 1973).

15. Emmanuel Levinas, "Is Ontology Fundamental?," in *Basic Philosophical Writings*, ed. Adriaan T. Peperzak, Simon Critchley, and Robert Bernasconi (Bloomington and Indianapolis: Indiana University Press, 1996).

16. Jean-Luc Marion, *In Excess: Studies in Saturated Phenomena*, trans. Robyn Horner and Vincent Berraud (New York: Fordham University Press, 2004).

17. Jacques Derrida, *The Politics of Friendship*, trans. George Collins (London: Verso, 1997).

18. Jean-Louis Chrétien, *The Call and the Response*, trans. Anne A. Davenport (New York: Fordham University Press, 2004).

19. Jean-Yves Lacoste, *Experience and the Absolute: Disputed Questions on the Humanity of Man*, trans. Mark Raftery-Skehan (New York: Fordham University Press, 2004).

We want to contend that such new phenomenological openings, though not themselves instances of theology, invite a direct appropriation of phenomenology as a resource for Christian thought and living. In particular, all of these new phenomenologists spend quite a bit of time thinking about the relationship of philosophy and theology from within a phenomenological approach. Although they offer a range of specific accounts that should not be collapsed into each other, they collectively see phenomenological philosophy to be a matter of possibility and phenomenological theology to be a matter of actuality. Phenomenological *philosophy* begins by saying "*if* X were the case, then what follows?" whereas phenomenological *theology* begins by saying "*since* X is the case, then this follows." So, without asserting the actuality of claims made by divine revelation (since that is a source of epistemic authority not immediately available to philosophy, nor are such claims immediately available to immanent experience), phenomenological philosophy can analyze the structure of the experience that such a possibility would entail. Alternatively, since theology takes special revelation as a primary source of epistemic authority, phenomenological theology begins with the assumption that revelatory claims are "actual" and then uses phenomenology as a tool to further investigate the experience. These different ways of approaching questions and drawing from a religious archive should not intimidate us. Instead, it should invite us to appreciate the need for philosophers and theologians to think together in order that phenomenology not miss what is given to us in religious traditions, experience, and texts.

PHENOMENOLOGY, THEOLOGY, AND BIBLICAL STUDIES

Scholars and practitioners engaged in the disciplines of theology and biblical studies are often aware that philosophy is always at work in the ways they approach their specific domains of inquiry. Theologians commonly draw from metaphysics to discuss the nature of God, the hypostatic union, or the inner life of the Trinity, or even to develop theories of the atonement. Biblical studies operates according to philosophical ideas about language, history, and interpretation in order to do textual analysis. Despite such appropriation, specifically phenomenological approaches have remained a largely untapped resource. Having given a basic overview of what phenomenology is, we will now show how it can be (and indeed already is) employed in current scholarship in ways that open up new avenues and even overcome long-standing impasses.

THEOLOGY

Often philosophical theology gets reduced to metaphysical claims about the God of classical theism. Phenomenology begins from a different starting point. Rather than starting with demonstrations of God's existence and claims about divine attributes (like Christian metaphysicians often do), phenomenology begins with our finite human existence and the way things disclose themselves to us in our experience. This approach is especially beneficial to Christian theology because it facilitates reflection in ways that allow us to attend more carefully to the implications of a doctrine of creation on epistemic life. Moreover, phenomenology can be deployed such that an understanding of theological selfhood can be seen as transformative for hermeneutic awareness. Furthermore, by speaking to the relational investment that accompanies affective life, phenomenology helps us see what it might mean to indwell truth through the life of faith.

Phenomenology prompts us to begin with the origins of our experience and to consider what that experience says about the kinds of created beings we are. As Oliver O'Donovan describes, the dawn of our experience is an awakening to find ourselves in a world of meaning – a creation already shaped by intentional engagement.[20] Analyzing the nature of this experience, we recognize that our existence is not self-initiated or self-willed, but *given*. We did not originally choose to exist; we already received our existence before we took it up as a matter of agency. Existential phenomenologists variously refer to this aspect as our "thrownness" (Heidegger), that we are always already "embarked" (Sartre), and that we are not simply born something but get made into who we are (Beauvoir). Such non-Christian accounts are not oppositional to Christian narratives of creation, but merely attempt to account for it without reference to divine activity. Phenomenological awareness suggests that even if we are radically free within existence, we are never fully autonomous in relation to existence itself. Our very existence is a response to a prior call – whether that call is from being, others, society, history, or God. Phenomenology, therefore, helps us recognize the contingency of our existence. When appropriated in specifically Christian ways, such a call is not simply an anonymous throwing, but a personal expression of generosity and love that calls us forth into faithfulness. It attends to the way in which we are situated in a specific time and place and to the way in which we are oriented to God, to the world, and to others. Our historical and embodied "situatedness," therefore, should not be understood as a limiting factor that precludes theology but actually as part of our status as contingent beings that calls for theological attention.

As the beings that we are, we find ourselves ensconced in a "world" – a world

20. Oliver O'Donovan, *Self, World, and Time*, Ethics as Theology 1 (Grand Rapids, Eerdmans, 2013), 1–17.

that has existed before us and that will continue on after us. In a theological register, we might say that we awaken to find ourselves in a world that is appropriately understood as where we come to know God as invested in the created order. Our creaturely "thrownness" suggests that we are not subjects that stand over the world as an object – an object that we master, manipulate, or exploit to serve our own agendas. By beginning with the conditions of experience, phenomenology allows us to recognize the gift like nature of human existence that then informs one's notion of experience as "religious."

Phenomenology can help us better understand how a posture of openness to God, to the world, and to one another leads to flourishing. It also discloses how a stance of self-importance, i.e., egoism, leads to the kind of violence and brokenness that also characterizes our world. Indeed, a theologian might turn phenomenological focus to the concept of sin in order to suggest that the sin that separates us from God is not our creaturely "thrownness" but the prideful attempt to "overthrow" our creaturely dependence in order to be our own criterion and master. Not only can phenomenology be used to explore the anatomy of sin, as Søren Kierkegaard does,[21] but, as Emmanuel Falque shows us, it can also be appropriated in order to describe the way the resurrection of Christ changes everything by opening closed horizons and inserting possibilities that did not previously operate.[22] Phenomenology facilitates understanding Christianity as a matter of openness to the unexpected and a refusal of naturalistic closure. It is for this reason that, as previously mentioned, Marion sees Christ, as expressed in liturgical enactments such as the Eucharist, as the "saturated phenomenon," *par excellence*.[23] That is, the Eucharist gives more than what is "presented" to our perceptual capacity. Grace and charity are "present" in the phenomenon and are experienced, despite not being "visible" to our visual cortex.

As another example of how phenomenology can get appropriated in such Christian respects, consider John Paul II's theology of the body, which, rather than defining what it means to be human in the world by abstract definitions, phenomenologically attends to the body in a way that discloses the deeper spiritual, and indeed eschatological, significance of embodied existence.[24] Following further on Merleau-Ponty's and Henry's specific focus on embodiment, we

---

21. See Søren Kierkegaard, *The Sickness unto Death*, ed. and trans. Howard V. Hong and Edna H. Hong (Princeton: Princeton University Press, 1980), 75–96.

22. This is Emmanuel Falque's central claim in *The Metamorphosis of Finitude: An Essay on Birth and Resurrection*, trans. George Hughes (New York: Fordham University Press, 2012).

23. Jean-Luc Marion, *In Excess: Studies in Saturated Phenomena*, trans. Robyn Horner and Vincent Berraud (New York: Fordham University Press, 2004).

24. John Paul II, *Man and Woman He Created Them: A Theology of the Body*, trans. Michael Waldstein (Boston: Pauline Books & Media, 2006).

could also look to Brian Brock's work on disabled bodies. Brock considers the way such bodies are fearfully rejected or lovingly included by the Church, and shows how they are nested in redemption narratives while being gifted to build up the Christian community.[25]

Another important implication of such phenomenological engagements with Christian theology is that each of these examples demonstrate how phenomenology can be used to challenge an assumed hierarchy between theoretical (systematic and biblical) theology and practical theology. The dichotomy between theory and practice is a problematic hallmark of modernity, and is often witnessed in the Church through a divorce between orthodoxy and orthopraxy. We often think that if we get our theory right, then it will trickle down into right practice. Christian life then seems really to be a matter of propositional assent that necessitates moral life. However, such a view is wildly out of step with the lived realities that attend embodied existence. Christian ministry, in particular, should be a site of radical invitation to think together in nurturant ways about mysteries that overrun us all, rather than a space of authoritative reinforcement of particular epistemological and political power structures that then get deployed as theological orthodoxy.[26]

The juxtaposition between theory and practice, whether in theology or other areas of human life, is a binary that phenomenology seeks to subvert as consistent with the disavowal of the inner/outer distinction that intentionality offers. By theologically taking up the first-person, experiential approach "from below" rather than the metaphysical approach "from above," phenomenology gives us a vantage point to understand the deeper significance of Christian doctrines within our embodied existence.

Phenomenology can benefit Christian theology by showing us that Christian truth is not simply something to know, but something to indwell, inhabit, and embody in word and deed. As Henry reminds us, Christ's claim was not to *know* the truth, but to *be* it.[27] Phenomenology is deeply interested in the ways that being and truth are co-implicated in each other. Christianity and phenomenology mutually inform us that truth is not simply something that is the case as expressed in sentences, but something into which we live in hope and humility.

---

25. Brian Brock, *Wondrously Wounded: Theology, Disability, and the Body of Christ* (Waco, TX: Baylor University Press, 2020).

26. For more on the distinction between nurturant and authoritative approaches to Christian theology, see John Sanders, *Embracing Prodigals: Overcoming Authoritative Religion by Embodying Jesus' Nurturing Grace* (Eugene, OR: Cascade, 2020).

27. Michel Henry, *I am the Truth: Toward a Philosophy of Christianity*, trans. Susan Emanuel (Stanford, CA: Stanford University Press, 2002). See also Michel Henry, *Words of Christ*, trans. Christina M. Gschwandtner (Grand Rapids: Eerdmans, 2012).

BIBLICAL STUDIES

The "rigorous science" of phenomenology is not the kind that would subject Christian scripture to the methods and presuppositions of natural science, which led to what many have called a "crisis" in biblical interpretation.[28] Instead, in line with the rejection of a strict dichotomy of theory and practice, phenomenology also serves to challenge the juxtaposition between "scientific" and "religious" readings of the Bible. Phenomenology does so in part by resisting the modern tendency to erect a strict division between fact and value. Modernity's emphasis on fact as always the criterion by which to judge value stands in stark contrast to phenomenology, which asks readers to attend to the givenness of the text by embracing a posture of openness and receptivity to it. In so doing, phenomenology highlights that description is always normatively laden. Alternatively, it illustrates how normative proclamations serve to elevate some descriptions while marginalizing others.

In the introduction to his edited volume, *Phenomenologies of Scripture*, Adam Wells situates phenomenology as a challenge to higher criticism, which he describes as a method that "reflects the Enlightenment ideal of an all-encompassing objective science" and that associates a true understanding of the Bible with a scientific rather than religious understanding.[29] As a fundamentally modernist enterprise, higher criticism's underlying assumption is that science and religion are juxtaposed opposites, the latter being a contaminate to the "objectivity" of the former. Wells offers a general taxonomy of the different ways that biblical scholars in the last three centuries have sought to navigate the supposed antagonism between reading the Bible scientifically as a historical artifact or religiously as Scripture. Some scholars have altogether rejected religious modes of understanding to adopt exclusively scientific modes. Others, especially those in ecclesial contexts, have rejected scientific modes of understanding to adopt exclusively religious modes. Still others have sought to reduce the antagonism by arguing that religious and scientific modes are simply two different hermeneutical lenses.[30] All three responses, however, maintain (and even reinforce) a binary logic which insists that science and

---

28. See Craig G. Bartholomew, "Uncharted Waters: Theology, Philosophy and the Crisis of Biblical Interpretation," in *Renewing Biblical Interpretation*, SAH Series 1, ed. Craig Bartholomew, Colin Greene, and Karl Möller (Grand Rapids: Zondervan, 2000) and Alvin Plantinga, "Two (or More) Kinds of Scripture Scholarship," in *"Behind" the Text: History and Biblical Interpretation*, SAH Series 4, ed. Craig Bartholomew et al. (Grand Rapids: Zondervan, 2003).

29. Adam Y. Wells, ed., *Phenomenologies of Scripture* (New York: Fordham University Press, 2017), 4.

30. Wells gives Wellhausen and Briggs as examples of the first category. He argues that fundamentalism is representative of the second category. And he cites Abraham Kuyper and Stephen J. Gould as examples of the third (*Phenomenologies of Scripture*, 2–5).

religion are not only entirely separate modes of inquiry but that science is the far superior option.[31]

It is worth noting that some scholars have sought to read Scripture in ways that are *both* historical *and* theological.[32] As fruitful as these scholars' approaches have proven to be, phenomenology's ability to subvert dichotomies makes it an especially valuable resource for contemporary biblical scholars interested in a more integrated approach. The problem with the modern notion of science, according to Husserl, is that it is insufficiently scientific insofar as it reduces all science to a specific empirical causal method. This method is fraught with naturalistic assumptions that predetermine and restrict the meaning of objects. In contrast, a truly rigorous science must "accept nothing in advance, accept nothing as a beginning that has been handed down, nor allow ourselves to be blinded by any names no matter how great."[33] While the scientific method reduces the complexity of phenomena by fitting them within a (constructed), naturalistic frame, the science of phenomenology aims to disclose phenomena in their very complexity. "Accordingly," Wells argues, "a phenomenology of scripture does not impose the methods of natural science onto scripture; rather, phenomenology starts with scripture itself, allowing scripture to 'give' itself freely . . . For, if we want to know *what scripture means* or *how it works*, we cannot begin our investigation by assuming answers to those very questions."[34]

A phenomenological approach to Scripture begins with a posture of radical openness to the way Scripture presents itself, and even an openness to the possibility of being addressed by it. We might say that phenomenology helps us to "listen" to the "call" that the Bible offers to its readers.[35] To read phenomenologically is to attend to the "givenness" of the biblical text – to pay attention to what is presented to us and to consider how our methods of reading (what we might call our "natural attitude" toward the text) might constrain the text, fitting it into predetermined categories of what its meaning must be. Sometimes this "natural attitude" simply assumes interpretive grids and expectations that

31. For a phenomenological account of the rationale and consequences of this turn toward scientism as a social logic, see Michel Henry, *Barbarism*, trans. Scott Davidson (London: Continuum, 2012).

32. For example, see the approaches of N. T. Wright, Michael Bird, Scot McKnight, and Beverly Roberts Gaventa, among others.

33. Edmund Husserl, "Philosophy as Rigorous Science," trans. Marcus Brainard, *New Yearbook for Phenomenology and Phenomenological Philosophy* 2 (2002): 293.

34. Wells, *Phenomenologies of Scripture*, 6 (emphasis original).

35. Here we are thinking especially of the work of Chrétien, who not only locates this call/response structure in the Bible but uses it more broadly as a mode of existential awareness. However, in *Under the Gaze of the Bible*, he specifically appropriates Kierkegaard's idea that the Bible invites us to see ourselves by hearing the voice of God within it. For more on the role of listening in philosophical inquiry, see Gemma Corradi Fiumara, *The Other Side of Language: A Philosophy of Listening*, trans. Charles Lambert (New York and London: Routledge, 1990).

we have adopted without being consciously aware of them. Other times this "natural attitude" may actually be read by Christians as an idolatrous imposition on the text or a way of approaching the Bible that makes it conform to our ideals, our preferred interpretations, and our pet issues.

A phenomenological approach to biblical hermeneutics allows us to attend to scriptural phenomena in ways that give rise to descriptions honoring the complexity and varied textures of the text. The aim for those in biblical studies is neither to make the text impenetrable nor to make it mean anything we want it to mean, but to allow its fullness to remind us that we are not masters of the texts that we read but receivers of them. In fact, as Chrétien urges, rather than seeking to master the biblical text (whether by reductive scientific explanations or by reductive religious explanations), we must allow it to master us.[36] This point is helpfully illustrated in Chrétien's newly translated essay "Martha and Mary, Hospitality's Twins," which is included in this volume. Therein he stresses the value of learning to listen as perhaps the easiest of all things and yet the most difficult given our normal mode of engagement in the world. Chrétien turns to the examples of Mary and Martha as two possible responses to the encounter with Christ (or the Word of God). He compellingly argues that hospitality is not exclusively an act of doing, but an act of receiving. We show hospitality by being open to the words of the Other. Learning to hear, to listen, to be silent, and to receive is crucial to receiving the kenotic message of Christ. Importantly, though, sound is impossible in a vacuum. We hear because we are already shaped by prior speech. Similarly, only in communities do we learn to listen.

In Chretien's account we can see that phenomenology again runs us headlong into hermeneutics. As Ricoeur says, we begin to see the value of "graft[ing] . . . the *hermeneutic problem* onto the *phenomenological method*."[37] Ricoeur is right to suggest that "every reading of a text always takes place within a community, a tradition, or a living current of thought, all of which display presuppositions and exigencies – regardless of how closely a reading may be tied to the *quid*, to 'that in view of which' the text was written."[38] Yet such hermeneutic awareness of the communal context or "world" of meaning, in which texts are written/presented and read/received, again points to the importance of being open to givenness. For those working in biblical studies, such givenness is even more complicated since it requires an awareness that phenomenal appearance

---

36. Jean-Louis Chrétien, *Under the Gaze of the Bible*, trans. John Marson Dunaway (New York: Fordham University Press, 2015). Joel Green also emphasizes this way of reading the Bible in *Seized by Truth: Reading the Bible as Scripture* (Nashville: Abingdon Press, 2007).

37. Ricoeur, *The Conflict of Interpretations*, 3 (emphasis original).

38. Ricoeur, *The Conflict of Interpretations*, 3 (emphasis original).

might actually give theological Revelation. However, affirming such revelation as Revelation always happens somewhere by someone such that we are returned to the importance of phenomenology as a tool for making sense of what is going on, not only *in* the text as a collection of written words but *with* the text as an expression of a particular Revelation around which the Christian community exists.

Phenomenology opens us onto the hermeneutic "world" of the text because it requires us to attend to the horizons by which the text is able to be read as meaningful. In this way, phenomenology makes the "invisible" visible by helping us to notice those aspects of the text that are ignored, overlooked, or that do not present themselves in ways we might have previously expected.[39] The patient attentiveness that phenomenological readings cultivate allows deeper patterns, connections, and relations to emerge which are not only significant for deeper theological reflection but also for transformed modes of being in the world.

CONCLUSION: MORE THAN METHODOLOGY

We have argued that phenomenology, and the hermeneutic awareness that it invites, are key resources for Christian scholarship – especially in theology and biblical studies. However, it is important to realize that phenomenology is about more than methodology. The new phenomenologists demonstrate that phenomenology is a matter of reflectively inhabiting openness as a way of life. Within a broadly Christian framework, this kind of openness could be described as the life of faith or a life of humble confidence that is receptive and responsive to God. As such, we might say that recognizing phenomenology as an important tool in our backpack is not enough – *we then have to go hiking.*

Phenomenology must avoid being reducible to a paint-by-Husserlian-numbers approach to thinking. Instead, doing phenomenology well means that we take ourselves up in the very world that becomes visible in our inquiry. Phenomenology makes detached speculation difficult because it reminds us that we are always implicated in that which we study. Similarly, Christianity makes detached objectivism problematic because it constantly calls for one to take up *one's* cross rather than simply writing commentary about crucicentrism. In this way, the first-person emphasis of phenomenology resonates deeply with

---

39. See for example Robyn Horner's essay, "Phenomenology as Lectio Divina: Jesus and the Woman Caught in Adultery," in *Phenomenologies of Scripture*, ed. Adam Y. Wells (New York: Fordham University Press, 2017), 114–24, in which she uses phenomenology to attend to the function of visibility in John 8:2–11.

the existential investment that should animate Christian living. Both remind us that although method matters, it is never ultimate.

So, take care that your scholarly backpack is well-thought-out and make sure to throw in some phenomenology and hermeneutics beside the map, water bottle, and firestarter, but then go outside and get on the trail. What finally matters about both phenomenology and Christianity must be expressed in the lives we live, not just in the books we write about living.

CHAPTER 5

Martha and Mary, Hospitality's Twins[1]

Jean-Louis Chrétien

Translated by Andrew Sackin-Poll

Dedicated to Br Camille de Belloy, O.P.

As much through its imperious stripped-back prose as its brief limpidity and clarity, the story of the hospitality given to Jesus by Martha and Mary in the village of Bethany as recounted in St Luke's gospel, and this gospel alone, seems to have disconcerted at the very start any prolix commentary and any interpretative subtlety. This inconspicuous narrative is a scene of few words and details, tending toward a single lesson: Jesus's assertion that little is required, indeed, only one thing, in order to hear and listen. The story initiates the reader into the simplicity of listening and hearing, which, it says, is an irreplaceable demand. Two warm welcomes, two ways of receiving, which are sisters to each other, like Martha and Mary, distinguish and confront one another here, upon the initiative of Martha. Mary will not break her silence. She will not respond, any more than Martha, and, in hearing the Word of the Lord, on Mary's part,

1. Unless otherwise stated, I have translated the quotes given in the French text into English. I would like to dedicate this translation to my wife, Rachel. Below is the original copyright from the French publisher.

who does not get up, begins to see this Word given to her by becoming the one who listens, too.

These two dimensions of hospitality are those of our hands and ears: our industrious hands, devoted to everything that one must do, that is, tidy up, prepare the table or cook a meal, ensure others have what they need, and, our ears "outstretched" and attentive (to these things) at the same time as our body bows or stands at rest, allowing the heavenly dew of the Word to descend upon him, according to the biblical image. As every church father has pointed out, Jesus's praise of Mary does not count as a criticism of Martha's work and tasks, even if the Latin translates *optima pars* as "the best part" while the Greek expression says only "the good (or right) part." But the very notion of "part" (or "portion") supposes that there is a single idea of hospitality that is split into two roles or tasks, which would be deformed if one were missing. Jesus does not begin with what Martha does, but how she does it – that is, the troubled and restless activity, the tense and unsettled mind in the midst of her task(s).

The opposition between multiple concerns and singular attention to the Word of the Lord, between the ephemeral nature of the former and the sustainable fructification of the latter, probably does not form the centre of the scene. This lesson on hospitality shows us that welcoming is, first of all, listening for what comes to light in the words of the one who enters your home, and everything must be in the service of this attention. What is most inapparent, the simple fact of paying attention, turns out to be most decisive, too. After all, who would want someone to care for their hunger and thirst without paying any attention? To nourish someone is, above all, to hear and to listen. To listen is, above all, to respect, even when this respect does not translate into standing to attention.

As profound as this teaching may be, and as long-standing its reverberations and resonances within us are, it does not in any way lend itself to interpretative controversies. How were these pages read in such a way as to give rise over the centuries to diverse interpretations, even going so far as reversing its obvious sense? How do we receive these words that tell us what reception means?

The importance of this scene in the Christian tradition draws, first of all, from its connection, from the time of Origen, with questions taken up again against pagan philosophers, while changing the terms, the meaning, and scope – that is, choosing our way of life. Beyond their respective conduct on that day, when they welcomed Jesus, Martha and Mary become the fundamental figures and types for two possibilities of human existence: the active life and the contemplative life. Ever since, any meditation on action, contemplation, their relation, and their value refers to this page, explaining and justifying itself on this basis. To praise Mary amounts to praise for the contemplative life. To insist upon the inferiority of Martha amounts to insisting upon the subordination of action to contemplation. By contrast, rehabilitating Martha, even against the patent sense of the story, granting her conduct a secret grandeur higher than that of Mary, amounts to placing the active life and its fecundity on the first rank. These are the key stakes at play throughout the rich and extensive diversity of interpretations.

On this basis, the scene depicted comes to concern us directly, the reader enters into the text, and we ourselves also enter into the house of Bethany. Which one are we? Who will we be? Will I be Martha or Mary? *Esto et tu Maria*, writes St Jerome to one of his correspondents, in order to encourage them to give up contemplation.[2] But the question does not pose itself only as a definitive alternative between two ways of life. It can also be formulated in temporal terms. Will I be Martha, first of all, in order to become Mary? Or Mary in order to become Martha? Or, even, can we be Martha and Mary at the same time? This is why St Peter Damian (tenth century), praising the hermetic life, writes that the solitary individual, "rushes forward, full of fervor and desire, toward the great works, whilst being careful not to neglect the small details. Such a life can reclaim the dignity of the two sisters of Lazarus, since, with Mary, seated at the feet of the Lord, she listens to his words, and, with Martha, she makes him taste the varied dishes of her great virtues."[3] When we speak about Martha and Mary, we speak about ourselves and the possibilities latent within our existence. The iconography inscribes the scene within this horizon: to accentuate, as, for example, Vélasquez did, the spatial separation between the two sisters, as between the foreground and a distant background depicts the radicality of the alternative; in contrast, drawing them together, as Vermeer does in his unique biblical tableau, brings to light the fact that these are not always two distinct states but rather the possibility of being otherwise, which offers itself to us at each moment. To this is added the comparison, notably made by St Augustine and St Gregory the Great, with other biblical figures, like the two wives of Jacob, Rachel and Leah, the one beautiful but sterile, the other less attractive but more fruitful. Such connections deepen the richness of the symbolism of these types of life.

Another element that comes to dominance in the West from St Gregory the Great (sixth century) onwards and will be decisive for the entirety of the Middle Ages and beyond, fills this very short story with all kinds of additions and resonances, giving it an almost dreamy, romantic temporal "density." This concerns

---

2. St Jerome, "Letter XXII to Eustochium," in *The Letters of St Jerome*, trans. W. H. Fremantle (London: Aeterna Press, 2016), 36–65.

3. St Peter Damian, *Du desert à l'action*, trans. L.-A. Lassus (Paris: Migne, 1992), 63 [my translation].

a fusion or confusion between the diverse figures of Mary in the Gospels: Mary, sister of Martha and Lazarus, is identified with Mary Magdalene, from whom Jesus chased seven demons (Luke 8) and to whom he appears risen (John 20). This is, in turn, confused with the anonymous sinner who bathed the feet of Jesus with her perfume and tears (Luke 7). Such identifications, which current scholarly interpretation rightly rejects, make these various scenes resonate and reverberate with one another, and forms the weft and weave of an ongoing history. The sister that symbolizes the contemplative life takes on another aspect when the reader thinks this concerns the one for whom much was forgiven because she loved too much! The celebrated Golden Legend of Jacobus de Varagine (tenth century) will synthesize these various perspectives by adding more parts and episodes that will impregnate the story with images and commentaries. Martha and Mary will become the Evangelists of Provence, which will earn them long-lasting devotion! As fragile and questionable as these may be in terms of scriptural support, it remains a source for the production and growth of sense and meaning in this tradition – a meaning which has itself nothing of the absurd.[4]

In the end, the liturgy of the Latin Church, up until Vatican II, read this page from the Gospel during the feast of the Assumption of the Blessed Virgin. This encouraged priests to meditate carefully on this passage, inviting them to pose and compare the incomparable and unique welcome that the Virgin Mary gave, in her body, to Jesus with the welcome and hospitality of Martha and Mary at Bethany. One was read in light of the other. It is thus, if only to cite it, that the admirable meditation of St Bernard of Clairvaux upon the two sisters, which continues throughout the five sermons, was done in this liturgical context.[5]

All of this only serves to highlight the breadth and variety of comments on this simple scene, where, following the famous formula of St Gregory the Great, Scripture seems to grow with those who read it. We will now explore them by following the interpretative choices of the time.

The first approach to this scene can be described as static: it sees in the contrast between Martha and Mary not two possibilities for existence, where each of us could be drawn according to circumstances, but two permanent states of life to which we would always belong. Good, then, is the part of the active, who lives according to Martha; better is the contemplative, who lives according to Mary. Two serious misinterpretations that arise from this reading must, however, be ruled out. In drawing the antithesis of *vita activa* and *vita contemplativa* from philosophy, commentators who see in Martha and Mary these two types

4. For a brief and clear case in point, see V. Saxer's article in *Catholicisme*, vol. VIII, 631–38.
5. St Bernard, *Sermons pour l'année*, trans. P. Y. Emery (Taizé, 1990), 643–81.

do not pour Greek or Roman wine into biblical wine glasses that they would have, first of all, emptied of their content: action is no longer, for them, a part of political life or the magnanimous self-love (*amour-propre*) of the philosopher; it becomes, rather, the love of and *service to the neighbour.* Thus, contemplation is no longer the *theoria* of Aristotle, but rather becomes the obedient listening of the Word of God.[6] It is very much Jesus that Martha and Mary, through action *and* contemplation, both welcome. St John Cassian (fourteenth century) thus writes: "It was to a very holy ministry that Martha devoted herself, since she served the Lord himself and his disciples. However, Mary, attentive only to spiritual doctrine, remained attached at the feet of Jesus, whom she covered with kisses, anointing them with the perfume of a good confession."[7] Cassian can only mix the two scenes together here, namely that of perfume and of Bethany, because he sees in Mary's silent confession of faith before Jesus another form of bathing in perfume, something which is profoundly biblical and has nothing in common with the contemplation of the Greeks. The very nature of "contemplation" is transformed and renewed.

The second false sense drawn from this static interpretation, close to but distinct from the first, consists in forgetting that it does not concern here action and contemplation in general, nor their respective value, but two forms of religious vocation. The future cardinal Newman underlines the point very well in a sermon from 1834 on this scene. Drawing upon many other "static" interpretations, he distinguishes "two categories of Christian: those who resemble Martha and those who resemble Mary," and goes on to say: "both glorify God in their way, either by work or by repose. In both cases, they demonstrate that they do not concern only themselves . . . if they work, it is for Him; if they worship, it is still out of love for Him."[8] In the eyes of Newman, a curious and selfish contemplation would be far less than the humblest service to the neighbour. If they use terms drawn from philosophy, they do not allow themselves to become disoriented; they keep closely to the orientation of Bethlehem and Calvary.

However, if the story is exempt from certain deviations that are wrongly attributed to it, the separation of the part of Martha from the part of Mary into two perfectly distinct ways of life does not come without raising questions and difficulties. In this way, it could be used to show the superiority of orderly over secular lives, monks over people of the world. Commenting on St Luke, St Ambrose of Milan (fourth century), the master of St Augustine, writes:

6. See J. H. Nicolas, *Contemplation et Vie contemplative en christianisme* (Paris-Fribourg, 1980), 331–32.

7. St John Cassian, *Conférences*, vol. I, I, VIII, ed. and trans. Eugène Pichery (Paris, 1955), 86.

8. St John Henry Newman, "The Good Part of Mary," in *Sermons Preached on Various Occasions* (Notre Dame, IN: University of Notre Dame Press, 2008).

"Jesus has many riches and is generous in many ways; thus, the wisest have chosen what they recognize to be first. Elsewhere, the Apostles did not consider it best to abandon the Word of God and serve at tables. (Acts 6:2); but both are works of wisdom, since Stephen was filled with wisdom and chosen as a servant. Therefore, whoever serves obeys the doctor, and the doctor exhorts and animates whoever serves. Since the body of the Church is one, so too are its diverse members; they each need one another."[9] Such a vision, resting upon a division of tasks, talents, and abilities, balances itself out. But it presents a strong shift with regard to the text that supports this vision, since Jesus has not instituted a statutory authority of Mary over Martha, nor said that the former must obey her sister. He only spoke about their conduct before him and their response to the situation that day. As for Newman, there is something embarrassing and troubling in the sermon quoted above when he puts on the side of Mary not only priests, but also children, the elderly, bachelors, etc., that is, anyone who is supposed to have more free time to dedicate to God, in opposition to those who, on the side of Martha, are absorbed in worldly affairs and concerns. It is too much to mix the distinct orders. Mary *has* no free time, she takes it, which is completely different and forms precisely the point of departure for indirect reproaches to Martha.

Can one, indeed must one, be ceaselessly, in whole and part, either Martha or Mary? This will be precisely the topic of debate, primarily concerning the work of monks. A charming and amusing tale about the Desert Fathers (fourth and fifth centuries) puts the problem in the spotlight with simplicity. A passing monk, seeing companions of Abba Silvain at work, opposes their activity with the Word of Christ for the better part that Mary had chosen. The abbot leads the monk into a cell with a book, and the old abbot ensured that the monk was not called for supper. When he emerges from his cell, he is surprised that no one called him to supper. Silvain replied: "Because you are a spiritual man and you do not need food. We, being of the flesh, we want to eat and, because of that, we work. You, you have chosen the best part by reading all day; you do not want to eat food." The monk asked for forgiveness and the old abbot concluded: "in truth, even Mary needed Martha. It is thanks to Martha, indeed, that we can praise Mary."[10] Jesus came to their home, not only to preach but also to be fed and to rest. The complementarity of Martha and Mary may also have a place in each of our lives. However, Silvain's reply must not be understood as a rejection of the preeminence of contemplation, but rather as a criticism of a human, all too human, way of understanding the Word of Jesus. It is through a lack of

9. St Ambrose, *Traité sur L'Évangile de saint Luc*, VII, 86, vol. 2, ed. and trans. by Tissot (Paris: Éditions du Cerf, 1976), 37.

10. Various, *Paroles des anciens. Apophtegmes des Pères du desert* (Paris, 1976), 157.

hospitality that he refers back to the spiritual foundations of this story, along with its diverse aspects.

It is Origen (third century) that historians often credit or reproach for introducing this interpretation of the figures of Martha and Mary as a function of the opposition between *praxis* and *theoria*, action and contemplation. This is at once true and false. True, when Origen writes: "one could admit with verisimilitude that Martha symbolizes action, Mary, contemplation."[11] False, since in this way, and others, Origen is not responsible for the rigid simplifications that later come to be imposed upon his mobile, undulating, and nuanced thought. Let us judge it more carefully. Immediately after the quoted sentence, Origen affirms that "the mystery of charity is taken from the active life, if the teaching and exhortation to action has not been for the purpose of contemplation." He continues, "since action and contemplation do not exist without each other." This expression is elliptical, since Origen, after arguing that action must necessarily be ordered to contemplation, then asserts their inseparability, which suggests that one could also show, which he is not doing here, how contemplation must be translated into action and radiate from it. Whatever the case, it clearly indicates that we must not consider Martha without Mary, nor Mary without Martha. To be ordered to the contemplation of God is what grants action its light, its liberty, its respiration and rhythm: the greatest activity is not confused with the highest charity. But, in an inverse sense, as Henri Crouzel excellently demonstrates, for Origen contemplation, which is biblical, must always flow from words, gestures, and deeds: whoever speaks of God without action does not speak of him in truth.[12] One does not contemplate for oneself alone, like an egoist.

Moreover, Origen's allegory is not static but evolutive, since Martha and Mary represent, first of all, two stages of religious education, two ways of listening to the Word, not two kinds of people. Martha welcomes the Word "in the house that is her soul," while Mary hears the Word "spiritually" by sitting at his feet. Mary is more advanced than Martha in her spiritual progress, but the symbolic value that Origen confers to this act of sitting at the feet of the Word shows that this does not only concern the highest contemplation.[13] Moreover, on the same page Origen proposes no fewer than three successive interpretations of the scene in question, which shows that the opposition between action and contemplation does not, for him, form a unique and exclusive framework for comprehension, contrary to what his critics have said. The second interpretation makes Martha the synagogue and Mary the Church of Nations. Origen, who

11. Origen, *Homélies sur saint Luc*, trad Crouzel et al (Paris: Cerf, 1962), 521.

12. Henri Crouzel, *Origène et la Connaissance mystique* (Bruges, 1961), 434–38.

13. Origen, *Homélies sur saint Luc*, 507, 511.

adopts the long version ("few things are needed, indeed, only one thing"), thus makes of the multiple concerns of Martha the symbol of "numerous ceremonies that require the letter of the Law," and the one thing necessary, the symbol, respectively, of the ten commandments and of the commandment of charity. It is in other contexts that Origen's commentary on Luke can give a more static interpretation of Martha and Mary, seeing, in the first, the figure of the simple Christian and, in the second, the figure of the perfect Christian. But it is clear that one cannot impute a unilateral or "hard" commentary to Origen, no more than one can reject action for the benefit of contemplation.

This is much more the case with other authors in the monastic line, where one can find this disequilibrium. St John Cassian is an eminent example of this kind of interpretation:

> What is, therefore, this unique thing, so incomparably superior to so many and so great goods, that one needs, in order to possess it, to suspect and reject everything? Without any doubt, this excellent part, namely the magnificent and everlasting part, which Mary will prefer to the duties and demands of hospitality, the part which was preached by the Lord. . . . The *theoria*, that is, the contemplation of God – this is the unique, necessary thing, the merit of which surpasses all the merits of holy actions, all the efforts of virtue.[14]

It is striking to note the context for this vibrant elegy to contemplation. Beyond all virtue and all good action, contemplation is, for Cassian, the evangelical pearl that one must gain at all costs. It is a question of determining, in the end, what will have been missing . . . from the apostle Paul! St Paul's apostolic zeal meant that he was gripped by multiple concerns and thus finds himself cast aside, along with Martha's labours, far from Mary, the contemplative. Csanyi ironizes this vision of St Paul, having not chosen the better part, speaking rightly of the "square circle" of this thought, whereby "the works of mercy are the antithesis of love."[15] But, as the following pages will show, such excesses are not common.

If St Augustine resumes the traditional symbolism, which makes Martha the symbol of action and Mary of contemplative life, this is not without making the scene undergo a profoundly original and transformative interpretation.[16]

14. St John Cassian, *Conférences*, vol. III, 141.

15. See Daniel Csanyi, "*Optima pars.* Die Auslegungsgeschichte von Lk 10, 38–42, bei den Kirchenvätern edr ersten vier Jahrhunderte," in *Studia monastica* (Montserrat, 1960), vol. II, 5–78.

16. See A. M. La Bonnardière, "Les deux vies, Marthe et Marie," in *Saint Augustine et la Bible* (Paris, 1986), 411–25.

In contrast to the static interpretation, he substitutes a dynamic and temporal one. What does this mean? Martha and Mary are not figures of two opposed possibilities that are present within life, but the opposition between the present life, which is necessarily active, and the future life, which will be the pure contemplation of God. Mary is kept in the present as a sign of the future, that is, as an eschatological sign: she announces this sign in her silence; she promises and figures, in her action, what we hope for in the life to come. Furthermore, as commentators have noted, this symbolism is not, first of all, individual, as if I had to choose between becoming Martha or becoming Mary, but essentially collective and ecclesial. Martha is the Church of the present, the one which makes its way in time, and Mary figures the Church of Heaven, the one of eternity. "You understand that these two women are the figures of two lives, the laborious life and the tranquil life, the life of turmoil and the life of happiness, the temporal life and the eternal life. Yes, these are two distinct lives: pay more attention to them."[17] This perspective renews the entire discussion.

It is thus that St Augustine does not engage in a dissertation on the respective merits of action and contemplation, which often makes the Gospel story no more than a pretext or a springboard. And when he discusses this problem in *The City of God*, he does not cite this episode. Between the contemplative life, the active life, and the mixed life, that is, composed of the previous two, "each can, without prejudice of faith, choose the one that he or she wants in order to lead his or her life and reach eternal reward, but it is important to consider what he or she preserves by their love for truth, and this of which the demand of charity leads him or her to undo."[18] In other words, action must not make me forget the search for truth, nor contemplation make me forget the needs and interests of other people. This seems to suppose the superiority of the mixed life, but, above all, underlines that no kind of human life is by itself more propitious for salvation than any other (which would be to deny grace). At the same time, St Augustine insists upon the fact that the distinction between Martha and Mary is good and better, not bad and good. This is part of a long line of interpretations, which defend Martha and rehabilitate her against the criticism that appears to emanate from the scene. "The act of Martha is not unworthy in virtue of the fact that Mary could do no better than abstain from taking any action."[19] In the house of Bethany, "there is a place only for two lives, both wholly innocent, both completely laudable: the one by work, the other by leisure, but one and the other

17. St Augustine, *Sermon 104*, trad Humeau, *Les Plus Beaux Sermons de saint Augustin* (Paris: Brepols, 1986), t. II, 147–52.

18. St Augustine, *The City of God*, XIX, 19.

19. St Augustine, *On the Good of Marriage*, VIII, 8.

are exempted from evil, free from laziness . . . there are in this house two lives, and the very source of life [*ipse fons vitae*]."[20] This beautiful expression shows that what is living in Martha and Mary flows from Christ himself.

Martha's life, with her numerous cares and concerns, is the life that we cannot *not* lead here, while the life of Mary is the life that we hope for ourselves at the end of time. This multiplicity is not bad. It pertains to the human condition itself as well as the diversity of tasks that we must assume for the love of another or others. St Augustine sees Martha within us, in whom the future Mary will grow; it is she that each of us will become by the grace of the Lord.

> Could [Martha] be blamed for putting all her joy in hosting such a guest? If she was really wrong, let men leave in this place everything they intended for the relief of the poor, so that they may choose the better part, which cannot be taken from them, so that they may be uniquely and singly attentive to the Word, that they may be left to gain the sweetness of the doctrine, that knowledge of salvation absorb them entirely, that they may not be troubled to know whether someone lacks bread or clothing, if they need to be visited, redeemed, or buried: in short, a cessation in the works of mercy. Let us abandon ourselves to the unique knowledge (*scientia*).

We see the ironic firmness with which St Augustine dismisses any praise of contemplation that would be made at the expense of charity. This general perspective in interpretation means that St Augustine, elsewhere, argues in favour of manual work for monks, as corresponding to a spiritual demand.

It is also on Martha's side that St Augustine, who was certainly a great contemplative and a great mystic, ranks himself. He does so on the basis of his own development, starting from the theme of nourishment: for him, the Word is essential nourishment, something as necessary to life as the needs of the body, which finds a biblical foundation. Martha and Mary in some sense stand on two sides of the table. "Mary abandons herself to the smoothness of the divine Word. Martha has only one concern: how to nourish the Lord; Mary has only one care: how to be nourished by Him. Martha prepares a feast for the Lord; another banquet has already been made and enjoyed by Mary." But at the end of his sermon, St Augustine applies this scene to his situation and that of his audience. The latter, separated, for a time, from the hassles, concerns, and affairs of daily life by the Divine Office, listening attentively to the sermon, are similar to Mary and receive via the mediation of the priest the food that is the Word of

20. St Augustine, *Sermon 104*, 147–52.

Christ. But what does St Augustine do? He is the one who prepares, offers, and serves this supper of the Word. He is, therefore, in his own view, on the side of Martha! That the Word arises from action and the active life, and may be, when it is preached, the part of Martha, poses an important philosophical question to which we will return later.

What authorizes St Augustine to make of Mary's silent listening a symbol of eternal life? His point of support is his own understanding of the Word of Jesus concerning "the better part, which will not be taken from her." He takes it in a strong and coherent sense. It does not signify for him that, since Mary has chosen the better part, there is no place, on that day, for her to be drawn away from him by being invited to help her sister, but that this part is better precisely because it will not be and never will be taken from her. "The Lord did not say that the activity of Martha is a bad part, but that the other part of us is the better one, which will not be withdrawn. Indeed, the part destined to the service of needs, once the need has passed, will be withdrawn. The good action which passes has precisely for recompense the repose which does not pass."[21] This "repose," *quies* or *requies*, is not at all passive nor idle for the thinker of *inquietudo*: it is the act of love embracing what it seeks. Here, Mary begins, therefore, the life of the blessed; she gives us a glimpse at the heavens, a glimpse of eternity. "It is this joy that Mary sat at the feet of the Lord symbolizes in advance, attentive to His Word – that is, free from all activity and entirely oriented toward the Truth, as much as this life permits; enough, however, to prefigure the future reality. Martha, her sister, was absorbed in a necessary activity, assuredly good and useful, but Mary, on the contrary, began to rest in the Word of the Lord." Or, as he writes elsewhere, regarding Martha: "for you, what you have chosen will be taken from you, but it will be for your good, and one will grant you better still. Labour will be taken from you; one will grant you rest and repose. You take still the high seas; your sister is already at port."[22] One sees how much St Augustine magnifies the modest domestic preparations of Martha by comparing them to the perils and fatigues of a grand sea voyage!

Where Origen saw in Mary's posture the sign that her contemplation was only beginning, far from the head and face of the Lord, St Augustine sees, on the contrary, what attracts her to such graces, according to a familiar comparison: "She was sat at the feet of the One who is our head, and the more she lowered and humbled herself in this posture, the more abundantly she received it. Water flows, indeed, into the base of valleys, but they quickly flow from the heights of the hills." We all tend and aspire toward this state of being the unique

21. St Augustine, *The Trinity*, X, 20.
22. St Augustine, *Sermon 104*, 147–52.

receptacle of Mary to the Word, according to St Augustine, throughout our various tasks and cares, which are not, therefore, understood in a pejorative sense.[23] What needs to be underlined in order to conclude, against any possible misunderstanding, is that if Martha signifies the Church in the present and Mary "the same Church, but in future centuries," one must evidently not deduce that, in the eyes of St Augustine, it would neither be possible nor required to contemplate God from now and in this life, but only that this contemplation cannot be the whole or sum, and that charity itself enjoins us often to turn away from it in order to put ourselves at the service of our neighbor. The Martha within us must sometimes reprimand the Mary in us, and one feels, in some pages of the *Confessions*, that this tension has sometimes been difficult or weighty for St Augustine himself, in his life as a Bishop, so busy and called upon by all kinds of tasks. The foretaste that contemplation gives us of eternal life cannot close our eyes and our ears to the calls and demands of the others.

The contemplative torn from his monastery for the arduous and complex duties of his pontifical responsibilities, St Gregory the Great felt deeply this tension. It is thus that at the start of his *Dialogues*, he describes his nostalgia for the contemplative in comparison to his tour, his boat, which would have left the calm and repose of the port in order to be thrown upon the ocean in a full storm. But his interpretation of the scene from Luke's Gospel, and, therefore, his understanding of the relation between action and contemplation is, likewise, in remarkable equilibrium. If he draws a certain number of affirmations from St Augustine, which marked him deeply, he also develops them in his own way, and tends, above all, to set the accent upon the necessary complementarity of Martha and Mary, action and contemplation. Following St Augustine, he insists upon the goodness of the part of Martha: "the Lord did not say that the part chosen by Mary is good, only that it is better, which ought to make us understand that the part of Martha is good,"[24] which clearly rests upon the Latin translation alone. He insists still upon the continuity between present contemplation, even though this may be inchoative and incomplete, and eternal life: "the contemplative life begins here below, in order to be perfected in the celestial kingdom, since the fire of love is set down and taken up here below, but when one sees the One who loves us, he will embrace from then on, the fire!" We are only at the very start of the fire!

But above all, bringing together, like St Augustine, Martha and Mary in comparison to the two wives of Jacob, Rachel and Leah, he opposes them as sterility and fecundity. We are far from the excesses of St John Cassian:

23. St Augustine, *Questiones Evangelicorum*, II, 20.

24. St Gregory the Great, *Homilies on Ezekiel*, vol. 2, II, II, 9.

> . . . the contemplative life is seductive for the heart; but desirous of rest and silence, it does not create sons by words and predication; it sees yet does not give birth; attached to repose, it does not have the desire to gather others together, and feels itself unable to find them in preaching everything that it sees within . . . The active life (on the contrary) is occupied entirely by work, sees badly, but enlightens the heart of the neighbor, sometimes through speech, sometimes by example, sometimes even the desire to imitate; it gives the whole day to numerous sons in view of good actions.

The contemplative life is good in itself, since its object is the highest; it is more noble and more penetrating than the active life, and shares in the freedom of action. But it cannot suffice here below, nor suffice for us, nor suffice for the other.

Thinker of charity, St Gregory the Great affirms that contemplation alone is not enough for salvation: "one can enter the heavenly kingdom without the contemplative life, if one does not neglect to do the good of which one is capable; without the active life, one cannot enter heaven, since one neglects to do good. The active life is, therefore, an obligation, the contemplative life is a choice."[25] We cannot not be Martha; her example necessarily behooves us to do the same. But what is, exactly, this part, and how is it so fecund? "The active life is giving bread to the hungry, instructing the ignorant through the words of wisdom, setting the lost back on the right track . . . giving to each what is useful to them, and providing subsistence to those for whom you are responsible."[26] These are the very words St Thomas Aquinas will cite in his *Summa Theologica* as an authority when he broaches the question of knowing whether to teach the active or the contemplative life.[27] It is a philosophical decision, heavy and pregnant with meaning. If to speak, to teach, and to preach arises from Martha's part, then Mary necessarily has need of Martha, or even to become Martha, on condition that it is worthy to transmit to the other what she herself knows. The beautiful Dominican motto *comtemplata aliis tradere* ("transmit to the other what one contemplates") implies, by this very fact, the complementarity of Martha and Mary. As cognizant as the Greeks were regarding the multiple powers of speech, they had not considered that a man may pass from contemplation to action, from a life of leisure to an active life, simply by teaching others what this contemplation has revealed to him. Speech, even the most spiritual, passes here from the side of *action*. It *is* the essence of action. And one will note

25. St Gregory the Great, *Homilies on Ezekiel*, vol. 1, I, III, 10.
26. St Gregory the Great, *Homilies on Ezekiel*, vol. 2, II, 8.
27. St Thomas Aquinas, *Summa Theologica*, IIa, IIae, ques. 181, art. 3.

that St Gregory does not separate in any way, in our duties of charity, the gift to the other of nourishment of the body and the gift to the other of the Word, itself nourishment.

Wholly in accordance with the order of St Augustine, that is, from action to contemplation, the present life to future life, St Gregory believes that the to-and-fro here from one to the other form of life is the highest and richest.

> The normal order tends to move from the active to the contemplative life, but one needs to know that there is often great profit in relating or drawing together the contemplative life with an active one; the soul, warmed and enflamed thanks to contemplation, will live more perfectly the active life. This active life must therefore be made first to pass to the contemplative life, but the contemplative life must lead us sometimes back to an active one that will render to the other better what the soul has within it.[28]

Throughout these lines can be felt the tension between the two models: the one that affirms clearly the superiority of contemplation, and the one which affirms, as Jérôme Nadal, one of the first of St Ignatius's followers, will do, that action and contemplation must ceaselessly enrich one another; in other words, that the better part is to be at once Martha and Mary, and, therefore, no longer be either Martha or Mary, according to a static interpretation, that is, to consider them as figures of a permanent state of life.

Furthermore, how does St Gregory the Great, who was one of the first thinkers, before followers of Victorinus from the twelfth century, to consider that love itself can be a source of knowledge, how could he insist unilaterally and definitively upon the myopia of Martha (or Leah)? Ludwig Binswanger, psychiatrist and phenomenologist, makes clear what he calls the "anthropological proportion" between horizontality and verticality in our existence: one must not strike higher than one can inhabit, nor hold ideas without any common measure, without any possible means of incarnating them. St Gregory, on his own account, formulated the understanding of the sign of the cross as the "theological proportion," if one dares to say: the horizontal is the extent and measure of love and service to the neighbour (the part of Martha), and the vertical is the height, that is, the knowledge of God (the part of Mary). The one grows in proportion to the other; the more I enlarge myself, the more I elevate myself; the more I love, the more I know: "as much as a soul will have grown to love the neighbor, so much it will show in the knowledge of God."[29] Even though St

28. St Gregory the Great, *Homilies on Ezekiel*, vol. 2, II, II, 11.

29. St Gregory the Great, vol. 2, II, II, 15.

Gregory does not expressly make this point, he assuredly prepares the way for the necessary step of the fusion in us of Martha and Mary. It is often, contrary to a prevailing prejudice, the great contemplatives who make clearest the necessity and grandeur of action. Those who criticize the traditional interpretation of Martha and Mary for being too "philosophical" forget that this tradition has engendered and produced its own correctives.

It is thus that St Teresa of Ávila, founder of a contemplative order if ever there was one, often returns to the episode at Bethany, and always in the same sense: the rehabilitation of Martha against undue or hasty criticisms, the demonstrations show that in our life Martha and Mary can and must be joined and completed. This draws together the perspectives of St Gregory the Great. St Teresa's interpretation of Martha's speech is original. "I sometimes reflect upon the complaint of Martha and say to myself that this holy woman does not complain only to her sister."[30] Her complaint, explains St Teresa, does not arise from her care and worries, but from a belief that she is less loved by Jesus than her sister, who does not seem to be concerned about her. "This appears clearly in the rest of the scene, since she does not address herself to her sister at all. It is to you alone, Lord, that she directs her complaint and her love hardens to the point of asking you why you do not concern yourself with what matters to her. The response you gave to her shows well that her question proceeds from the motif that I will come to speak about." This loving complaint has therefore nothing cantankerous about it, and does not concern domestic matters. The response of Jesus signifies, for St Teresa, that "love alone gives value to things, and the one thing that is necessary; it is that love may be so ardent that nothing can stop it." The mystical life is the freedom of love and love alone.

In states of prayer, writes St Teresa, the will may be "wholly and entirely occupied with God, incapable of leaving itself for another object and applying itself there," but that the other powers of the soul (the understanding and the senses) "remain free to deal with affairs and what concerns the service of God; in the end, Martha and Mary go together [*en fin andan juntas Marta y Maria*]."[31] We are very much, then, one and the other at once. St Teresa says it again elsewhere, commenting on the *Song of Songs*: "in this new state, i.e., where one renounces certain inner delights for the service of the other, Martha and Mary almost always go together, because, during action and in the midst of what appears to be external, inner life remains at work. Moreover, active works, when they arise from so excellent a root, are like beautiful flowers and delicious

30. St Teresa of Ávila, *Exclamations*, 5, *Oeuvres complètes*, vol. 2., trad Carmelites of Paris-Clamart (Paris: Cerf, 1963), 428.

31. St Teresa of Ávila, *Relations spirituelles*, 54. *Oeuvres complètes*, vol. 1, 456.

perfume – they come from the tree of divine love."[32] And humility demands, she says in her *Life of Teresa of Jesus*, "not to want, in the end, to be Mary before having worked with Martha."[33]

The assured discernment of the great St Teresa motivates one to read St Luke's passage (and live according to it!) starting from the central notion of hospitality. In the very last pages of the *Castle of the Soul*, one of the highest treatises of mystical theology, she writes: "believe me, in order to give hospitality to our Lord, in order to keep Him with us, in order to treat and nourish Him as needed, Martha and Mary must join together. And how would Mary, always sat at His feet, manage to feed Him without the help of her sister? But do you know what is her food? It is that, by all means at our disposal, we are being given our souls . . ."[34] One returns to the center of St Augustine's thought: the essential is that the root of our actions is love, and, as for the rest, each must act according to their vocation.

"Let the Master of the house do it," writes again St Teresa. "Therefore, if you contemplate, doing mental or vocal prayer, caring for the sick, serving in the employ of a household, even the most vile, then you are doing nothing else than rendering your duties to the divine Host who comes to dwell within, to eat and relax with us, what does it matter to serve in this way or another?"[35] Hospitality, the welcome of the other, presides above all, and the diversity of vocations is nothing other than the diversity of modes of hospitality rendered to God and to the neighbor, who is the icon of him. St Teresa, who cannot be accused of misunderstanding contemplation, refuses the unilateral interpretation of the "better part" of Mary.[36]

Founder of the Carmelites in France, Cardinal Pierre Bérulle (from the end of the sixteenth to the beginning of the seventeenth century), who was not only a great spiritual thinker, founder of what one might call, rightly or wrongly, the French School, but also a great writer, too much misunderstood, places himself, in his interpretation of the scene from Bethany, in continuity with St Teresa with respect to his praise of Martha. He did, indeed, in his *Oeuvres de piétié*, dedicate a little treatise, less well known and celebrated than his astonishing *Élévation sur sainte Madelaine* (confused, again, with Martha's sister).

Bérulle's Christocentrism means that he interprets Jesus's visit to the home of the two sisters as a true act of foundation: the issue is no longer to scrutinize

---

32. St Teresa of Ávila, *Pensées sur le Cantique*, 7, *Oeuvres complètes*, vol. 2, 406.
33. St Teresa of Ávila, *Ma vie*, 22, *Oeuvres complètes*, vol. 1, 204.
34. St Teresa of Ávila, *Le Château intérieure*, VII, 4, *Oeuvres complètes*, vol. 2, 697.
35. St Teresa of Ávila, *Le Chemin de la perfection*, 17, *Oeuvres complètes*, vol. 2, 314.
36. St Teresa of Ávila, *Le Château intérieure*, 697.

Mary and Martha's response to Jesus, but what in and by them Jesus, in the strict sense, institutes. "You are the Life, Lord, and the author of Life, and you want to establish two kinds of life in Your Church, and we portray them in two sisters, both together holy, venerable, and most signaled in your grace, in your procession, and in your Gospel."[37] One finds again, certainly, the classical distinction between action and contemplation as the affirmation of their complementary and inseparable character, but in a new light. Before Olivier Messiaen and his *Vingt regards sur l'Enfant-Jésus*, Bérulle sees in Martha and Mary two ways of seeing, two modes of attention becoming two lives: "these two sisters honored by their common service of piety towards the same object, that is, towards the same Jesus Christ, teach us that these two lives must be conjoined in charity, one with the other, like twin sisters, and conjoined by an affinity in the same Jesus Christ that the two different lives regard and honor with the same intention and piety, as well as by actions and roles that are very different."

The accent is strongly set on the parity and equal dignity of Martha and Mary: each forms for us a model and a way towards Christ, and it is no longer a matter of knowing which must be preferred to the other. "[He] wants to weave together and give birth from this place [i.e., Bethany] two kinds of life . . . constituting the primacy and domain of one in Martha and the other in Mary. The happy lot of these two sisters, who share life, in order to have welcomed Jesus, who is the Life and a new way of living in the world – divine Life and human life, all together!" Here one can see as much the depth and the originality of Bérulle. Jesus, for him, makes all things new; the incarnation of the Word changes human life. Martha and Mary are not symbols or figures of an active life and a contemplative life, which had previously been the subject of philosophical debate: they are the very place where Christ inaugurates a new sense of action and a new sense of contemplation. "As the Son of God through His coming elevated human nature, he also revealed the roles and actions of human life. The status of the active life is very different after the Son of God came to the world in a way it was not before." The same applies to contemplation. Contemplation and action, for which Jesus is the source, object, and end, are not the same as that of pagan philosophy.

Jesus Christ, says Bérulle, "must be the example that we look at and imitate in these two lives," which was at once active and contemplative. When he washes the feet of his disciples, Jesus is very much on Martha's side, holding her posture. This active Christian life has its first model, before Martha, in the Virgin Mary. This, for Bérulle, marks its dignity. And it is no less mystical than the

37. Pierre de Bérulle, "De sainte Marthe et de la vie active," in *Oeuvres de piété*, vol. 3 (Paris, 1995), 410–16; all quotations are drawn from this passage.

contemplative life, for Bérulle, *a propos* Martha, uses the term *adherence*, which is like his signature: it has "a kind of adherence to and participation in Jesus." For him, "adherence" constitutes an intimate conformation of our being in the incarnate Christ, not in a general and vague way, but, through the active or contemplative state, we participate in something of his life. And Bérulle finally finds the insistence of St Teresa of Ávila on hospitality: Jesus will receive us as we received him (and it is together that Martha and Mary receive him). "Let us house Him and He will house us, and we will house Him in Himself and in His Father." Bérulle goes so far in his claim for the parity of the two sisters that the saying according to which Mary has received the best part ends up fading from his considerations, even if it does not follow, as will be made clearer than others have done, until the perspective is reversed.

As mentioned above, the liturgy of the past chose this page from St Luke as the reading for the feast of the Assumption. The link between the two has nothing to do with the immediately apparent but rather the ingenuity of preachers, who explored this page in such a way as to clarify and bring out this additional textual detail, which has not yet been properly used. The first sentence of the story says that Jesus "entered a village." The word "village" or "town" translates the Greek *kômè*. This was rendered in Latin by the word *castellum*. This is the origin of the word "château" used in the French language, but its common meaning is "village." It can also mean a stronghold or fort, even if this is not the case in the Gospel. But some medieval people understood the term in this way, and took Jesus to be entering a fortress in which the house of Martha and Mary could be found. From then on, a whole network of symbols could be established. The *tertium comparationis* between the reception in Bethany and the Virgin Mary is none other than hospitality: Martha and Mary received Jesus in their home, the Virgin initially received him in her body. Martha and Mary lived in a fortress; the body of the Virgin was a very strongly protected fortress. How was this hospitality our business and concern?

Aelred de Rievaulx (eleventh century), a fine figure of spirituality of English origin, takes this question as his starting point and the central theme of his sermon for the Assumption on Martha and Mary.[38] As much in the life of Jesus as in our lives today, it is not only a question of receiving Christ bodily, but also spiritually. We must, then, here and now, grant hospitality and welcome to Christ, and prepare ourselves for his arrival. Many centuries before Kierkegaard, Aelred criticizes the alleged privilege of contemporaries of Jesus. This preparation consists, according to Aelred, in making our soul a *castellum*, a fortress.

38. Aelred de Rievaulx, "Sermon 19," *Sermons pour l'année*, trad Briey (Oka, Québec: Abbaye cistercienne Notre-Dame-du-Lac, 1999), t. II, 49–61.

This includes a moat, a wall, and a tower. The deep moat is the humility that we reach by confessing our faults and our human frailty. The wall to be built is that of chastity and integrity. As for the tower, the very high tower, it is charity. The "song of the highest tower" is love. These three elements protect each other, and the castle is only strong so long as they are united. It goes without saying that the Virgin Mary shines with these three lights. It is only in such a castle that Jesus can be received in truth.

The "castle of the soul" thus appears long before St Teresa of Ávila. It is interesting to note that the modest home of the two sisters counts among the origins of this castle. In addition to Aelred, both St Bernard of Clairvaux and Meister Eckhart bring into play, albeit in different directions, the same symbolism.[39] In the first sermon he dedicated to this passage from St Luke, Meister Eckhart does not mention Martha and Mary at all, only that Jesus is received by a woman, that the soul must become woman – that is, fertile – and receive him in a strong castle; indeed, through what is highest in ourselves, we must become such a castle. Eckhart develops these two points in a striking and singular manner.

Returning to Aelred de Rievaulx, how does he understand the figures of Martha and Mary? He insists that their hospitality is shared and enacted conjointly, and that it is in their single house that they both receive Jesus together. Neither would suffice alone, neither is sufficient without the other. "Therefore, brothers, as long as Christ is poor, walks on foot, hungers, thirsts, finds Himself tempted, then one and the other of these women must be in the same house, i.e., that both of these activities coexist in the same soul." This permanent peregrination of Jesus clearly extended itself to the members of his body; that is, virtually everyone, as in Pascal's famous phrase that "Jesus will be in agony until the end of the world" and his invitation "not to sleep during this time." Our house, that is, our soul, must always be ready, with its own Martha and Mary. On this point, Aelred joins this scene with the Marian theme, the Virgin Mary set a supreme example, being both the one who served Jesus in body and the one who kept his words in her heart. The liturgical circumstances thus further emphasise the necessary unity of action and contemplation as something we should strive for in our lives.

However, when it comes to the interpretation of the figures of Martha and Mary, the most astonishing thing still awaits us. Not content with rehabilitating Martha against a tradition that sometimes overshadows her for the benefit

39. St Bernard, *Sermons pour l'année*, trans. P. Y. Emery (Taizé, 1990), 643–81; Meister Eckhart, "Sermon 2" (*Intravit Jesus in quoddam castellum*) in *Sermons*, trad Ancelet-Hustache (Paris: Seuil, 1974), t. I, 43–56.

of Mary, or, as many did, place them on the same footing, granting them equal dignity, there are two mystical authors, one well known and the other less so, who have read this passage and turned the obvious meaning upside down. At the cost of a rich and profound meditation, which literally reverse the text, they have concluded that Martha is superior to Mary: it is Martha, against the word of Jesus, who would have received the better part! The two proponents of this reading are Meister Eckhart, in one of his German sermons, and Louis Chardon, Dominican of the seventeenth century, author of a spiritual and literary masterpiece, rediscovered by Abbot Brémond in his *Histoire literature du sentiment religieux en France, La Croix de Jésus*. How is this paradoxical reversal, to say the least, possible? What meaning does it make clear to us?

It must be stated at the outset that there is much more at stake than a simple reversal of the values of action and contemplation: Eckhart and Chardon decipher the attitudes of Martha and of Mary in light of their own spiritual principles, and seek to discern them, as though they were directed by them, in a kind of contemporaneity. Here again, the question is posed: should we be Martha or Mary? But it is taken in a different light. The fusion of Mary of Bethany with Mary Magdalene certainly plays a role, but it is not the most decisive. Eckhart's Sermon 86 is long and sometimes very difficult, but it is possible to identify the main axes.[40] Eckhart, first of all, builds on the difference between the two sisters in terms of their age and life experience. Mary is wholly enjoyment, consolation, and joy as she sits at Christ's feet, drinking in his words. This joy lies in an "inexpressible desire" (*unsprechelfchiu begirde*): she does not know what she desires. But this "je ne sais quoi," which will stand out in the history of spirituality, and then in aesthetics, does not, in Eckhart's mouth, have the value of praise; when he uses the same expressions a little further on, he adds: "we suspect her, dear Mary, to be sitting there more for her own pleasure than for her spiritual benefit."[41]

Eckhart distinguishes here between two pleasures, one according to sensibility, the other according to spirit. In the latter, "the highest peak of the soul is not lowered by pleasure, does not become overwhelmed and drowned in pleasure, but remains powerfully above it," as well as suffering. Mary's danger can be found in becoming absorbed in her desire to the point of extinguishing her freedom. In Eckhart's eyes, it signals the danger for a novice, which contrasts with Martha's maturity: only her "mature age and solid ground [that is, of her

40. Meister Eckhart, "Sermon 86," in *Sermons*, t. III, 472–503.

41. Jean-Louis Chrétien writes in the footnote to this sentence that the French translation chooses to translate the German *Lust* by « plaisir », writing that this "sometimes 'euphemizes' the Eckhartian critique of Mary." For this reason, I have followed the French translation using the English cognate 'pleasure'.

being] exercised to the utmost" means that it seemed to him that activity was not suitable for anyone other than her. She knows the perils that threaten her, the youngest daughter, because of her life experience, "since life gives the noblest one knowledge" (*leben gibet daz edelste bekennen*). How then should we understand her complaint to Jesus?

Here, Eckhart's reading is, as was once said, more admirable than imitable insofar as he takes the opposite view of the text: "Martha does not say this out of discontent. Rather, affection compelled her to do so. We ought to consider her words as affectionate or as gentle teasing." In this disguised form, she expresses her concern for the spiritual future of her sister to Jesus, as amongst adults, in a discrete way. "She is concerned that she might remain in pleasure and not advance." In his response to her, evoking the best part of Mary, which will not be taken away from her, Jesus is actually reassuring her about Mary's future. "Christ thus spoke to Martha, not as a rebuke, but rather gave her a comforting reply that Mary would become as she so desired." Eckhart then reflects on the fact that Jesus, in his reply, repeats Martha's name, taking seriously the act of being named twice by the divine Word. For Eckhart, Jesus's reply is not made in the tone of an admonition, but the mark of the double perfection of Martha, according to the temporal good and the eternal good. Martha's superiority is, therefore, clear in everything: she forms the model for an accomplished spiritual life of the people in contrast to her younger sister! But how should this unusual perspective following Jesus's words – "you are concerned about many things" – be understood? Here again, Eckhart inverts the meaning of the text, even if it is ingenious. *Dû bist sorcsam:* this concern or this care[42] is the mark, not of restless absorption in the small details, but spiritual freedom. "He meant: you are close to things (*dû stâst bî den dingen*), and things are not in you. Those who remain careful are without obstacles in all their activities. Those who are without obstacle do all their works according to the image of the eternal light, and these people are close to things and not absorbed by things [*bî den dingen und niht in den dingen*]."

This beautiful distinction opens up the free space of solicitude that is neither concern nor preoccupation and the space for action that is not businesslike. Inwardly clear, strengthened in a love that does not seek consolation, elevated above what she senses, which does not mean, as Eckhart insists, she feels and experiences nothing. Martha can be with things, with luminous efficiency, without things possessing her and without being swallowed up by them. This is Christian freedom, where action and contemplation, duty and flexibility are

42. The German *sorcsam* is close to the French for "careful" or "thorough" – *soigneux* – but also includes the sense of "vigilance."

tightly bound together. Turning toward what one must do is not the same as being absorbed by them. This is Eckhart's lesson, the validity of which remains distinct from the questionable character of its hermeneutic. This can be entirely supported by St Paul's invitation to "use the world as though not using it" (1 Cor 7). "Martha," writes Eckhart, "was so accomplished that her action did not hinder her: her work and her action led her to eternal beatitude," since "she was separated from things and things were separated from her," as far as she ensured it. This is real separation, which no ivory tower will replace. "Her light is her action, and her action her light." Eckhart adds: "Martha was in a state of mature and solid virtue, with a free spirit that nothing hindered." Her freedom is bathed in the density of the time of life.

Mary does not yet know how to live, does not have this knowledge that comes from life, overwhelmed as she is by joy: "when she sat in joy and gentleness, she was, first of all, at school, and learnt to live." Whatever violence may be done to the text, the sermon is magnificent: Martha is no longer a figure of the active life opposed to contemplative life, she is the unity of action and contemplation in a higher and stronger life than the one that would separate them. But Mary, at the end of the long road that Eckhart took her, will learn how to serve and to deepen her clarity.

As for Louis Chardon, a Dominican, like Eckhart, he considers the scene at Bethany at the end of his sumptuous *Croix de Jésus* via a series of biblical examples intended to show that "crosses [i.e., tests] are more perfect means of union [with God] than consolations." Such examples include Abraham, Elijah, Jacob, and which, after the chapter on Martha and Mary, concludes with "Mary Magdalene alone." The view Chardon takes of Mary, more severe and rougher than Eckhart's, and, furthermore, merged with Magdalene, should not make us forget that it leads to a higher praise. The transition from the two last chapters is clear: "it is time for Magdalene to leave childhood."[43]

Between Martha and Mary, Louis Chardon plays the opposition of their age, but also of their condition, one innocent, the other repentant, and finally sees in it, like Eckhart (and Origen before them, but in reverse), the figures of the beginning and the completion of the spiritual life. The refusal of sentimentality and psychologism, which menaces religious movements at this time, and which eventually culminates, alas, in Jansenism, gives Chardon a very sombre vision of Mary at the feet of Jesus (by making him forget that the Gospel does not specify the mode of her listening, but only says she is listening). "This new convert is full of contentment, sitting at his feet, in rest and deep silence, intoxicated

43. Louis Chardon, *La Croix de Jésus*, ed. Florand (Paris, 1937), III, 30, 543–49; all quotations are drawn from this passage.

by the sweet words from Him, whose words are the happy channels that carry eternal life." That she gorges on these words and becomes drunk on them does not augur well! In addition, Chardon goes on to say, with rare violence (if one remembers that Mary is identified with the repentant sinner in Luke 7!): "this is why Martha is wrapped in her troubles and pains, whilst Mary swims in the pleasures of not having to do anything . . ." And this final touch, which confirms that we are in the *Grand Siècle*: "the most caressed are not always the best loved . . . the sweet treats of the youngest have no weight at all compared with the mores of the one who is more advanced in age, loyalty, and perfection."

Like Eckhart, but with different arguments, Louis Chardon becomes Martha's ardent advocate, and dispels, word by word, in Jesus's speech, anything that might seem to be criticism of her in the narrow sense (yet it is certainly a criticism, albeit affectionate, the only question being what is precisely its object). "The reproach to Martha is harsh only in appearance and, indeed, a powerful act and favour of His love." Jesus begins by repeating her name: "this repetition of a name [is] usually used in Scripture to express tenderness and the strength of the affection of the one who pronounces it." In order to illustrate this point, Chardon gives a series of examples where one could also see the urgency of an appeal. "He says she is full of solicitude: what is there to blame? He adds that she is troubled; but is it not written that the Mother of Jesus had been troubled, and even Jesus Himself had been disturbed?" And finally here is the reversal in the sense and meaning of the many things that concern Martha via a *petition principii*: "the multitude she embraces has more the character of union than of dissipation. She carries on more through drawing things together than through distraction, and makes us see that her charity is greater, more extended, more eminent as she takes, for her principal subject, the unity that joins together divine nature and human nature in a single repository [*suppôt*]."

Beyond the sophistication of some of the arguments, the last phrase indicates the real spiritual foundation of the elegy to Martha. She appears to Chardon as the model of devotion to the Incarnation through her concern for the needs – hunger, thirst, fatigue – that Jesus feels in the only way one can in their body, and by consenting to be separated from him, out of love, in order to go about her business instead of being near him. Martha is sacrificial. "Mary contemplates Jesus in His greatness; but Martha looks at all His greatness in His baseness. Mary rejoices in His bounty; Martha sympathises with His poverty. The one, in loving, does not add anything to the perfections of the Beloved; but the other, by working, relieves the miseries of the Beloved." It is this emphasis on the hunger and distress of the incarnate Word that signals the originality of Chardon with regard to Meister Eckhart. But he joins him in seeing in Martha the unity of action and contemplation: "Martha's love has the advantage that it is not without contemplation, which in this world is for action and must obey charity. . . . Martha, moreover, is not divided in her action and contemplation; one is in accord with the other. Since, if she leaves her contemplation to make herself attentive to her action, she does not leave, however, in any way, the object of her contemplation. If she changes its exercise, she does not change the subject of its exercise."

A first reading of the scene in Bethany can make us see in Mary a more personal and intimate connection to Jesus. Chardon shows that by moving away from Jesus to better serve him, by integrating the absence, and the pain of absence, to love itself, Martha is also an exemplary model and a luminous figure. By putting Martha above Mary, Eckhart and Chardon are not content with a simple reversal of traditional interpretation, as though out of a mere taste for the contrary and paradoxical: they transform the framework of this interpretation, since Martha stops being the role and the symbol of active life and signals now the symbol of the unity between the active and the contemplative life. One need only make a simple effort of translation in order to see that the rupture between them and others is more apparent than real: transposed into usual language, their thesis would be that we ought to be Martha and Mary at the same time; that is, contemplatives in action, which is in line with some of the views of St Teresa of Ávila and St Gregory the Great, to name only a few. The significant difference concerns how they see in Mary the figure of an immature contemplative practice that is still only in its infancy. Lowering esteem for this contemplation is, therefore, not so much to despise it but rather to meditate on its various steps.

At the end of this journey, which is by no means exhaustive but has traced the major interpretative decisions in reading St Luke's scene, several conclusions emerge. The first is a matter of hermeneutics. Seeing how such elevated spirits have drawn various, and sometimes even opposing, meanings from this simple story, one might be tempted towards an interpretative scepticism, as if the text had only been a pretext to affirm decisions about the possibilities for human existence taken before even reading it and that go beyond its content. Fighting back against the use of citations is often a dubious struggle. But this would be to miss the essential point: the diversity of interpretations of this scene, which puts at stake the welcoming of the other and the eminence of the other, can be read as various responses to a call that grips our very existence and troubles it. St Augustine liked to say that Holy Scripture is a mirror which reveals us to ourselves. In order to see ourselves in it, we must also allow ourselves to be worked upon by it, in our own lives, through the questions it asks of us. The tain of this mirror is also something of our flesh. And this page of St Luke cannot be anything other than a question: who will we be, how will we act for the one who comes? How to go before the one who comes? It questions our vocation, and it is only with our vocation, albeit uncertain and trembling, that we respond. By bringing out this dual hospitality, two modes of reception, the page itself opens up a space for play and trouble. All authors agree that there would have been no hospitality if there had only been Mary or Martha. But the lesson needs to be drawn from our own life, and thus brought to our life, in its unity and singularity, with the timbre of its voice and the shape of its hands. By welcoming the other, I reveal who I am and that I, too, am becoming one in truth. Can we not hear the reproach made to Martha as a reminder to her that there is no one way to welcome, that is, his own coming, and that it is wrong to forget that everyone receives with what they are?

The second conclusion is spiritual, and in continuity with the first. By bringing back the terms, certainly of philosophical origin, action and contemplation, the choices of Martha and Mary before Jesus, the Fathers and the mystics certainly did not "Hellenize" the Bible nor compromise faith with purely human knowledge (if there is such a thing). They never lost sight of the fact that this contemplation was a listening to God in his Word, and that this action is service to the neighbour and to God, through the one who is hungry or tired. They do not talk about the contemplation of the laws of the universe or political action. With Martha and Mary, there is a personal relationship to the one who comes, and who only arrives by being received. And this hospitality is not that of a past gathering, something which can no longer be repeated, for Jesus himself tells us (Matt 25) that in receiving or refusing to receive any man in distress or need, it is Jesus whom we welcome or refuse. The ancient Greeks had, in their own way, done the same by making Zeus the protector of foreigners, then, and not only then, without rights, and implying that the stranger knocking at our door is, perhaps, a god in disguise, veiled in anonymity. The greatness of hospitality is also not wanting to know too much about the guest, not to measure in advance the dimensions of his or her being. Let them always remain in some way unknown, so that we allow them the freedom to make themselves known!

Finally, even in a profane and modest way, Martha and Mary are luminous: sometimes one goes to such lengths, as one says in popular French "*en quartre*," in order to receive and satisfy us ("you trouble yourself with many things!"), that we no longer have anyone opposite us, only someone occupied by a series of tasks and concerns which makes us feel as though we might be a burden for the other. St Cyril of Alexandria, though a speculative thinker, drew from this scene the simple lesson that if we receive missionaries of the Word (and what person cannot be himself, if we listen to him?), then a kitchen and a reception, without pomp and luxury, will be, if they are worthy, sufficiently appropriate.[44] To receive is, first of all, to listen. But, inversely, a listening that would like us to talk for hours without troubling to find out whether we are hungry, thirsty, tired, or simply wanting us to be quiet for a little while, would no longer be attentive or hospitable.

It does not suffice to be Martha and Mary. One must be Mary reaching for the best in Martha, Martha reaching for the best in Mary, a listening which acts and hands that listen. The unity of the two does not form the synthesis of two concepts, but the convergence of and encounter with two possibilities for existence, each of which only reaches its full flame by worrying about receiving a scolding from the other. If the one who comes is always to come (*à venir*), then hospitality, with its two faces, two sides, is, likewise, always to come (*à venir*); one must ensure that one is always prepared to receive this visitor, which means that the trouble and pains of hospitality must never be eased.

---

44. St Cyril of Alexandria, *Homélies sur Luc* 69, trad Tonneau (Louvain, France: Secretariat du Corpus Scriptorum Christianorum Orientalium, 1953), 189.

Language

CHAPTER 6

Four Promising Issues for the Future

Reflections on *After Pentecost*

Anthony C. Thiselton

Of all the questions raised in the volume *After Pentecost*, four are among the most urgent, which have still not been adequately answered. What distinguishes the first three of these four is that they pose a dilemma concerning which we may be attracted to both of two opposite points of view. When a dilemma seems insoluble, this may constitute an invitation to proceed to a new stage beyond the dilemma.

First, Raymond Van Leeuwen raised the deeply troubling dilemma which concerns biblical translation. Do we try to remain with the more traditional method of decoding the source language and recoding into the target language by means of as transparent a process of equivalence as would be possible? Or do we succumb to the increasingly fashionable and often insightful method of "functional equivalence," used nowadays by many or perhaps most modern English versions of the Bible? The dilemma is a serious one. I have long wrestled with it, especially when translating for published commentaries. In my case these included 1 Corinthians, Colossians, and in part 2 Corinthians. I am persuaded by many of Van Leeuwen's arguments, but I find myself also admiring some of the renderings in those modern versions of the Bible which appear to follow the method of functional equivalence.

Second, Neil B. MacDonald raises the question of whether Hans Frei's splitting apart the world of literal speech from the referential world of historical reality is always valid. It may seem to be all gain to allow a disjunction between referential discourse and examples of narrative language, such as we find in the

Book of Jonah and in accounts of the sequence of the temptations in the Gospels. Jonah functions primarily but not entirely as satire. The release from bondage to "defend" examples of historical accuracy when the writer may not have intended this is immense. My research into narrative time immediately released me from trying to harmonize the chronology of the temptations in the Synoptic Gospels, and probably from the cleansing of the temple in the Synoptics and John.

This no doubt accounts for the immense popularity of Frei's work, and it has become almost a fashion for biblical scholars to praise it. But in spite of these undoubted positive factors, MacDonald expresses grave reservations about Frei's hermeneutics. His convincing criticisms deserve respect and may serve to slow the disproportionate praise which Frei's work has attracted. Here, again, the invitation to advance beyond the dilemma suggests that further work may be desirable.

Third, the value and limitation of metaphor and symbol is much discussed, but this conversation is still in process. I believe that it requires further progress. Gordon McConville addressed the use of metaphor and symbol in Deuteronomy, and Ian Paul has more broadly addressed the problem of metaphor and exegesis. In my recent book *The Power of Pictures in Christian Thought*, I highly evaluated the use of pictorial, metaphorical, and symbolic language. But I also argued that such language could seduce us and lead us astray. I used various examples from Wittgenstein in philosophy and from early Gnostic texts and some medieval mystics to make this point. This third example is not perhaps a paradox or contradiction, but it does call for careful and balanced judgment, which may not always be apparent in recent arguments.

Fourth, several writers in *After Pentecost* addressed different aspects of speech-act theory, including Kevin Vanhoozer, Dan Stiver, and Nicholas Wolterstorff. Further, related aspects of illocutions emerged in MacDonald's critique of Hans Frei. I have discussed this problem at length in my book *Promise and Prayer: The Biblical Writings in the Light of Speech-Act Theory* (2020). Closely related to this is the further issue of the multidisciplinary nature of hermeneutics. Biblical studies should not be isolated from systematic theology, philosophy, linguistics, and social sciences. These four issues seem to me to invite further exploration and progress.

1. THE DILEMMA POSED BY DIFFERENT METHODS OF BIBLICAL TRANSLATION

Ray Van Leeuwen contributed not only his essay in *After Pentecost* but also his article, "Translation," in *Dictionary for Theological Interpretation of the Bible*, edited by Kevin Vanhoozer. The dilemma of translation faces us almost every day. On the one hand the translations or paraphrases of the NJB and J. B. Phillips may often hold us spellbound. Phillips translates (or paraphrases) Paul's "sentence of death" to "reached the end of our tether" in 2 Corinthians 1:9. On the other hand, the warnings of Van Leeuwen must be heeded. Is querying the spell of "functional equivalence" constructively swimming against the stream? We might feel some anxiety about this, except that wanting to say "yes" to two opposing sides of a debate often marks an advance in thought.

To begin, I select seven points made by Van Leeuwen which I find convincing. (1) He points out that whereas most Muslims and Jews read their holy scriptures in Arabic or Hebrew, the majority of Christians remain content to rely on translations in their mother tongue. Even clergy training colleges are nowadays teaching Hebrew and Greek to fewer and fewer ordinands. The call to use original sources for a needed renewal of preaching is widely ignored, partly for financial reasons. This makes the issue of translation all the more urgent.[1]

(2) Van Leeuwen does not argue that functional equivalence in translation is wrong, but that it should be supplanted by translations which are more transparent and direct.[2]

(3) The functional equivalence method has tended to replace biblical metaphors with abstractions. This is because many biblical metaphors are judged to be part of an ancient culture, so their meaning will not be immediately apparent to many modern readers.

(4) Dynamic or functional equivalence often relies on what H. Paul Grice called conversational implicature. According to this view, the receiver of the translation is expected to possess adequate tacit or implicit contextual and cultural assumptions. This procedure is made explicit by Dan Sperber and Deidre Wilson.[3] This constitutes a major factor, to which we shall return.

(5) Van Leeuwen prefers the term "transparent" to "literal" when we speak of literal rather than functional meaning. The original source language, he says, shines through to the extent permitted by the target language. Admittedly we may need pastors and teachers to assist the process, but God has appointed them for this purpose: "Individualistic reading of the Bible is unbiblical."

(6) The abandonment of biblical metaphors impoverishes translation. Secular traditions need to listen, rather than seeking to master the other.

---

1. Raymond C. Van Leeuwen, "On the Bible: Translation and Hermeneutics," in *After Pentecost: Language and Biblical Interpretation*, SAH Series 2, ed. Craig G. Bartholomew, Colin Greene, and Karl Möller (Grand Rapids: Zondervan, 2001), 284.

2. Van Leeuwen, "On the Bible," 284.

3. Dan Sperber and Deidre Wilson, *Relevance: Communication and Cognition*, 2nd ed. (Oxford: Blackwell, 1995).

Metaphors make us stop and think. For example, we may compare "God is my rock" with "God is my firm support."

(7) Efforts to make the Bible "readable," Van Leeuwen says, "sometimes domesticate and flatten the Bible for an audience of people whose expectations are shaped by TV, pulp fiction, the blandishments of consumerism, remnants of pagan Greek thought in theology, American individualism and the post-Kantian dichotomy of 'facts and values.'"[4]

Van Leeuwen appeals to what I wrote in 1999, "Hermeneutics nourishes respect as respect for the otherness of the Other . . . [citing Gadamer] It is the Other who breaks into my echo-centredness and gives me something to understand." I continued,

> Interpreters conditioned by their own embeddedness in specific times, cultures, and theological or secular traditions need to *listen*, rather than seeking to "master" the Other by netting it within their own prior system of concepts and categories. This premature assimilation of the Other into one's own prior grooves of habituated thought constitutes the "control" and advance commandeering that Gadamer calls "Method."[5]

One major problem concerns implicature. An implicature is a contextual assumption or implication which a speaker or author intended to make known to the hearer or reader. Andrew Goatly discusses metaphor and relevance, concluding after examining examples, "There is some doubt involved in this inferential process; in other words many of the implicatures are very weak."[6] For example, there is uncertainty over which are the relevant contextual assumptions to access, as well as uncertainty about the factuality of the assumptions assessed.

Too many contextual assumptions are derived from cultural assumptions rather than from the context. Goatly comments further, "An important criticism of Relevance Theory is that it is not sufficiently explicit about purpose. Relevance only becomes meaningful if we can decide on the answer to the question 'Relevant to what?'"[7] He gives the further example of trying to explain electricity through water flow: voltage becomes water pressure; resistance the width of the pipe; and amperage the rate of flow. But alongside the similarities between electricity and water flow, dissimilarities should also be stressed. Where

4. Van Leeuwen, "On the Bible," 293.

5. Anthony C. Thiselton, "Communicative Action and Promise in Interdisciplinary, Biblical, and Theological Hermeneutics," in Roger Lundin, Clarence Walhout, and Anthony C. Thiselton, *The Promise of Hermeneutics* (Grand Rapids: Eerdmans, 1999), 133–34 (emphasis original).

6. Andrew Goatly, *The Language of Metaphors* (London: Routledge, 1997), 144.

7. Goatly, *The Language of Metaphors*, 148.

there is a chain of implications the total effect becomes increasingly speculative. Van Leeuwen is right to ask whether these are derived wholly from biblical contexts or sometimes from modern secular culture.

Van Leeuwen is also right to stress the part played by Christian pastors and teachers in shaping this set of assumptions. Goatly calls this "a construction of reality through a categorization entailing the selection of some features as critical and other factors as non-critical."[8] In hermeneutics this might be called preliminary understanding (*Vorverständnis*). Yet Van Leeuwen does not argue for the rejection of so-called functional equivalence, but only for its supplementation by more traditional methods.

Nevertheless, a straightforward comparison between some functional equivalence versions and traditional translations does make us stop and think. Bruce Metzger has selected these samples. The Good News Bible reformulates "anointed my head with oil" (Ps 23:5) as "welcome me as an honored guest." In place of "Thy throne shall be established for ever" (2 Sam 7:16) this version has, "Your dynasty will never end." It even borrows American slang in its effort to render functional equivalence. So it actually has, "She nagged him" (Judg 14:17) and "You smart aleck, you!" (1 Sam 17:28). "For his name's sake" (Ps 23:3) becomes "as he has promised."[9] If we follow functional equivalence, something is missing for mature or informed users of the Bible. Even Sperber and Wilson acknowledge, "Relevance is not just an all-or-none matter but a matter of degree."[10]

2. THE ISSUE OF REFERENCE, ESPECIALLY IN RELATION TO THE WORK OF HANS FREI

Hans Frei has received acclaim as offering a virtual breakthrough in hermeneutics. I suspect that his undoubted popularity is due to his disentangling biblical narrative and extralinguistic reference in a way that allowed interpreters to value biblical narratives without feeling an obligation to defend their historical reliability in all circumstances. In many cases this move is fully justifiable not on the basis of nineteenth century hermeneutics but of rightly more sophisticated narrative theory.

---

8. Goatly, *The Language of Metaphors*, 155.

9. Bruce M. Metzger, *The Bible in Translation: Ancient and English Versions* (Grand Rapids: Baker Academic, 2001), 168.

10. Deidre Wilson and Dan Sperber, "Relevance Theory," in *The Handbook of Pragmatics*, ed. Laurence R. Horn and Gregory L. Ward (Malden, MA: Blackwell, 2004), 608.

In *After Pentecost*, Neil B. MacDonald rightly joined Kevin Vanhoozer in raising questions about Frei's book *The Eclipse of Biblical Narrative: A Study of Eighteenth and Nineteenth Century Hermeneutics* (1974). MacDonald wrote, "In essence I argue that Frei's framework has to be augmented with the illocutionary stance of historical truth-claiming, specifically the concept of belief understood in terms of epistemic stance."[11] In particular, MacDonald queried the alleged contrast between precritical and critical readings of biblical narratives, in which the former read these narratives "literally" as referring to historical occurrences while the latter interpreted them very differently.[12] The logic of the narrative took over from questions of historical extralinguistic reference.

One of the most important advances in narrative theory, which seems to confirm the critical stance, concerns the advance made in our understanding of narrative time. Through the research of Gérard Genette, Wesley Kort, and many others, it became clear that narrative plots often (although certainly not always) revolved around sequences of time which served the purposes of the author rather than astronomical chronology. For example, the use of flashbacks in many detective stories is often necessary. In the biblical writings the Gospel of Mark constitutes a classic example. In the first few chapters events occur very quickly, often introduced by the Greek term *euthus*, frequently translated "immediately." The middle chapters then proceed at a normal pace, while the Passion narrative recounts events in slow motion.[13] Interpreters largely agree that Mark wants to present the events of the cross as the central focus of the Gospel narrative. The sociologist Robert Lauer also points out that "social" time is different from chronological time.

This appreciation of different accounts of time relieves interpreters of having to harmonize, for example, the sequence of the temptations or the cleansing of the temple. It becomes unnecessary to resort to theories about pre-critical interpretation. MacDonald writes, "*Where Frei goes wrong is in his account of the transition from pre-critical to critical biblical hermeneutics* . . . He gets it wrong on the critical period."[14] MacDonald argues that Frei confuses two conceptual categories: "history-likeness" or meaning, and historicity or truth-value. He also appeals to Nicholas Wolterstorff in his *Divine Discourse* on "realistic fiction."

---

11. Neil B. MacDonald, "Illocutionary Stance in Hans Frei's *The Eclipse of Biblical Narrative: An Exercise in Conceptual Redescription and Normative Analysis*," in Bartholomew, Greene, and Möller, *After Pentecost*, 313.

12. Hans Frei, *The Eclipse of Biblical Narrative: A Study in Eighteenth and Nineteenth Century Hermeneutics* (New Haven: Yale, 1974), 2–3.

13. Cf. Wesley A. Kort, *Story, Text, and Scripture: Literary Interests in Biblical Narratives* (University Park, PA: Pennsylvania State University Press, 1988), 44.

14. MacDonald, "Illocutionary Stance," 319 (emphasis original).

MacDonald concludes, "Historical truth-claiming cannot be avoided."[15] He appeals to the theory of knowledge and "basic" beliefs that constitute themes in Reformed epistemology. Frei, he insists, needs a broader conceptual framework than that which he uses.

Referring has a complex history in philosophy and in linguistics. In philosophy it features in Gottlob Frege (reference in contrast to sense), in Bertrand Russell (in his theory of descriptions, denotation, and existential quantifiers), and in P. F. Strawson (in relation to presuppositions). The distinction between sentences and statements plays its part. In linguistics John Lyons discusses reference in relation to synonymy, cognitive and affective meaning, connotation and denotation, definite and indefinite reference, and reference and truth.[16] A discussion of these terms might have taken us further than exploring a supposed gulf between precritical and critical hermeneutics and might have engaged with epistemological issues identified by MacDonald. Paul Ricoeur bridges the difference between philosophy and linguistics, and is more positive than Frei about the relation of reference to truth.[17]

3. THE VALUE AND LIMITATIONS OF METAPHOR

This is the third of the four issues that I am urging needs further attention. It would be odd if I asked us to give more attention to specific issues but was doing nothing about them. Thus, it comes as no surprise to learn that I have written already on the third and fourth issues. On metaphor, I have recently published *The Power of Pictures in Christian Thought: The Use and Abuse of Images in the Bible and Theology*.[18] I shall say more later about the fourth point, speech-act theory.

Meanwhile, in *After Pentecost* J. Gordon McConville has written on metaphor and symbol in Deuteronomy and Ian Paul on metaphor and exegesis. McConville considers the function of kingship, Zion, Horeb, "the place that the Lord shall choose," and land inheritance, together with the narrative metaphors of journey and brotherhood, in the wider canonical setting of Deuteronomy.[19]

15. MacDonald, "Illocutionary Stance," 323.

16. John Lyons, *Introduction to Theoretical Linguistics* (Cambridge: Cambridge University Press, 1968), 424–35; John Lyons, *Semantics*, vol. 1 (Cambridge: Cambridge University Press, 1977), 174–97.

17. Paul Ricoeur, *The Rule of Metaphor: Multi-Disciplinary Studies of the Creation of Meaning in Language* (London: Routledge, 1978), 216–56; Paul Ricoeur, *Hermeneutics and the Human Sciences* (Cambridge: Cambridge University Press, 1981), 287–96.

18. Anthony C. Thiselton, *The Power of Pictures in Christian Thought: The Use and Abuse of Images in the Bible and Theology* (London: SPCK, 2018).

19. J. Gordon McConville, "Metaphor, Symbol, and the Interpretation of Deuteronomy," in Bartholomew, Greene, and Möller, *After Pentecost*, 329–51.

Ian Paul points out how widely biblical writers use metaphor in hymns, songs, and elsewhere. He traces the problems of metaphor in Aristotle and Locke, the creative power of metaphor in Paul Ricoeur, the traditional notions of vehicle and tenor, and interactive metaphor in Max Black. This leads to the notion of "surprise" and "impertinence" as ways of making us think.[20]

In *The Power of Pictures* I first underlined the importance of metaphor for biblical writers. The Old Testament, the Gospels, Paul, and the book of Revelation abound in creative metaphors. Raymond van Leeuwen also made this point. Metaphors give us freshness, intensity, evocative power, and participation.[21] Like symbols, they can also extend meanings beyond cognitive concepts. I considered Bevan, Dillistone, Tracy, and Ricoeur on symbols, just as I considered Lakoff and Johnson; Nietzsche, Derrida, and Locke; and Wheelwright, Black, Barfield, Jüngel, Ricoeur, and Soskice on metaphors. These provide positive evaluations and negative critiques of metaphor.[22]

A fascinating conjunction of the two opposite views comes in the writings of Wittgenstein. In his early work he regarded a proposition as a picture of reality. But he later realized that how we interpret a metaphor or picture depends on the system or frame within which we interpret it. He wrote, "The same thing can come before our minds when we hear the word, and the application will be different."[23] "System" becomes an interpretive frame. Hence, given the right system, we may revel in the power and creativity of metaphor. But within an inappropriate frame metaphor can bring disastrous misunderstanding.

I illustrated the latter from many of the gnostic writings. Bertil Gārtner writes, "[the Gnostics] make irresponsible alterations, rephrasing and rearranging our Lord's words, changing their meaning altogether," while Samuel Laeuchli and Jean Doresse say that they use the words of Jesus but attach a different meaning to them.[24] I also showed how pictures and images could vary in their accuracy and helpfulness in examples from the mediaeval mystics. Today, however, one of the most serious dangers comes from misguided people who claim that God has given them a "picture," from which can arise many misleading directives or applications.[25] On the other hand, we see an abundance of

20. Ian Paul, "Metaphor and Exegesis," in Bartholomew, Greene, and Möller, *After Pentecost*, 387–402.

21. Thiselton, *The Power of Pictures*, 19.

22. Thiselton, *The Power of Pictures*, 39–51.

23. Ludwig Wittgenstein, *Philosophical Investigations* (Oxford: Blackwell, 1958), para. 140; and Ludwig Wittgenstein, *Zettel* (Oxford: Blackwell, 1967), 195, 201, 228.

24. Jean Doresse, *The Secret Books of the Egyptian Gnostics* (London: Hollis & Carter, 1960), 342–43; Bertil Gārtner, *The Theology of the Gospel of Thomas* (London: Collins, 1961), 78; Samuel Laeuchli, *The Language of Faith: An Introduction to the Semantic Dilemma of the Early Church* (London: Epworth Press, 1965), 16, 19

25. Thiselton, *The Power of Pictures*, 195–223.

metaphors and images generated by Old Testament writers, the Gospels, Paul, and Revelation, which, interpreted within the framework of the biblical canon and the cross, are life-giving, creative, and indispensable.[26] We have only to think of God's throne room in the book of Revelation, or the trees that were for the healing of the nations, to see what we should miss without metaphor.

4. THE FRUITFULNESS OF SPEECH-ACT THEORY FOR BIBLICAL INTERPRETATION

Nicholas Wolterstorff contributed "The Promise of Speech-act Theory for Biblical Interpretation" in *After Pentecost*.[27] Here Wolterstorff extends and reapplies what he has said previously about speech acts in his full-length book *Divine Discourse: Philosophical Reflections on the Claim That God Speaks* (1995). The heart of the argument is that illocutionary language exposes the phenomenon of "double-agency discourse" and "deputized discourse."[28] He says, "one person performs some illocutionary act by way of another person performing either some locutionary or some illocutionary act."[29] The respective roles of secretaries and ambassadors are obvious examples. "Paradigmatic cases are those in which one person has been deputized to speak on behalf of another."[30] In the same way God speaks through the variety of different human authors involved in producing the sixty-six books of the canon of Scripture. "God speaks by way of Scripture."[31]

This also provides a way of "breaking out of the sterile impasse," Wolterstorff says, "among defenders of authorial-intention interpretation, of textual-sense interpretation, and of performance interpretation."[32] These two approaches are represented, respectively, by two of the greatest pioneers of hermeneutics, namely Friedrich Schleiermacher and Hans-Georg Gadamer. Thus, a second huge leap forward in hermeneutics is made by this reflection on speech-act theory. Mary Hesse takes this forward in a subsequent essay in the *After Pentecost volume*. The canon of Scripture, Wolterstorff says, provides something like the hermeneutical circle whereby we interpret the parts in the light of the whole, and the whole in

26. Thiselton, *The Power of Pictures*, 69–193.

27. Nicholas Wolterstorff, "The Promise of Speech-act Theory for Biblical Interpretation," in Bartholomew, Greene, and Möller, *After Pentecost*, 73–90.

28. Wolterstorff, "The Promise of Speech-act Theory," 82–85.

29. Wolterstorff, "The Promise of Speech-act Theory," 83.

30. Wolterstorff, "The Promise of Speech-act Theory," 83.

31. Wolterstorff, "The Promise of Speech-act Theory," 84.

32. Wolterstorff, "The Promise of Speech-act Theory," 83.

the light of the parts.[33] Clearly, *Divine Discourse* includes more on the mechanics of speech acts than can be included in an essay. There is much more on "counting as" and counting one act as representing another.

Vanhoozer's essay rightly regards promise as "the paradigmatic speech act," which is a major theme of my book *Promise and Prayer: The Biblical Writings in the Light of Speech-Act Theory*.[34] Most of all, he correctly underlines the concept of the covenant, as I do in my book. Speech acts rest on institutional facts and commitments, which behind God's biblical promise is covenant. Since prayer is also deeply interpersonal, it is good that Vanhoozer also discusses Grice and conversational implicature in the context of communicative action.

Dan Stiver considers the relationship between history and fiction, which offers a further critique of Hans Frei. He then, perhaps surprisingly, attempts to bring together J. L. Austin and Paul Ricoeur from very different traditions. Speech acts, he believes, can facilitate this task.[35]

In *Promise and Prayer*, after an introduction which sets out the importance of God's promise in Paul, Hebrews, Luther, Tyndale, Pannenberg, and Moltmann, I explain prayer as a Trinitarian dialogue initiated by the Holy Spirit and mediated through Christ (Rom 8:26–27). It is marvellous and extraordinary that Almighty God is willing to bind his options by promising to be faithful to his promises. His promise in Scripture rests on the institution of the covenant, as Vanhoozer and John Searle have also argued. If statements simply describe the world, speech acts (including promises) change the world. They constitute an act of commitment; they are performative commissive utterances. God or the speaker "stands behind them." Searle illustrates this point by speaking of a "difference of fit" between words and the world. Assertions merely describe the world; speech acts change the world.

This is a far better explanation than "word magic" to understand why Isaac and Balaam (Gen 27:33, 37; Num 23:20) could not recall their blessings. There was no operative institutional mechanism for doing so, any more than there is a liturgical formula for "I unbaptize you"![36] Moreover, as Austin points out, an implied promise is not explicit. "I will come to you" or "I will be with you" is just as much a promise as "I promise to come to you." God's promises rest on

33. Wolterstorff, "The Promise of Speech-act Theory," 86.

34. Anthony C. Thiselton, *Promise and Prayer: The Biblical Writings in the Light of Speech-Act Theory* (Eugene, OR: Cascade Books, 2020); Kevin J. Vanhoozer, "From Speech Acts to Scripture Acts: The Covenant of Discourse and the Discourse of Covenant," in Bartholomew, Greene, and Möller, *After Pentecost*, 1–49.

35. Dan Stiver, "Ricoeur, Speech-act Theory, and the Gospels as History," in Bartholomew, Greene, and Möller, *After Pentecost*, 62–69.

36. Anthony C. Thiselton, "The Supposed Power of Words in the Biblical Writings," *Journal of Theological Studies* 25 (1974): 283–99.

the covenant. As Walther Eichrodt expresses it, "With this God, men know exactly where they stand; an atmosphere of trust and security is created."[37] I have explored promise not only in Austin and Searle, but also in Zimmerli, von Rad, and others. Austin includes along with promise such terms as "bind myself," "vow," "give my word," and "covenant" as commissives.[38] In biblical literature, Hebrews 6:13, 6:16, 7:21, and 9:15, together with Romans 4:20–21 and Galatians 3:16 and 3:22, are among many references which underline the importance of God's promise. The whole of Paul's argument in Romans 9–11 depends on God's promise.

Promise is clearly a speech act. But what types of prayer can function as speech acts? Part of the problem is that Austin seems to blur the contrast between statements and illocutions by including among speech acts not only commissives, verdictives, exercitives, and behabitives, but also expositives or constatives. I traced the promises of God through the Old and New Testaments and found that they change situations, whether or not they are conditional. Even unfulfilled promises may have fulfilments as yet reserved for the future.

Prayer cannot be a speech act if it is restricted to what Kant called rational prayer – i.e., subjective prayer which Vincent Brümmer calls "therapeutic meditation."[39] Speech acts demand a genuine interaction between two agents, of the kind which Martin Buber called the I-Thou relationship. Donald D. Evans calls active prayer self-involvement. Austin included among his performatives "to apologize" (vaguely parallel with confession of sins), "thanking" (akin to thanksgiving to God), "congratulating" and "blessing" (vaguely akin to adoration or veneration), and even "deploring" (vaguely akin to repenting). Clearly Austin's "behabitives" are not as clear-cut as his commissives. But, as G. J. Warnock has argued, we can distinguish between degrees of strength in different speech acts. Austin's commissives, verdictives, and exercitives, are "strong" compared with his behabitives and expositives.[40]

As we examine the examples of prayers in Genesis, we find that prayers for Hagar's son, Ishmael, and Eliezer's prayer for guidance to find a wife for Isaac both concern changes in specific situations (Gen 21:16 and 24:12–14). The same is true of Jacob and Esau (32:9–12), along with the prayers of Moses in Exodus 32:11–13 and 32:31–32 as well as his prayer for Miriam (Num 12:13). Moses prays for the right leader (Num 27:16–17), and in Judges Gideon (6:22), Manoah (13:8–9), and Samson (16:28) pray, seeking changes in situations. In

37. Walther Eichrodt, *The Theology of the Old Testament*, vol. 1 (London: SCM, 1961), 38.
38. J. L. Austin, *How to Do Things with Words* (Oxford: Clarendon, 1962 and 1970), 156–58.
39. Vincent Brümmer, *What Are We Doing When We Pray?* (Aldershot: Ashgate, 2008), 20–21.
40. Austin, *How to Do Things with Words*, 152–63.

Promise and Prayer, we cited sixteen examples of prayer from Genesis to Isaiah which relate to changes in situations. In addition to these prayers of petition or intercession, we also considered prayers of blessing. Donald Evans argues for these to be regarded as speech acts, even if they are "weaker" than other prayers. Patrick Miller also regards them as "a kind of performative and declarative speech act." At the very least they are not less so than Austin's behabitives (e.g., "I approve") or Evans's self-involving utterances. In Catholic traditions a priestly blessing certainly has illocutionary force.

Searle points out that such institutions as the church, the law, private property, and the state (e.g., declaring war), provide the institutional background for speech acts.[41] In the final chapter of *Promise and Prayer*, I examined developments in speech-act theory in so far as these impinged on biblical interpretation. I discussed Evans, Recanati, Wolterstorff, Vanhoozer, Briggs, Neufeld, White, and Botha. I am especially drawn to Wolterstorff, Briggs, and Neufeld.[42] Briggs applies speech-act theory to forgiveness of sins, to credal confession, and even to teaching. Neufeld uses speech-act theory to bring 1 John to life.

I cannot imagine that very much more need be said about exploring speech-act theory to shed light on biblical interpretation. Nevertheless, new horizons beckon us on. These four issues together may signal where fresh discussion is needed and fresh energies may take us further ahead.

41. John Searle, *Expression and Meaning: Studies in the Theory of Speech Acts* (Cambridge: Cambridge University Press, 1979), 18.

42. Richard S. Briggs, *Words in Action: Speech-Act Theory and Biblical Interpretation* (Edinburgh: T&T Clark, 2001); Dieter Neufeld, *Reconceiving Texts as Speech Acts: An Analysis of 1 John* (Leiden: Brill, 1994).

Ethics

CHAPTER 7

Technology

The Mastery of Human and Non-Human Nature

John Wyatt

INTRODUCTION

We live in confused and confusing times. The threats that face the human race in the third decade of the twenty-first century can appear overwhelming and intractable. Climate change, growing inequality, political polarisation, the rise of totalitarian regimes, and sexual identity politics pose challenges to orthodox biblical theology and ethics. In this chapter I shall focus on one particular ethical challenge which appears to be often overlooked by Christians, that of technology.

There is no doubt that all-pervasive but frequently invisible technology is transforming our world at breakneck speed.[1] The COVID-19 pandemic, in particular, has led to a marked acceleration in the growth, penetration, and power of online technologies across the world. And yet there has been surprisingly little reflection on the biblical and theological implications of the rapid technological advances which are irreversibly changing our human experience. How easily Christians have adapted to the marvels of Zoom and online streaming services, and yet how little serious theological thought has been spent on the deeper implications of this strange new way of living and being!

---

1. For one recent example, see John Wyatt and Stephen Williams, eds., *The Robot Will See You Now: Artificial Intelligence and the Christian Faith* (London: SPCK, 2021).

Oliver O'Donovan is an honourable exception as an influential theologian who has thought deeply about technology from an Augustinian theological perspective. His groundbreaking little book *Begotten or Made?*,[2] published in 1984, is a model of Christian engagement with the complex issues of reproductive technology which were emerging at the time, and remains highly relevant to the technological challenges that we are facing today.

In my work as a Christian paediatrician and ethicist, I have frequently wrestled with the difficulties of applying the biblical text with integrity to the moral complexities raised by advances in biomedical technology.[3] Of course the world of the Bible is unfamiliar with the technological world of late modernity, and the development of biblically informed wisdom which engages with the complexities and ambiguities of our modern age is an essential need. An ecology of theological ethics must contain multiple elements and, of course, Scripture is a central and normative element in such an ecology. The central importance and fruitful contribution of hermeneutics is demonstrated throughout this volume.

In this chapter, as I attempt to reflect on the nature and challenges of modern technology, I will focus mainly on historical and philosophical contributions to an ecology of ethical engagement. In my role as a Christian physician and academic researcher, O'Donovan's insights into the nature of technology and the theological anthropology of his work *Resurrection and Moral Order*,[4] published in 1986, have been profoundly formative. In what follows I will examine how O'Donovan and the philosophers George Grant and Charles Taylor have provided fruitful perspectives which can guide us in developing authentically Christian responses to the strange new world in which we find ourselves.

THE CO-PENETRATION OF KNOWING AND MAKING

The word "technology" is of relatively recent origin, used in the modern sense from the 1860s when the Massachusetts Institute of Technology was formed. What Canadian philosopher George Grant termed "the very American

2. Oliver O'Donovan, *Begotten or Made? Human Procreation and Medical Technique* (Oxford: Oxford University Press, 1984), 3.

3. John Wyatt, *Matters of Life and Death: Human Dilemmas in the Light of the Christian Faith*, 2nd ed. (London: IVP, 2009).

4. Oliver O'Donovan, *Resurrection and Moral Order: An Outline for Evangelical Ethics* (Grand Rapids: Eerdmans, 1986).

neologism" highlights "the idea that modern civilisation is distinguished from all previous civilisations because our activities of knowing and making have been brought together in a way which does not allow the once-clear distinguishing of them. In fact, the coining of the word 'technology' catches the novelty of that co-penetration of knowing and making."[5]

Grant argued that modern technology was not just a more effective form of ancient *techne*. Instead, in its flowering both knowing and making had become intermingled or "co-penetrated" in ways which transformed both activities. As technology advanced in the modern age it provided a new account of what it was both to know and to make. But, the novelty of this situation was hidden from us by the very transformation in knowing which technology brought.

As the familiar aphorism has it, "If you want to understand what water is, don't ask a fish." In the same way, if we want to understand what technology is, don't ask a person whose life is lived within a technological civilization. The metaphor can be pushed further. The only visual perception of reality the fish ever experiences is inextricably altered, refracted, and distorted by the effects of water. It would be simply impossible for a fish to detect the refraction and warping imposed on its vision by water, or to imagine what the world would look like to dwellers on the shore. And so for us moderns too, an accurate perception and undistorted analysis of technology poses unique challenges.

In George Grant's words, "technology is the ontology of the age."[6] In other words, technology is the way being appears to us. But, as we have seen, this means that the historical novelty of technological knowing is hidden from us. As Grant puts it, "We hide the difficulty of thinking that novelty, because in our implied 'histories' it is assumed that we can understand the novelty only from within its own account of knowing, which has itself become a kind of making."[7]

In reflecting on this new way of knowing, Charles Taylor highlights the importance of instrumental reason, which he defines as "the kind of rationality we draw on when we calculate the most economical application of means to a given end."[8] The supreme importance of maximising output for minimum cost becomes an invisible and all-pervasive way of thinking. One illustration of this is in the universally adopted cost-benefit approach for social and healthcare planning. "If we put in a traffic overpass at a cost of X millions, how many lives per year will be saved? Is it cost-effective?" "If we adopt this new medical treatment, what will be the overall economic cost per life-year saved?"

5. George Grant, *Technology and Justice* (Concord, Ontario: Anansi, 1986), 12.
6. Grant, *Technology and Justice*, 32.
7. Grant, *Technology and Justice*, 13.
8. Charles Taylor, *The Malaise of Modernity* (Concord, Ontario: Anansi, 2003), 5.

FRANCIS BACON AND THE MASTERY OF NATURE

Grant characterised the ultimate goal of technology as the mastery of nature – both non-human and human nature. This concept is, of course, often historically traced back to the deeply complex and ambiguous figure of Francis Bacon. Bacon lived on the cusp between the Renaissance and the Enlightenment, during an age in which there was rapid development of machines and inventions which fostered a new sense of humanity's power over nature. Taking the medieval concept of God's two books, the book of Scripture and the book of Nature, Bacon developed a utopian vision of humanity overcoming the miseries of existence exacerbated by the fall in order to recover an Edenic prosperity and well-being for the entire human race.[9]

But in order to persuade Nature (universally conceived of as female) to reveal her secrets, it was necessary to subject her to investigation, which Bacon conceived of in the manner of seventeenth-century judicial investigation, interrogating a witness under duress. Although it seems that he himself did not use the phrases attributed to him, "putting nature on the rack" or "torturing nature to reveal her secrets," there is no doubt that these phrases reflected his underlying guiding metaphor of judicial investigation. It is highly relevant that at the time Francis Bacon was the leader of the feared Star Chamber, the supreme judicial court that met in secret in the Palace of Westminster, which had the power to subject witnesses to torture in order to seek out the truth.

But Bacon's ultimate objective in subjecting Nature to the duress of experimentation was to recover that "dominion over creation" that, he claimed, was always humanity's prerogative. The interpretation of the early Genesis passages was central to Bacon's promotion of the modern scientific method. It is striking that a central argument employed by Bacon to defend humanity's right to exercise a controlling dominion over the rest of creation was Adam's naming of the animals in Genesis 2:19–20. Modern discussion of this crucial passage has drawn out more profound and nuanced implications than a right to coercive domination over the animal kingdom. For example, Jean-Louis Chrétien in his book *The Ark of Speech* argues that naming the animals may be seen as an act of hospitality:

> Much more essential, and worthy of consideration, is the fact that this story makes human speech into the *first ark*. The animals have been gathered for

9. Carolyn Merchant, "The Violence of Impediments: Francis Bacon and the Origins of Experimentation," *Isis* 99 (2008): 731–60.

> human speech and brought together in this speech, which names them long before they are brought together . . . in Noah's ark to be saved from the flood and the destruction it brings.[10]

Quoting Chrétien, Ashford and Bartholomew argue that naming the animals does not place animals as objects within a human-centred world, but protects their God-given identity within the creation.[11]

Bacon, however, chose to interpret the text through the lens of human domination over weaker subjects, of which he was a feared judicial exponent, and his distorted hermeneutic would become highly influential in the thought world of early modernity. The God-given human dominion over creation had been lost at the fall, but it could be recovered through the constraint and "vexation" of Nature by technology. In this way, all humanity could overcome the malign material consequences of the fall. The aim of technology was not mastery for its own sake; it was to "relieve the condition of mankind."

Bacon ushers in a new and characteristically modern perspective in which the goals of technological intervention are no longer the betterment of a few individuals. Now it is the entire world of starving, suffering, and impoverished humanity that comes into view, and what is to be achieved is the betterment of the "condition of mankind." The boundless ambition and utopian dreams that had always motivated a few dreamers were now becoming a sober reality for the new technocrats of the 17th century.

Charles Taylor has emphasised the link between the rise of the new science and what was seen as a practical way to overcome the consequences of the fall. "The thrust behind this new science was not only epistemological but moral."[12] It was a compelling and attractive vision of practical and universal beneficence. As Taylor argues, our modern international campaigns for famine relief or for those affected by climate change are illustrations of how we are all heirs of Bacon's vision. "We have come to accept a universal solidarity today . . . and we accept this under the premise of an active interventionism in nature. We don't accept that people should continue to be potential victims of hurricanes or famines. We think of these as, in principle, preventable evils,"[13] but only through the application of advanced technology. We naturally and

---

10. Jean-Louis Chrétien, *The Ark of Speech*, trans. Andrew Brown, quoted in Bruce R. Ashford and Craig Bartholomew, *The Doctrine of Creation: A Constructive Kuyperian Approach* (Downers Grove: IVP Academic, 2020), 200 (emphasis original).
11. Ashford and Bartholomew, *The Doctrine of Creation*, 200.
12. Taylor, *The Malaise of Modernity*, 104.
13. Taylor, *The Malaise of Modernity*, 104.

unthinkingly turn to technology to overcome the evils with which we are confronted.

This has been very evident in the progression of international responses to the COVID-19 pandemic in 2020–22. As news of the pandemic first broke, the immediate response was to highlight the urgency of finding technological solutions to what was recognised as an existential threat. First, the focus was on obtaining a complete genetic sequence of the novel coronavirus. Then the focus turned to vaccine manufacturers, who used advanced molecular genetic techniques to design and commence production of entirely innovative vaccines. And then the pressing need was to design and carry out double-blind clinical trials in order to demonstrate the safety and efficacy of the vaccines. And, finally, there was the design of a practical vaccination programme that had the potential to reach every person on the planet.

Because of the existential global threat to lives and livelihoods, there was unprecedented international collaboration between scientific investigators, commercial companies, regulators, and governments, all focused on developing and disseminating advanced technological solutions to a very ancient problem – pandemic infections. Here is a very tangible demonstration of the Baconian vision of practical and universal beneficence. And despite the very obvious failures and shortcomings of the international response to the pandemic, the benefits achieved by cutting-edge technology have been spectacular and will continue to save millions of lives into the future.

In my work as a clinical paediatrician over more than twenty-five years, I have observed firsthand the extraordinary power of the application of "instrumental reason" (as defined by Charles Taylor) and biomedical technology in saving the lives of extremely vulnerable and premature newborn infants. When the new discipline of neonatology first came into existence in the 1970s, the survival rate of infants born at less than twenty-eight weeks of gestation was less than 10 percent, and the majority of survivors had severe neurological impairments. Now, the survival rate of the same group of babies is approaching 90 percent, and the large majority of survivors will live normal lives. And this revolution in outcome has been achieved by incremental advances in scientific understanding, preclinical experimentation, and the application of new pharmaceuticals and novel bioengineering technology.

The global impact of healthcare and public health technologies on the lives of children across the world is staggering. According to the WHO, the total number of children under the age of 5 dying across the world has declined from 12.6 million in 1990 to 5.2 million in 2019. Since 1990, the global under-5 mortality rate has dropped by 59 percent, from 93 deaths per 1,000 live births in

1990 to 38 in 2019. This is equivalent to 1 in 11 children dying before reaching age 5 in 1990, compared to 1 in 27 in 2019.[14]

Similar stories can be recounted in terms of combating global famine. It is said that for the first time in the history of the world, food technology has meant that there is now more than enough food being created to satisfy every person on the planet. Tragically, famines still occur in many places, but this is due to human factors such as warfare, insecurity, and mass migrations of refugees, not food insufficiency.

What are we to make of all this from the perspective of the Bible and the Christian faith? It appears that at least some of the works of the kingdom are being carried out across the world as never before; the blind are seeing, the lame are walking, the infected are being healed, and the hungry are being fed. But much of this is being achieved not by the children of the kingdom, but by the technological mastery of nature. And the malign consequences of this form of mastery are also all too evident, not least in climate change.[15] But the response of many to impending climate disaster is to seek further technological solutions. As the ecologist Stewart Brand said, "We are as gods and have to get good at it."[16]

The statement has disturbing resonances to the words of the builders of Babel ". . . let us make a name for ourselves, lest we be dispersed over the face of the whole earth" (Gen 11:4 ESV). Leon Kass, in his monumental reading of Genesis, perceptively comments on this passage that:

> To make a new name for oneself is to remake the meaning of one's life so that it deserves a new name. To change the meaning of human being is to remake the content and character of human life. The city, fully understood, achieves precisely that.[17]

Space does not allow a detailed examination of the early Genesis texts which must be engaged with any biblical hermeneutic of technology. But there is clearly a spectrum of perspectives from the positive tone of the cultural mandates of Genesis 1 and 2 and the patriarch Tubal-cain: "the forger of all instruments of bronze and iron" (Gen 4:22 ESV) through to the fearsome possibilities of

---

14. "Child Mortality and Causes of Death," World Health Organization, 2022, https://www.who.int/data/gho/data/themes/topics/topic-details/GHO/child-mortality-and-causes-of-death.

15. See the penetrating analysis of climate change in Bob Goudzwaard and Craig Bartholomew, *Beyond the Modern Age: An Archaeology of Modern Culture* (Downers Grove: IVP Academic, 2017), 255–73.

16. Stewart Brand, "We Are as Gods and Have to Get Good at It," *Edge*, August 18, 2009, https://www.edge.org/conversation/stewart_brand-we-are-as-gods-and-have-to-get-good-at-it.

17. Leon Kass, *The Beginning of Wisdom* (Chicago: University of Chicago Press, 2003), 231.

Genesis 11:6 (ESV): "Behold, they are one people, and they all have one language, and this is only the beginning of what they will do. And nothing that they propose to do will now be impossible for them." The coming-to-be in the last decade of a unified global language of digital technology suggests that this divine prediction may have new contemporary relevance.

THE MASTERY OF HUMAN NATURE

Technology does not only offer mastery of Nature external to our humanity. A new and potent dream first emerged in the French Enlightenment: the mastering and transformation of human nature through technology. In 1769, Denis Diderot, editor of the *Encyclopédie*, wrote three imaginative essays known as "D'Alembert's Dream,"[18] recounting imaginary dialogues between himself and a few friends. Since science has revealed that the human mind is a product of brain matter, it will become possible for the conscious mind to be deconstructed and manipulated. Science will bring the dead back to life. Animals and machines can be redesigned with greater intelligence, and humanity will be able to redesign itself into a great variety of types "whose changes and whose future and final organic structure it's impossible to predict."[19]

More than 250 years have passed since Diderot's speculations were first published, and it is only in the last few decades that technology has advanced to a level which makes these fantasies start to seem realistic. Indeed, what might be termed "low-tech transhumanism" is becoming a commonplace occurrence within our healthcare systems. Cosmetic surgery, gender-reassignment treatments, and pharmaceutical and neurosurgical modulation of brain function are becoming unexceptional features of the delivery of healthcare, not just in the rich world but in many middle-income countries as well.

Many transhumanists confidently predict that over the remaining years of the century, as pharmacology, artificial intelligence, nanotechnology, and biotechnology converge, human enhancement will become commonplace. Our senses will extend to perceive sights, sounds, and sensations beyond our current abilities. We will remember more of our lives, with greater fidelity. We will master fatigue, arousal, and attention, and give ourselves more working intelligence. We will have greater control over our emotions, and be less subject to depression, compulsion, and mental illness. We will enhance our moral capacities and

18. Denis Diderot, *D'Alembert's Dream and Rammeau's Nephew*, trans. Ian Johnston (Arlington, VA: Richer Resources, 2014).

19. Diderot, *D'Alembert's Dream*, Kindle edition, 320.

diminish antisocial and self-destructive behaviours. Just as Diderot predicted, we will use these technologies to redesign ourselves, our children, and animals into varieties of intelligent life impossible to predict.

This vision of the future, whether regarded with optimism or horror, seems to represent in some sense the apotheosis of the Baconian project. The interpenetration of knowing and making will have achieved technological mastery and re-engineering of our human nature. But how, as biblically informed Christians, can we respond to these developments? Here we turn to the prescient vision of C. S. Lewis.

THE ABOLITION OF MAN

Lewis's seminal short work, *The Abolition of Man*, written in the aftermath of the Second World War, foresaw the ultimate direction of the Baconian project.

> What we call Man's power over nature turns out to be a power exercised by some men over other men with nature as its instrument . . . Man's conquest of nature, if the dreams of some scientific planners are realized, means the rule of a few hundreds of men over billions upon billions of men. . . . Each new power won *by* man is a power *over* man as well. Each advance leaves him weaker as well as stronger. In every victory, besides being the general who triumphs, he is also the prisoner who follows the triumphal car . . . The final stage is come when Man by eugenics, by pre-natal conditioning, and by an education and propaganda based on a perfect applied psychology, has obtained full control over himself. *Human* nature will be the last part of Nature to surrender to Man. The battle will then be won. We shall . . . be henceforth free to make our species whatever we wish it to be. The battle will indeed be won. But who, precisely, will have won it?[20]

Lewis points to the power dynamics that lie behind the attempt to remodel and enhance our human capacities. It is surely no coincidence that the US military is currently the biggest funder of technological research into human enhancement. But Lewis also draws out a fundamental incoherence at the heart of the project to remake our own humanity. When 'I' choose to remodel my own body, precisely who is the agent in this activity? Who is doing the choosing? What is the nature of the 'I' who determines what it is to be human?

---

20. C. S. Lewis, *The Abolition of Man* (New York: Macmillan, 1947), 28 (emphasis original).

TECHNOLOGY AS A WAY OF KNOWING

How has technological mastery of our own human nature become an apparently obvious goal for our scientific endeavours? In *Begotten or Made* Oliver O'Donovan, drawing on Heidegger and Grant, states:

> When every activity is understood as making, then every situation into which we act is seen as a raw material, waiting to have something made out of it. If there is no category in thought for an action which is not artifactual, then there is no restraint in action which can preserve phenomena which are not artificial . . . what marks this culture out . . . is not anything that it does, but what it thinks. It is not 'technological' because its instruments of making are extraordinarily sophisticated . . .[21]

After all, other historic cultures have also constructed artefacts and tools of extraordinary beauty and complexity. O'Donovan argues that what marks out our culture is that ". . . it thinks of everything it does as a form of instrumental making. Politics is talked of as making a better world, love is building a successful relationship."[22]

The force of O'Donovan's argument is that a society which can only think of everything in terms of a project of making or constructing fails to think appropriately about human activities, which are "natural" and non-artefactual. He then employs a delightful and homely illustration of the inescapability of the natural order. However much we

> surround ourselves with our artifacts, banish every bird from the sky and every fish from the river, tidy every blade of grass . . . however blind we may become to the given-ness of the natural order on which our culture is erected, nevertheless, when we take off our clothes to have a bath we confront something as natural, as given, as completely non-artifactual as anything in this universe: we confront our own bodily existence."[23]

I have always loved this image ever since I first read *Begotten or Made* in the 1980s. When most of us lie down in our baths we are thinking "Oh dear, I've put on weight" or "I really must cut my toenails." But the Reverend Professor

21. O'Donovan, *Begotten or Made?*, 3.
22. O'Donovan, *Begotten or Made?*, 3.
23. O'Donovan, *Begotten or Made?*, 5.

is contemplating the mystery of bodily existence . . . and he uses the experience of the bath to remind us that we must cherish the natural order revealed in our bodily structure; we must "defer to its immanent laws" and we must plan our activities in cooperation with those laws.

Stanley Hauerwas reflects a similar attitude of reverence for the human body as it is given to us. He applies this to the relationship between patient and physician based on respect for "the wisdom of the body":

> The best way of thinking about the medical relation is to see it as fundamentally an educational process for both doctor and patient in which each is both teacher and learner. It is from patients that physicians learn the wisdom of the body. Both physicians and patients must learn that each of them is subject to a prior authority – the authority of the body. . . . Medicine thus represents a transcultural practice of learning to live with finitude.[24]

Elsewhere O'Donovan speaks of "a divinely given order of things in which human nature itself is located. . . . The order of things that God has made is there. It is objective and mankind has a place within it. . . . The way the universe is determines how man ought to behave himself in it."[25] God locates human nature within a greater order and makes his image-bearers rational and morally responsible, capable of both understanding and responding freely to God's commands. The concept of a created moral order is central to an authentically biblical worldview. Most secular philosophers adopt some version of "voluntarism"; morality is imposed on reality by the human mind. Ethical values are a human invention, part of human storytelling. But in biblical thought the moral order is a part of objective reality. It is an aspect of the way that the world is made. This, of course, is why the fact/value distinction, so beloved of much contemporary liberal thought, fails to cohere with the orthodox Christian perspective which O'Donovan exegetes. Both "facts" – the physical structure of the universe, including the structures of our embodied humanity, and "values" – the moral order – cohere in an integrated and mutually dependent whole. Since both come ultimately from the mind and intentions of God, the physical structure and the moral order of the cosmos are coherent and interpenetrated.

---

24. Stanley Hauerwas, *Suffering Presence: Theological Reflections on Medicine, the Mentally Handicapped, and the Church* (Edinburgh: T&T Clark, 1988), 48.

25. O'Donovan, *Resurrection and Moral Order*, 16.

RESURRECTION AND MORAL ORDER

Oliver O'Donovan's defence of the goodness of created human nature is not in the last resort based solely upon creation order. He argues that it is the physical resurrection of Jesus that provides the final and irrevocable divine endorsement of human embodiment.

> It might have been possible, we could say, before Christ rose from the dead, for someone to wonder whether creation was a lost cause. If the creature consistently acted to uncreate itself, and with itself to uncreate the rest of creation, did this not mean that God's handiwork was flawed beyond hope of repair? It might have been possible before Christ rose from the dead to answer in good faith, Yes. Before God raised Jesus from the dead, the hope that we call "gnostic," the hope for redemption *from* creation rather than for the redemption *of* creation, might have appeared to be the only possible hope. "But in fact Christ has been raised from the dead . . ." ([1 Cor] 15:20). That fact rules out those other possibilities, for in the second Adam the first is rescued. The deviance of his will, its fateful leaning towards death, has not been allowed to uncreate what God created.[26]

When Christ is raised as a physical, touchable, recognizable human being, God proclaims his vote of confidence, his final Yes to "original model" humanity. Our embodied humanity is not overturned but instead subsumed into a greater and richer reality. In Jesus, the Second Adam, we see both a perfect human being (what the original Adam was meant to be) and the pioneer, the blueprint for a new type of human being, the one in whose likeness a new creation will spring, the first fruits of those who are to come (1 Cor 15:20).

Hence from the perspective of orthodox Trinitarian Christology, we must draw a distinction between mastery of nature in its non-human and human forms. Technological mastery of non-human nature, although it always carries the risk of instrumentalisation and abusive domination of the created order, can play an important role in the fulfillment of our human calling to "subdue nature" for the good of humankind. As we have already seen, technological mastery and the application of instrumental reasoning in healthcare and agriculture have resulted in remarkable improvements in the lives of human beings across the world.

But when it comes to mastery over our own human nature, it can be argued

26. O'Donovan, *Resurrection and Moral Order*, 14 (emphasis original).

that we cross an important Rubicon. However limited and restricted we perceive our embodied humanity to be, it may be argued that a true understanding of the dignity of our humanity expressed in the incarnation and resurrection urges restraint. In effect we say, "We don't need to create a better, stronger, brighter kind of humanity. If this kind of original-model humanity was good enough for Jesus, then it's good enough for us."

FLAWED MASTERPIECES AND THE ETHICS OF ART RESTORATION

I have previously argued that the analogy of art restoration is helpful when it comes to assessing the role and limits of healthcare technology.[27] Each human body can be conceived as a "flawed masterpiece." The original masterpiece, created with such love and embodying such artistry, has become flawed and defaced through the consequences of evil and the fallenness with which it is invaded. The image of God is distorted and partially obscured. But through the imperfections we can still see the outlines of the original masterpiece. What is the responsibility that we owe to this flawed masterpiece? We are to act both as art preservers and restorers. Our duties are to protect flawed masterpieces from further harm, and to attempt to restore them in line with the original artist's intentions.

It is helpful to look at the code of ethics that art restorers operate under. According to the UK Institution of Conservation Guidelines, "Conservation is the means whereby the original and true nature of an artistic object is maintained." The true nature of an object is determined by "evidence of its origins, its original constitution, the materials of which it is composed and information which it may embody as to its maker's intentions and the technology used in its manufacture."[28]

So, when it comes to ethical restoration the intention of the original creator or artist is normative. The restorer must use all the information at his or her disposal – X-ray and photometric analysis, historical records, sophisticated chemical tests, and so on – to determine the object's original "constitution" and to assess what information the object itself embodies regarding the maker's intention. Only when the original creator's intention is revealed can the restorer decide what form of intervention is appropriate. Unethical restoration is the use

27. Wyatt, *Matters of Life and Death*, 98.

28. John Ashley-Smith, "The Ethics of Conservation," in *Care of Collections*, ed. F. Knell (Abingdon: Routledge 1984), quoted in John Wyatt, *Matters of Life and Death*, 99.

of technology to alter, improve, or enhance the appearance of the artistic piece. The ethical restorer must refuse any request to enhance the object, even if it means that valuable business is lost.

Art restorers are not free to change or improve the masterpiece as they like. They are not at liberty to improve on the original by adding an extra bit here or there. The restorer is free only to operate within the parameters fixed by the artist's original intention. Of course, provided they are operating within these constraints, restorers may decide to employ highly artificial and invasive technology. The precise nature and the invasiveness of the procedures are less important than the aims of the restorer: to protect and maintain the "original and true nature of the object."

Similarly, I have argued that the task of the ethical health professional is to protect and restore the masterpieces entrusted to their care, in line with the original creator's intentions.[29] We must use technology in a way which is appropriate to preserve and protect the original design, to maintain and preserve the creation order embodied in the structure of the human body. However tempting it may be, however spectacular the consequences which might result, we must not resort to unethical restoration. We are not free to improve on the fundamental design. The original Creator's intentions are normative.

With each new advance in technology, we have to ask the basic question: "Does the use of this technology allow the artist's intention to be fulfilled, or is it changing the design at a fundamental level?" This analogy, of course, highlights the traditional distinction drawn between restorative and enhancing interventions. It is not possible here to address the many theoretical and practical ethical issues that arise in distinguishing between restorative and enhancing technologies, but these have been addressed in greater detail elsewhere.[30]

We conclude this chapter by considering the role of technology in forming and changing our human future.

FASHIONING THE FUTURE

As we saw earlier, Oliver O'Donovan highlighted that a key mark of our culture is that "it thinks of everything it does as a form of instrumental making." And

29. Wyatt, *Matters of Life and Death*, 99.

30. See Wyatt, *Matters of Life and Death*, chapters 3, 5. See also Gerald McKenny, *Biotechnology, Human Nature, and Christian Ethics* (Cambridge: Cambridge University Press, 2018); Neil Messer, "Human Genetics and Theological Ethics," *The Expository Times*, 124, no. 12: 573–81; and Michael Sandel, *The Case Against Perfection: Ethics in the Age of Genetic Engineering* (Cambridge, MA: Belknap Press of Harvard University Press, 2007).

so the future too is increasingly regarded as an artefact. With our technological mastery we are "fashioning the future." The future is a production created out of the present by human choices and actions. It is constructed brick by brick, as each of us chooses how to act. The future is what we make it. And, of course, this means that we as humans assume a burdensome and "totalistic" responsibility for the future. If at any time we fail and err in our choices and actions, the future may become hopelessly deformed and dystopic.

Oliver O'Donovan contrasts this way of thinking with a traditional understanding of human freedom within the constraints of the created order.

> An action is an event which has a beginning and an end. And when one completes what one is doing one launches it as it were, upon the stream of history. What happens to it then is out of one's own control. Something will happen to it, certainly, and it will make some impact on the future because deeds have extended repercussions, through their chains of consequences. Yet we cannot perform the consequences as one performs the deed itself. They are, as it were, a cargo of unexplored possibilities which one lets the deed slip out from under one's hand, and one must simply entrust one's bark to a course of events which one cannot rule. . . . But to "fashion the future," is to refuse to let one's act go. It is to strive to extend one's control, even to direct the stream of history . . .[31]

So, human freedom is always expressed within the wider context of God's providence, his wise and beneficent rule and ordering of the stream of history. As human beings we are called to employ our technology with wisdom, care, and appropriate restraint, aware of the possible downstream consequences of our actions, but we submit to the wider domain of God's providence; we cannot take on hubristic responsibility for fashioning the future.

This is beautifully illustrated in the creation ordinance of the Sabbath. We are called to work for six days, but our work is not all-consuming. We can dare to rest and celebrate the goodness of creation, knowing that the future will not collapse without us, and in doing so we look forward to the eschatological fulfilment of creation. As O'Donovan puts it, "The sign which celebrates the completeness of creation looks forward also to the fulfilment of history."[32] We are ultimately called to enter the Sabbath rest which God in his creative and providential action has prepared for us.

---

31. O'Donovan, *Begotten or Made?*, 7.
32. O'Donovan, *Resurrection and Moral Order*, 61.

CONCLUSION

We have been reflecting on George Grant's insightful observation that technology represents the co-penetration of knowing and making, orientated towards the mastery of nature – both non-human and human nature. There is a deep ambiguity in technological visions which can be traced all the way back to the thought of Francis Bacon, and beyond that to the first eleven chapters of Genesis. On the one hand there is a compelling vision of employing novel technology in practical and universal beneficence, to "relieve the condition of mankind." On the other hand there is the terrible alternative vision of despotic mastery, which extends to domination of our own human nature – "power exerted by some man over other men." But, as Oliver O'Donovan has emphasised, in the risen Christ we catch a glimpse of an alternative future for embodied humanity. In Jesus, the Second Adam, we see both a perfect "original-model" human being and the pioneer, the blueprint, for a new type of human being, the one from whose likeness a new creation will spring. Redeemed technology has a part to play in the journey to the new heaven and the new earth, but in the end we recognize that the future is not ours to fashion and humanity is not ours to mould to our will. The future lies secure in the providential purposes which God has for the natural order and in our embodied humanity, which is both vindicated and celebrated in the person of the risen Christ.

CHAPTER 8

The Task of Reading the Bible for a Culturally Diverse North American Church

Bo H. Lim

In this essay, I address whether the hermeneutical task as conceived by the contributors to the Scripture and Hermeneutics series, which was published between 2000 and 2007, is adequate to address the needs of a culturally diverse North American church in the twenty-first century. Since this series is primarily devoted to methodological issues, the contributors engaged what they perceived to be the most significant challenges to theological interpretation. I will argue that due to current challenges and opportunities facing the North American church, the theological task of reading Scripture ought to be expanded. By limiting my concerns to North America, I by no means am suggesting that this continent is more important than, or ought to set the agenda for, other regions. It is simply my attempt to identify the needs of my context and acknowledge the significant religious, social, cultural, and political differences among ecclesial communities that span seas and borders. I recognize describing the church as "culturally diverse" is redundant, but I do so because public discourse about Christianity in the US is too often in reference solely to white Christians. I do believe the concerns I raise apply to other contexts, and I leave it to readers to discern how this application happens.

BIBLICAL INTERPRETATION BETWEEN THE TIMES

The gravity of Christianity has shifted from Europe and North America to Africa, Asia, and Latin America. White persons will soon be racial minorities in the US, and these same demographic trends are occurring within US congregations. In response to these changes, models of theological education are undergoing significant rethinking and revisioning as described in many of the volumes in the series Theological Education Between the Times. Amos Yong in his contribution to this series observes, "If the 'browning' of the church across this continent involves not only its ongoing Latinization but also Africanization and Asianization, then the demands for theological education will stretch to include these contextual realities."[1] What is striking about this series is that five of the seven volumes currently in print directly address the task of theological education in nonwhite contexts. Willie Jennings reimagines theological education when it is not centered on the white self-sufficient male; Chloe Sun describes the history and contribution of a US seminary founded to serve the Chinese diaspora; Amos Yong addresses the rise of evangelical and charismatic Christianity in the Global South and East but also within North America; Elizabeth Conde-Frazier narrates the diverse range of theological models and opportunities facing the Latinx church; and Keri Day testifies to her lived experience as a black Pentecostal woman in predominantly white institutions. Recurring themes throughout these volumes are the need for theological education to address the lived experience of women and persons of color; the hegemony of white persons; the unique dynamics in Asian, African, and Latinx Christianity; and the explosive growth of evangelical and charismatic spiritualities. What is noteworthy is that all these authors reside and teach in the US, not in the Global South nor East, highlighting that these are concerns for the Global North and West.

These issues and concerns have been raised in certain sectors of the church and academy for some time, but they were perceived to be marginal to the concerns of Trinitarian and evangelical Christianity in the West. Mainline Protestants affiliated with the ecumenical wing of the World Council of Churches have oriented their theology around postcolonial issues and have foregrounded interfaith, feminist, socioeconomic, political, and sexuality issues in their theology for some time. For decades the Bible has been studied in the academy through the lens of liberation theologies, sociology, cultural and critical studies, literary criticism, postcolonialism, gender and sexuality, and race and

---

1. Amos Yong, *Renewing the Church by the Spirit: Theological Education after Pentecost* (Grand Rapids: Eerdmans, 2020), 28.

ethnic studies. Since it has been almost half a century since the launch of a journal dedicated to such studies – *Semeia* in 1974 – one cannot say that these ideological approaches are new. Most postcolonial interpretations do not possess a commitment to theological orthodoxy or the evangelical witness of the church, use solely humanistic methods, and are suspicious of ecclesial traditions and institutions. Trinitarian and evangelical Christian scholars have largely ignored these studies and approaches because they considered them a threat to their theology and ministerial practice. For example, Anthony Thiselton acknowledges some of the contributions of reader-response theory yet adds, "But I am still doubtful whether a sufficient number of biblical scholars see that the Bible concerns engagement with the Other, and does not constitute primarily a mirror in which the wishes and desires of the self are bounced back, clothed with pseudo-divine authority."[2] He interprets the cessation of the journal *Semeia* in 2002 as the demise of these approaches, when in fact they have simply been absorbed into mainstream biblical studies as evidenced in the recent publication of the article "Multiracial Biblical Studies"[3] in the *Journal of Biblical Literature*, known historically as a journal dedicated to historical criticism.

In the US, the culture wars involving race, gender, sexuality, immigration, the treatment of indigenous populations, and anti-Muslim sentiment are waged not only in the public square but also in the church. Many pastors and church leaders have felt paralyzed due to their inability to engage such matters, resulting in the perception of a church that is impotent or implicated. Many seminaries have responded to this racial crisis by mandating courses on racism in seminary. Keri Day consequently observes, "Requiring courses in race/ethnicity demonstrates that race and racism are *theological* issues. . . . *What good is it to produce leaders for churches, social movements, and other faith communities who can interpret Barth or Tillich but cannot interpret their communities that are plagued by racial anger, frustration, and violence?*"[4] The current cultural crisis has led to a theological crisis, compelling Christian educators to rethink how to train clergy. Seminaries are mandating that reading lists include works authored by women and people of color, calls to "decolonize" one's faith are coming from the mouths of evangelicals, and protests against the underrepresentation and mistreatment of faculty of color are occurring at seminaries and colleges. Students of color and women are accusing white male faculty of reading the Bible, "pri-

---

2. Anthony C. Thiselton, "The Future of Biblical Interpretation and Responsible Plurality in Hermeneutics," in *The Future of Biblical Interpretation: Responsible Plurality in Biblical Hermeneutics*, ed. Stanley E. Porter and Matthew R. Malcolm (Downers Grove: IVP, 2013), 25.

3. Wongi Park, "Multiracial Biblical Studies," *Journal of Biblical Literature* 140, no. 3 (2021): 435–59.

4. Keri Day, *Notes of a Native Daughter: Testifying in Theological Education* (Grand Rapids: Eerdmans, 2021), 53 (emphasis original).

marily [as] a mirror in which the wishes and desires of the [white male] self are bounced back, clothed with pseudo-divine authority."[5] The suspicion Thiselton projects towards reader-response biblical scholarship is now projected towards its traditional forms. Certainly one may view these cultural trends as faddish, ignore them, and choose to focus on traditional forms of theology and biblical interpretation. However, the inability of ministers to address issues of systemic injustice mars the church's public witness, and the continued growth of non-white Christians in the US suggests that addressing ideological concerns will be a necessary aspect of Christian ministry. If the Bible is to bear upon the life of a church intent on ministering to our changing times, its interpreters will need to be conversant with these issues.

Because of its Jewish-Gentile identity, cross-cultural biblical interpretation and theology have been at the heart of the church from its inception.[6] However, within the Christian academy cross-cultural engagement was solely the interest of departments of missiology and intercultural studies until recently. The rapid and exponential growth of Christianity in the Global South and East has led to Christian theologians in every field acknowledging the contributions of Christian scholars in the Majority World. This has led to a proliferation of so-called contextual theologies and forms of contextual biblical interpretation. While I will use the term "contextual" for practical purposes, it is important to acknowledge that it is problematic because its use often assumes Eurocentric models where scholarship is legitimated on its ability to address the intellectual interests and cultural norms of white audiences.[7] A wide range of these contextual theologies exist, ranging from highly sophisticated forms done by academics, grassroots and populist versions that often exist solely in oral traditions, and liberationist forms that arise from scholars, Christians from lower classes, or through a combination of both. The interest in these so-called global theologies and biblical interpretations in both the Majority World and the West has led to the proliferation of contextual interpretations.

Langham Partnership, a ministry begun by John Stott to support the evangelical ministries in the Global South and East, has created a publishing house dedicated to resourcing the Majority World church. The scale of its publications is staggering, having three imprints as well as an additional imprint solely dedicated to African resources, ten series, and texts in multiple languages. At

5. Thiselton, "The Future of Biblical Interpretation," 25.

6. Lamin Sanneh, *Translating the Message: The Missionary Impact on Culture* (Maryknoll: Orbis, 1989), 13–55.

7. Courtney T. Goto, *Taking on Practical Theology: The Idolization of Context and the Hope of Community* (Leiden: Brill, 2018).

the time of this writing, Langham's imprint dedicated to publishing theological monographs contains seventy-two titles, and one-volume commentaries on the entire Bible have been written for Africa, South Asia, Eastern Europe, Latin America, and the Middle East. In addition, five volumes have been written in the Africa Bible Commentary Series and nineteen in the Asia Bible Commentary series. These resources demonstrate the different needs between Christians of color in Western contexts and Christians in the Majority World, although globalization, transnationalism, and immigration to the West make these distinctions fluid. Recent works in mainstream scholarship have begun to incorporate these interpretive approaches as evidenced in two recent textbooks. *Scripture and Its Interpretation: A Global, Ecumenical Introduction to the Bible* includes chapters on African American, Latino/a American, and Asian and Asian American biblical interpretation.[8] A recent textbook introducing the Old Testament adopts the following format for each chapter: Part 1: Introduction; Part 2: Interpretation: Early Christianity, Medieval Christianity, Reformation Christianity, Modern Christianity, and Global Christianity; Part 3: Application.[9] In response to the changing demographics of the church, biblical scholarship has begun to include diverse approaches, but the nature of their contribution remains unclear. Are they included for the sake of representation? Are they an alternative to traditional forms? Are they to challenge traditional scholarship? In such publications, not only does the rubric of "global" interpretation include authors spanning vast differences based on geography and culture, but it includes a myriad of approaches from indigenous, liberationist, postcolonial, and other readings that are oftentimes at odds with each other. Used in this manner, the terminology "global" simply means non-Western, and it is a reminder that theological discourse remains Eurocentric.

THE RISE OF THEOLOGICAL INTERPRETATION OF SCRIPTURE AND THE SCRIPTURE AND HERMENEUTICS SERIES

What is the task of academic biblical interpretation in service for the North American church? For some, the definition of the discipline of biblical studies is obvious. They view biblical studies as a linguistic and historical task aimed

8. Michael J. Gorman, ed., *Scripture and Its Interpretation: A Global Ecumenical Introduction to the Bible* (Grand Rapids: Baker, 2017).

9. Hywel Clifford et al., *Companion to the Old Testament: Introduction, Interpretation, Application* (London: SCM, 2016).

at understanding the ancient texts of the Old and New Testaments. Skills and knowledge required for biblical interpretation include facility with the languages of the Bible and comparative texts, textual criticism, various forms of historical criticism, ancient Near East and Greco-Roman backgrounds, and early Jewish and Christian studies. Within the Western academic tradition biblical studies is a humanistic enterprise, and as such it is not only housed in seminaries and schools of religion or theology, but within colleges of arts of sciences. It is not uncommon for biblical studies professors to have their terminal degree in a discipline other than the Bible itself, such as in Egyptology or classics. Professors of Bible might move between secular and religious universities because their research is not perceived to be ideologically driven. While some of these scholars populate seminaries and train clergy, others teach in departments of history, ancient Near East studies, or classics and contribute to the liberal arts.

Because of Christianity's legacy in Europe and North America, the church and academy have continued to grant the Bible privileged status as both an icon within Western culture and sacred Scripture for Jews and Christians. In a context where the Bible holds religious, cultural, and political influence, biblical scholarship served multiple purposes with varied audiences. It served to nourish the spiritual life of the church, but it also directly or indirectly contributed to various nonreligious functions. For example, Gregory Cuellar observes how the archaeological scholarship of B. F. Westcott and S. R. Driver, based on the artifacts housed in the British Museum, not only advanced their careers but helped establish the academic reputation of the British Museum, which in turn helped legitimate the colonial policies of the British Empire.[10] The fact that the American Academy of Religion continues to hold joint meetings with the Society of Biblical Literature and the recent opening of the supposedly nonsectarian Museum of the Bible in Washington, D.C., both demonstrate the Bible's ongoing cultural influence in North American life. The Bible has held both sacred and secular roles, and therefore biblical studies has similarly served multiple functions.

When forms of biblical scholarship, particularly higher criticism, were perceived as a threat to the sacredness of the Scriptures, Christian and Jewish communities either rejected academic study of the Bible or created sectarian scholarly societies, schools, and publications, many of which continue today. For example, several scholarly societies exist that parallel the Society of Biblical Literature (SBL) in its programming but require all their participants to uphold specific doctrines. In more recent years the SBL has wrestled with its own values

10. Gregory L. Cuéllar, *Empire, the British Museum, and the Making of the Biblical Scholar in the Nineteenth Century* (London: Palgrave Macmillan, 2019).

to be inclusive in its approval of study groups that focus on religious forms of interpretation, such as the Pentecostal, missional, and theological study groups. Some members of the SBL argued that such forms of purportedly sectarian approaches ought to be rejected and the SBL ought to maintain a sole focus on humanistic forms of interpretation such as literary and historical analysis. The problem with this objection is that so many study groups with specific ideological commitments have been approved within the SBL (e.g., feminist, Latinx, postcolonial) that academic biblical study is no longer merely a linguistic, literary, and historical enterprise. In a postmodern context, the lines between ideology, theology, confessionalism, and sectarianism are more difficult to draw. If the SBL is going to accept ideological approaches, it must also accept theological ones.

It is against this cultural and historic backdrop that the discipline of theological interpretation of Scripture (TIS) emerged. The discipline is primarily populated by English-speaking scholars from the UK, Australia, New Zealand, Canada, and the US. Catholic, Eastern Orthodox, Protestant, and Jewish scholars have sought to decenter Scripture study from historic concerns to theological foci and employ the resources of Christian and Jewish religious traditions rather than solely the tools of historical criticism. Scholars retrieved the rule of faith, a set of theological commitments that centered, unified, and bounded Christian belief and practice. These commitments determined biblical interpretation until the sixteenth century, and TIS seeks to revive these hermeneutical principles to read Scripture for the church today.

Theologians had never abandoned the Bible, nor had biblical scholars ever completely eschewed theology in modernity, but the novelty of TIS was its claim as a legitimate academic discipline. For some, TIS posed a threat to delegitimize biblical studies' claim to be nonsectarian within the secular academy. Some worried that calling attention to the Bible's religious claims might awaken people to question the Bible's privileged cultural status, and others fretted that such a hermeneutic would jeopardize what they deemed to be the objective results of biblical scholarship. Some accused TIS as an attempt to insulate the Bible from critique, whether in the form of historical or ideological criticism, and to privilege certain religious groups as interpreters of the Bible. Practitioners of TIS claim that theological interpretation is an attempt to retrieve biblical interpretation for the sake of the church, and implied in such statements is the belief that Bible scholars have too long attended to the agenda of the academy. Theologians have welcomed the opportunity to engage in biblical interpretation, as demonstrated by the proliferation of theological commentaries, and biblical scholars have enjoyed the freedom to be overt about their faith assumptions. It seems the jury is still out whether clergy and congregations will benefit more from the contributions of TIS than from traditional forms of biblical scholarship.

It is against this cultural backdrop that the Scripture and Hermeneutics (SAH) Series was conceived and written. I will not attempt to provide a comprehensive overview or critique of the eight volumes in this series, but I wish to sketch in broad outlines how the editors and authors conceived of the task of TIS. Of the eight volumes in the SAH Series, six works were devoted to methodology and two volumes were constructive works, one on reading the Gospel of Luke and the other on engaging the political theology of Oliver O'Donovan. The very first volume, titled *Renewing Biblical Interpretation*, provided the framework for subsequent volumes. In its introduction, understandings of historical, literary, and theological issues were identified as the three key elements necessary for a theologically informed model of biblical hermeneutics. Craig Bartholomew argued that biblical interpretation was shaped by philosophy, so the philosophy of history, literature, and theology had to be engaged to define and determine a theological hermeneutic for Scripture.[11] Of the ten essays in the initial volume, four were devoted to history, four addressed literature, and two were focused on theology. While the volumes in the series are not neatly divided into the categories of history, literature, and theology, one can observe from the series' topics and titles that these elements shape the series as a whole:

Vol. 1 *Renewing Biblical Interpretation*
Vol. 2 *After Pentecost: Language and Biblical Interpretation*
Vol. 3 *A Royal Priesthood? The Use of the Bible Ethically and Politically: A Dialogue with Oliver O'Donovan*
Vol. 4 *"Behind" the Text: History and Biblical Interpretation*
Vol. 5 *Out of Egypt: Biblical Theology and Biblical Interpretation*
Vol. 6 *Reading Luke: Interpretation, Reflection, Formation*
Vol. 7 *Canon and Biblical Interpretation*
Vol. 8 *The Bible and the University*

The SAH Series was written to respond to the intellectual challenges of modernity and postmodernity. Historical criticism was the legacy of modernity and it continued to confine the Bible to the past, while the danger postmodernity posed to the Bible was "to make it so contemporary that all we hear are the echoes of our own voices."[12] Clearly Trinitarian theology and evangelical witness

11. Craig G. Bartholomew, "Introduction," in *Renewing Biblical Interpretation*, SAH Series 1, ed. Craig Bartholomew, Colin Green, and Karl Möller (Grand Rapids: Zondervan, 2000), xxvii.

12. Bartholomew, "Introduction," xxv.

were ongoing concerns for all the series' contributors. Whereas the purported objectivity that historical criticism assumed rendered the Bible irrelevant for the present, the rampant subjectivity of the current contemporary scene threatened the church's ability to hear God's word among a multitude of contemporary interpretations. The SAH Series was written in a moment of significant cultural and intellectual transition and was intended to address vital issues of the past, present, and future. Regarding diversity, few women and persons of color contributed essays throughout the entire eight volumes. Three essays in the series were devoted to missional hermeneutics. One of these appeared in the introductory volume, in which Harry Beeby wrote, "Missionaries and evangelists have used the Bible with a missionary understanding but missionary hermeneutics seem to have little if any place in the publication of biblical scholars. This I find disturbing."[13] It seems Beeby's concerns for a missional hermeneutic, which has been defined by James Brownson as multicultural interpretation,[14] was considered of marginal importance to the series.

THE FUTURE OF THEOLOGICAL INTERPRETATION

I have taken time to provide a sketch of the SAH Series, since this edited volume functions as a retrospect and prospect. I write to address the question, "Should theological hermeneutics continue to be primarily focused on the topics of history, literature, and theology?" I propose that if theological interpretation is to equip ministers of the gospel, then its hermeneutical and theological foci must broaden. If the church is *semper reformanda* and biblical and theological interpretation is to serve the church, then biblical and theological studies too must be *semper reformanda*. I am in no way suggesting that TIS scholarship be displaced by contextual interpretation. Rather, I am arguing for more reflexive discourse between the two so that they might mutually benefit and be transformed through the interchange.

I acknowledge that the interchange that I propose involves risk. Both the church and academy share an anxiety over the fragmentation of biblical interpretation should the various contexts or communities of interpretation become too numerous or narrowly defined. While diversity is valued in Christianity, too much of it threatens the Church's catholicity. Should biblical readings become

13. H. D. Beeby, "A Missional Approach to Renewed Interpretation," in Bartholomew, Greene, and Möller, *Renewing Biblical Interpretation*, 282.

14. James V. Brownson, *Speaking the Truth in Love: New Testament Resources for a Missional Hermeneutic* (Harrisburg, PA: Trinity Press International, 1998), 22.

too disparate in the academy, the definition of biblical studies as a discipline may become incoherent. Stephen Moore and Yvonne Sherwood observe that even R. S. Sugirtharajah, a champion for diverse contextual readings of the Bible, laments:

> While identity hermeneutics has allowed people to empathize with social movements which try to rectify the injustices of the past, the obsessive focus on narrow identity issues may result in the neglect of shared values. . . . One needs to be alert to the likely adverse consequences of the splintering of marginal hermeneutics. It is unlikely that such a fragmented status will radically trouble mainstream biblical study.[15]

What is revealing in Sugirtharajah's comment is what many Christian scholars suspected; that is, the motive behind diverse and contextual readings is to decenter mainstream scholarship from its privileged status. Sugirtharajah acknowledges that identity politics animated and motivated these readings, yet also laments that if this is taken too far the discipline itself will dissipate. While his concerns are academic, it is fair to say similar forms of identity politics are operative in the church. As acknowledged above, an overemphasis on cultural difference and social identity can threaten the unity of the church and lead to sectarianism. Thus, how one responds to the diversity within the church and how Christians are to engage diversity in the culture are some of the most pressing theological tasks facing the church today. Cultural diversity and catholicity have been theological and pastoral issues from the church's inception, and so engaging diverse biblical interpretation ought not to be perceived as something peripheral or *avant garde* for theologians. If the cacophony of Pentecost did not deter the apostles from ministering to people from every nation, theologians today who confess to believe in one, holy, catholic, and apostolic church ought to follow suit.

Trinitarian and evangelical scholars have been open to diverse forms of intercultural and missional interpretation, indigenous forms of biblical interpretation, and some evangelical forms of liberationist interpretation, but by and large they are wary of postcolonial theologies and interpretations.[16] For

---

15. R. S. Sugirtharajah, "Muddling Along at the Margins," in R. S. Sugirtharajah, *Still at the Margins: Biblical Scholarship Fifteen Years after the Voices from the Margin* (London: T&T Clark, 2008), 11, as quoted in Stephen D. Moore and Yvonne Sherwood, *The Invention of the Biblical Scholar: A Critical Manifesto* (Minneapolis: Fortress, 2011), 120.

16. An exception would be Kay Higuera Smith, Jayachitra Lalitha, and L. Daniel Hawk, eds., *Evangelical Postcolonial Conversations: Global Awakenings in Theology and Praxis* (Downers Grove: IVP, 2014).

example, *Scripture and Its Interpretation* lacks any chapters dedicated to liberationist or postcolonial interpretation.[17] These methods are contested because, for some postcolonial scholars such as Sugirtharajah, "the Bible itself is part of the conundrum rather than a panacea for all the ills of the postmodern/postcolonial world."[18] Trinitarian and evangelical communities will acknowledge problematic readings of the Bible, but typically will not problematize the Bible itself. The question to be asked is whether all forms of postcolonial or decolonial study ought to be rejected. Robert Romero observes that Latina/o Christians have engaged in decolonial and culturally contextualized self-reflection since the 1960s.[19] He, along with countless other theologians of color and women, finds it necessary to engage critical studies and contextual theologies due to the church's entanglements with slavery, racism, sexism, and the oppression of indigenous populations. Doing so results in tensions for Christians who hold to orthodox teachings and identify with evangelical and charismatic movements. It is no secret that sectors of the academy are suspicious of the church and vice versa. While some white male theologians may consider engagement with critical studies and contextual theologies as marginal to their personal and professional lives, for many women and theologians of color these issues are front and center for their identities and vocations, particularly when they live and work in predominantly white contexts.

Theological interpretation has also helped fuel the renewed interest in the Bible's reception within the church. TIS scholars acknowledge that the church read the Bible christocentrically, figurally, and sacramentally until modernity, and argue that we ought to recover such readings rather than allow historical criticism to dictate Scriptural study. Often neglected in this retrieval of the church's tradition is the attention given by past interpreters to apologetic issues. Many of the church's critics raised historical or textual difficulties, but much of the criticism leveled against the Bible was regarding moral and ethical matters. Moore and Sherwood offer the reminder that early in the Enlightenment the primary objection to the Bible was moral, but historical and scientific questions would go on to dominate biblical study for the next several centuries.[20] Ethical objections to the Bible's teachings resurfaced at the end of the twentieth and beginning of the twenty-first centuries in the form of ideological criticism.

---

17. It ought to be noted that liberationist and postcolonial forms of biblical interpretation are addressed in various chapters.

18. R. S. Sugirtharajah, *Postcolonial Criticism and Biblical Interpretation* (New York: Oxford University Press, 2002), 100.

19. Robert Chao Romero, *Brown Church: Five Centuries of Latina/o Social Justice, Theology, and Identity* (Downers Grove: IVP, 2020).

20. Moore and Sherwood, *The Invention of the Biblical Scholar*, 49–64.

Theological interpreters must return to the church's historic task of addressing these ethical and ideological concerns rather than focus solely on historical or scientific objections.[21]

Those engaged in theological interpretation and biblical scholarship from Trinitarian and evangelical perspectives have increasingly acknowledged the importance of diverse readings of Scripture.[22] While white scholars recognize their theological contribution, they have produced few examples themselves. They have extensively written on the methodology of biblical and theological interpretation regarding historical, literary, and theological matters, but very little has been done on the topic of cultural diversity. Darren Sarisky, in his recent work on theological interpretation, observes that the lacuna in TIS scholarship has been theological reflection on reading and readers. He writes, "The hermeneutic proposed here assumed that it is neither actually possible nor genuinely desirable for readers 'to strip off all our particularities – particularities of gender, race, nationality, religion, social class, age – and enter [upon proper inquiry] purely as normal adult human beings.'"[23] So, while in theory diverse contextual interpretation is the domain of TIS, the practice of it has not lived up to its claims. In the remainder of this essay, I will begin to explore what a methodology for reading the Bible theologically in diverse cultural contexts might look like.[24]

A PROPOSAL FOR THEOLOGICAL AND CONTEXTUAL INTERPRETATION OF SCRIPTURE

In a recent essay within an edited volume devoted to the topics of Scripture, theology, and culture, Joel Green outlines the three most dominant models of engagement between the ancient biblical text and the contemporary context.[25] In what he deems the "scientific frame," the historical study of the biblical

21. John L. Thompson, *Reading the Bible with the Dead* (Grand Rapids: Eerdmans, 2007), is one of the few works on the history of reception that engages contemporary ideological criticism.

22. See Bo H. Lim, "Critical Methods and Critiques: Theological Interpretation," in *The T&T Clark Handbook to Asian American Biblical Hermeneutics*, ed. Uriah Y. Kim and Seung Ai Yang (New York: T&T Clark, 2019), 141–59.

23. Darren Sarisky, *Reading the Bible Theologically*, Current Issues in Theology 13 (Cambridge: Cambridge University Press, 2019), 188–89, quoting Nicholas Wolterstorff, "The Travail of Theology in the Modern Academy," in *The Future of Theology: Essays in Honor of Jürgen Moltmann*, ed. Miroslav Volf, Carmen Krieg, and Thomas Dörken-Kucharz (Grand Rapids: Eerdmans, 1996), 38.

24. See also my proposal in Lim, "Critical Methods and Critiques," 141–59.

25. Joel B. Green, "A Discursive Frame for Reading Scripture," in *Acts of Interpretation: Scripture, Theology, and Culture*, ed. S. A. Cummins and Jens Zimmermann (Grand Rapids: Eerdmans, 2018), 46–62.

text is so prioritized that little concern is given to the significance of the Bible for today. In the "contextual frame" serious attention is given to understand the Bible's message in its ancient context, and once that is determined its relevance for modern life is explored. Green criticizes the "scientific frame" for leaving the Bible in the past and the "contextual frame" for failing to take into consideration all that modern readers bring to the interpretive process. He then proposes a "discursive frame" where readers acknowledge the questions and assumptions they bring to the text and a circular dialogue is created between texts and readers. In the first model no path exists between ancient text and modern reader; the second model provides only a one-way street; and in the third model the communication travels in both directions. Theological interpretation has been forthright in acknowledging its ecclesial location and interests in this two-way engagement with the Scriptures. If Green's "discourse frame" is a model for TIS, then reading the Bible theologically for diverse ecclesial communities begins by intentionally and explicitly naming the unique cultural characteristics and interests of communities of faith. What makes these readings theological is that they are practiced by communities *of faith*, so various critical and cultural interpretations of the Bible are read along with the church's tradition.

While Green and other TIS scholars affirm a discursive methodology, very few examples of its practice for diverse ecclesial communities of faith exist. The question remains, what would it look like for communities of faith that are underrepresented in the academy to read the Bible theologically? I consider the recent work *God, Sexuality, and the Self* by Sarah Coakley to provide a theological model for reading the Bible for diverse communities. Her theological methods are traditional, as she views Trinitarian doctrines emerging "in primary interaction with Scripture, become intensified and contested in early Christian tradition, and are purified in the crucible of prayer."[26] Like many TIS scholars who argue that theology is a spiritual practice rooted in the Christian virtues, Coakley considers ascetic practices as the precondition for doing Trinitarian theology. She writes, "Simply put, and conversely: if one is resolutely *not* engaged in the practices of prayer, contemplation, and worship, then there are certain sorts of philosophical insight that are unlikely, if not impossible, to come available to one."[27] As an ascetical exercise, theology involves the metaphysical and epistemological, personal and political, bodily practice and intellectual engagement, and disorienting response and the transformation of one's thoughts and desires.

26. Sarah Coakley, *God, Sexuality, and the Self: An Essay "On the Trinity"* (Cambridge: Cambridge University Press, 2013), 2.

27. Coakley, *God, Sexuality, and the Self*, 16 (emphasis original).

This theological method, which Coakley calls "*théologie totale*," "puts contemplation at is [sic] heart, but spirals out to acknowledge the complexity of the entanglement of the secular and the spiritual realms for those who dare to practise it"[28] and "insists on the sweated-out significance of embodied (and thus gendered, and socially located) contemplation, not mere verbal play or abstract thought."[29] This is an embodied and lived theology. This theology is discursive in that it involves an utter submission to God so that the desire for God is to supersede other human desires. However, rather than render topics such as gender, class, or race as secondary or peripheral, it presses into them. Coakley summarizes, "In short, *théologie totale* makes the bold claim that the more systematic one's intentions, the more necessary the exploration of such dark and neglected corners; and that, precisely as a theology *in via*, *théologie totale* continually risks destabilization and redirection."[30] If Coakley is correct, then the absence of theological interpretation for diverse communities of faith is due to two factors. First, its practitioners simply are not diverse themselves, and if they are nonmajority persons they have not sufficiently reflected theologically on the ways their faith is embodied. Coakley herself includes ethnography in her theological method to acknowledge the ways theology is always embodied. Second, it is possible that the desire for stability and safety may stifle an honest engagement with culture. Her work *God, Sexuality, and the Self* is a Trinitarian engagement of sexuality and equally a sexual engagement of the Trinity. It is this kind of reflexive, genuinely discursive, and oftentimes risky interaction between the Scriptures and contemporary life that ought to characterize the theological interpretation of the Bible for persons on the margins. It ought to be noted that even ascetical practices, oftentimes commended by practitioners of TIS as necessary for the task of reading the Scriptures faithfully for the people of God, may not produce salutary effects. Lauren Winner narrates occasions of how the practices of the Eucharist, prayer, and baptism themselves may be damaged and consequently injure the lives of people and distort doctrine, so these too involve risk.[31]

If theological interpretation is to serve a culturally diverse church, a *théologie totale* will require the participation of an *église totale*. Given that academic biblical interpretation and theology are embedded within Western social structures, it will take more than the addition of a few diverse voices to engage in

---

28. Coakley, *God, Sexuality, and the Self*, 59.
29. Coakley, *God, Sexuality, and the Self*, 59.
30. Coakley, *God, Sexuality, and the Self*, 48.
31. Lauren F. Winner, *The Dangers of Christian Practice: On Wayward Gifts, Characteristic Damage, and Sin* (New Haven: Yale University Press, 2018).

authentic, mutually informing, and transformative discourse. Given that scholars of color are tasked to master two or more kinds of academic discourses, it will take time for them to integrate contextual and traditional approaches to theology. What remains to be seen is how traditional forms of theology will respond to this cultural diversity.

History

CHAPTER 9

Christian Faith and History

Murray Rae

In the prologue of Luke's gospel (Luke 1:1–4 NRSV) we are advised of the author's intention to set out an orderly account of "the events that have been fulfilled among us."[1] Luke advises further that he has investigated everything carefully from the beginning and that he is dependent upon the reports of those who "from the beginning were eyewitnesses" and "servants of the word." Confident of the reliability of his sources, Luke explains to Theophilus, to whom the prologue is addressed, that his orderly account is offered "so that you may know the truth concerning the things about which you have been instructed."

Luke's prologue establishes two important principles for Christian theology, first, that the gospel is founded upon "events that have been fulfilled among us," and, second, that we should strive to develop an orderly and truthful account of those events. The integrity and truthfulness of Luke's gospel depends, it would seem, upon the appropriate observance of these two principles. Put simply, history matters, and knowing the truth matters.[2] This ought to be agreed upon by biblical scholars and Christian theologians alike. The difficulty, of course, is that developing an orderly and truthful account of past events is no easy matter. We have difficulty enough finding agreement about the events of our own time. Consider, for example, how we might develop an orderly and truthful

1. All citations of the Bible are from the NRSV.

2. I use the term "history" here to designate the series of "events that have actually happened." The phrase is taken from I. Howard Marshall, who notes that the term "history" is also used to refer to an "account (written or otherwise) of past events." Marshall advises further that "we may use the word 'historiography' to describe the study of what historians do, or to refer to history writing itself." I. Howard Marshall, *Luke – Historian and Theologian* (Exeter: The Paternoster Press, 1970), 21.

account of the presidency of Donald Trump. Whose perspective can we regard as authoritative? How should the evidence be weighed? How are we to determine and evaluate the causal factors at work in the unfolding of events? To what degree was Trump's rhetoric a decisive factor in the storming of the US Capitol building on 6 January 2021? What impact did the president have on the way the COVID-19 pandemic developed in the United States? The writing of history is a highly contested enterprise, and it is no easy matter to piece together an orderly and truthful account of the things that have happened among us.

The task of constructing an orderly and truthful account of the events comprising the career of Jesus of Nazareth is equally difficult. Whose testimony should be regarded as authoritative? How should the significance of the available data be assessed? What are the causal factors at play and how are they related to one another? What interpretative lenses should be used in order to bring the reality with which we are concerned into sharpest focus? It is not possible to answer any of these questions from some ideologically neutral or detached, objective perspective. The judgments each of us make and the judgments that expert historians make in response to all such questions are shaped in part by a prior set of convictions about the way reality is constituted and, crucially, in the case of Jesus, by a prior set of convictions about God and God's relation to the world.

That the judgments made about past events and their significance are shaped to some extent by the beliefs, interests, and personal convictions of the inquirer is widely acknowledged now. As Søren Kierkegaard pointed out in the first half of the nineteenth century when D. F. Strauss and others were setting out upon their quest for the historical Jesus, we do not view the world *sub specie aeternitatis*. The particularities of our own context and the constraints of our own point of view mean that we cannot be detached, neutral, and wholly objective observers of what goes on in the world. This is no less true in the realm of biblical hermeneutics than it is in any other sphere of human inquiry. All of us approach the texts with a particular understanding of how the world works and with particular convictions about God, whether we think of God as existing or not. The Christian might, indeed ought to, approach the Bible with a readiness to have those convictions challenged and modified, but no reader can engage with the text or indeed with the reality to which the text bears witness except within some interpretive framework or other that determines to some extent what we make of the testimony to be found therein. Therefore, it is important for us to consider the impacts that particular perspectives and hermeneutical frameworks have on our reading of Scripture and upon our apprehension of the things to which the biblical authors seek to draw our attention. We are also bound to consider whether some interpretive frameworks are more helpful than others. It is with these observations in mind that I propose to consider in what follows the relation between historical and theological judgements in the reading of the Bible and in our efforts to learn the truth about the events of which the Biblical authors speak.

Within the cultural and the intellectual milieu established by the Enlightenment, biblical scholarship has typically presumed that our concern to learn the truth will be served best by privileging the methods of inquiry loosely grouped under the title of historical criticism, otherwise referred to as the historical-critical method.[3] While the term "historical criticism" has served as a generic term for a varied range of approaches, there are some common features among those approaches that justify their inclusion in the general category.[4] These especially include a commitment to investigate both the reliability of a text's witness to what has gone on in the past and the historical circumstances that account for the text's production and transmission. Richard Burnett advises that "historical criticism seeks to answer a basic question: to what historical circumstances does the text refer and out of what historical circumstances did it emerge?"[5] Historical critics have endeavoured thereby to furnish us with an account of "what really happened," or, perhaps more accurately, an account of what in their judgment seems to be most plausible. The orderly accounts duly provided are typically distinguished by one further notable feature: God is not involved, either as an active agent in the sequence of events under consideration or as one who might be involved in our knowing the truth about those events. As Craig Bartholomew has pointed out, it became a rule of historical criticism that theology "must stay away from this operation lest it contaminate it."[6] The invocation of God either as a guide to our knowing or as one who is involved in the unfolding of events is ruled out a priori. The historiography in play here,

3. Although the historical-critical method is largely a modern Western development, it is not without precedent. As N. T. Wright has pointed out, "The historical study of the Bible which often to this day pretends at least on the surface to an 'objective' or detached stance has itself been radically shaped by the variegated revivals of Epicureanism, which encouraged people to study the world without reference to God . . ." N. T. Wright, *History and Eschatology* (Waco: Baylor University Press, 2019), xv.

4. Craig Bartholomew points out that "there is a variety of historical criticisms and all sorts of developments within this period" in which historical criticism has held sway. Craig Bartholomew, "Uncharted Waters: Philosophy, Theology and the Crisis in Biblical Interpretation," in *Renewing Biblical Interpretation*, SAH Series 1, ed. Craig Bartholomew, Colin Greene, and Karl Möller (Grand Rapids: Zondervan, 2000), 4. See also in the same volume, Karl Möller, "Renewing Historical Criticism," 150 n. 34, along with the chapter by Alvin Plantinga, "Two (or More) Kinds of Scripture Scholarship," in *"Behind" the Text: History and Biblical Interpretation*, SAH Series 4, ed. Craig Bartholomew et al. (Grand Rapids: Zondervan, 2003).

5. Richard E. Burnett, "Historical Criticism," in *Dictionary for Theological Interpretation of the Bible*, ed. Kevin J. Vanhoozer et al. (Grand Rapids: Baker Academic, 2005), 290.

6. Bartholomew, "Uncharted Waters," 25.

sometimes called methodological naturalism,[7] is functionally agnostic at best and often tends toward what Francis Watson describes as "a kind of de facto atheism."[8] Well might we heed therefore the advice given by Pope John Paul II, who reminds us, "Those who devote themselves to the study of Sacred Scripture should always remember that the various hermeneutical approaches have their own philosophical underpinnings, which need to be carefully evaluated before they are applied to the sacred texts."[9]

The Scripture and Hermeneutics Seminar has recognised from the outset that the philosophical underpinnings of historical criticism and the privileging of such criticism in the world of biblical scholarship requires further scrutiny. Bartholomew observed at the first consultation in 1998 that while the historical-critical method, in its varying forms, has been the favoured hermeneutical approach of the majority of biblical scholars through the course of the past 150 years, the accompanying claims of objectivity, freedom from dogma, scholarly neutrality, and the like have become much less convincing than they may once have been. "One of the effects of postmodernism," Bartholomew writes, "is that we have become increasingly aware that the above way of understanding historical criticism – and many other issues – is itself traditioned and has its own 'prejudices,' to use Gadamer's term."[10]

Given that all human inquiry and every hermeneutical framework that is applied to the reading of the Bible necessarily rests upon a set of beliefs about the nature of the world and about the reality under investigation, we need to be as transparent as we can about the particular beliefs and prior commitments that inform our inquiry. Such commitments ought to be made public, but we must be clear: the "public" is not a neutral arbiter of the legitimacy or otherwise of those commitments. The legitimacy of any hermeneutical strategy and of the beliefs that undergird it is not determined in the end by public agreement, valuable though public scrutiny may be in sifting out wildly implausible strategies and

7. A helpful account of methodological naturalism can be found in Robert L. Webb, "The Historical Enterprise and Historical Jesus Research," in *Key Events in the Life of the Historical Jesus*, ed. Darrell L. Bock and Robert L. Webb (Grand Rapids: Eerdmans, 2010). I have offered a critique of Webb's approach in "Theological Interpretation and Historical Criticism," in *A Manifesto for Theological Interpretation*, ed. Craig Bartholomew and Heath Thomas (Grand Rapids: Baker Academic, 2016).

8. Francis Watson, "*Veritas Christi*: How to Get from the Jesus of History to the Christ of Faith without Losing One's Way," in *Seeking the Identity of Jesus*, ed. Beverly Roberts Gaventa and Richard B. Hays (Grand Rapids: Eerdmans, 2008), 114.

9. John Paul II, *Faith and Reason* (London: The Incorporated Catholic Truth Society, 1998), 85. Cited by Bartholomew in "Uncharted Waters," 1.

10. Bartholomew, "Uncharted Waters," 25. Again, see also Möller, "Renewing Historical Criticism," 150–53. Further attention is given in volume 4 of the SAH Series to the philosophical underpinnings of the historical-critical method. See especially the essay by Iain W. Provan, "Knowing and Believing: Faith in the Past," in Bartholomew et al., *"Behind" the Text*, 229–66.

beliefs, but by the degree to which particular beliefs and methodological strategies conform to the reality with which we are concerned. In other words, the appropriateness of the beliefs and strategies of the methodological naturalist who proceeds as if God *is not* involved in the events to which the Bible bears witness and the contrasting beliefs and strategies of the theologically committed enquirer who proceeds as if God *is* involved are validated in the end simply in virtue of whether God was and is involved or not. There is, of course, no neutral arbiter of that dispute and no means to determine for sure which approach is to be preferred. Recognition of this fact should make clear, however, that the privileging of methodological naturalism in the realm of historical inquiry has no self-evident warrant. There is no good reason to reject at the outset the legitimacy of appeals to divine agency in the accounts we might give of what has gone on through the course of history.

A possible objection to this claim is that the discipline of "history" is simply the study of *human actions* in the past. Divine action may occur, but it lies outside the scope of historical investigation. Robert Webb, appealing to the authority of R. G. Collingwood, offers this justification for the adoption of methodological naturalism.[11] We must be clear, however, that this approach may come at a cost. If God *is* involved in the events which the biblical authors narrate, then the account of events offered by the methodological naturalist is bound to be inadequate at best and possibly seriously misleading. The biblical testimony to the resurrection of Jesus is an obvious case in point. The range of explanations offered by methodological naturalists is well known: the body of Jesus was removed from the tomb, perhaps in service of a conspiracy; Jesus didn't really die but fainted and was later revived; the biblical authors who speak of resurrection are not referring to something that happened to Jesus himself but to a revival of faith among the disciples; and so on. Those methodological naturalists who are prepared to say that something momentous did happen but we are not able to explain what it was are to be commended for their greater reserve, but this admission gives further cause to question the appropriateness of prohibiting at the outset any appeal to divine agency. Referring particularly to the search for the "historical Jesus," Sarah Coakley observes that the historical approach "*shrinks* what can be said of Jesus to what secular historians regard as appropriate to their task and duty and so necessarily consigns him to the past."[12]

---

11. Webb, "The Historical Enterprise and Historical Jesus Research," 16–17. Webb cites Collingwood, who says, "What kinds of things does history find out? I answer, *res gestae*: actions of human beings that have been done in the past." R. G. Collingwood, *The Idea of History: With Lectures 1926–1928*, rev. ed., ed. Jan van der Dussen (1946; repr., Oxford: Oxford University Press, 1993), 9.

12. Sarah Coakley, "The Identity of the Risen Jesus: Finding Jesus Christ in the Poor," in Gaventa and Hays, *Seeking the Identity of Jesus*, 306 (emphasis mine). Coakley's observation that historical criticism

This does not mean that historical criticism yields nothing of value for the student of the Bible. It can and does offer, for example, valuable insight into the political, cultural, and social contexts of the events narrated by the biblical authors. Historical criticism has also shed much light upon the way in which texts reflect their cultural milieu, and so on. Coakley's observation does mean, however, that the study of the events which the Bible narrates is improperly constrained if the explanatory categories to be employed in that study are confined to those deemed to be acceptable by the exponents of historical-critical inquiry. Inasmuch as the events narrated by the biblical authors involve divine agency, their true character and significance remains inaccessible to historical inquiry as typically practiced in the modern Western academy.

It is also important to note that the methodological commitment to exclude any appeal to divine action and to keep theological concerns at arm's length is a commitment not shared by the biblical authors themselves. The gospel writers, for instance, clearly believed that we cannot possibly give an orderly and truthful account of the events comprising the career of Jesus without full immersion in a theological understanding of the world and of the God of Israel. Watson observes that "the Gospels assume that we are to speak not of Jesus alone but of Jesus in relation to God and of God in relation to Jesus; and there is no good reason not to take that assumption seriously."[13] We must be very clear, therefore, that those historical critics who insist upon excluding from their orderly accounts all theological categories and causes have determined to read the texts not on their own terms but on terms dictated by a "modern" secular mindset that has emerged within Western traditions of thought following the Enlightenment.[14]

Along with the methodological decision to suspend belief in the assumption that God is involved in the events narrated by the biblical authors, the historical-critical method has typically proceeded under the conviction that the historian should be given first access to the biblical text in order to determine what counts as reliable historical data. These "assured results" of historical scholarship are then pieced together to deliver an account of what really happened, or of who Jesus really was.

Two possible justifications might be offered for this procedure. The first is related to the principle already agreed upon that history matters for Christian

consigns Jesus to the past highlights a further consequence of the method. It cannot admit the possibility that Jesus has risen from the dead and may still be involved in our knowing of him.

13. Watson, "*Veritas Christi*," 114.

14. Any serious engagement with indigenous cultures and with their particular ways of conceiving the nature of what is going on in the world gives cause to wonder why a peculiarly Western and increasingly secular understanding of the world such as is represented in the historical-critical method should be privileged in the reading of Scripture.

faith. The gospel is not reducible to a set of abstract ideas or eternal truths, but rather involves a set of claims about certain things having taken place. Paul therefore says that if Christ has not been raised then our faith is in vain (1 Cor 15:14). Given this dependence upon history, it surely makes sense for historians to assess the available evidence and to determine, with whatever degree of certainty the evidence permits, what has in fact taken place. Theologians may then be invited to reflect upon the theological import and significance of those events. The difficulty, of course, with this proposal is that it takes no account of the impact that the personal convictions of the historian might have on his or her inquiries. It presumes that the work of establishing the "facts" can be done in a wholly objective and theologically neutral fashion. As N. T. Wright has quite rightly pointed out, however, "all reading involves the reader as an active participant. To say that one is merely studying objective history, without other presuppositions, is no longer an option."[15]

The exclusion of theology from the investigation of what has gone on in the past could also be justified if we knew for sure either that God does not exist or that God does not involve himself in the sequence of events that historians set out to study. The obvious difficulty here is that we do not know either of these things to be true. At the very least, therefore, we ought to keep an open mind on such questions. Keeping an open mind will require that we attend to two further questions: 1) by what means may we come to recognise the work of God in the events of past history, if indeed God has been at work? And, relatedly, 2) what kind of historiography would be required in order to accommodate the possibility of divine causality in history? The term "historiography" has two senses here. I mean to refer first to an account of what history is. Is history, for instance, merely one damn thing after another, as Henry Ford is alleged to have remarked, a sequence of events utterly bereft of any meaning or purpose, or might it be the fruit of some divine intention that is still being worked out and will one day be brought to fulfilment? These are but two among numerous possibilities, but the question of how history should be understood is surely important as we seek to understand what is going on in and through the sequence of events that historians set out to investigate.

A second sense of the term "historiography" also applies here; the term may be applied to whatever it is that historians do. Thus, the question "what kind of historiography would be required in order to accommodate the possibility of divine causality in history?" invites consideration of the tools and the explanatory categories that may be available for the task. These, I think, are the critical

15. N. T. Wright, *The New Testament and the People of God* (London: SPCK, 1992), 121.

questions that those interested in reading the Bible on its own terms must continue to explore, for, as I noted earlier, the biblical authors themselves take it as axiomatic that the provision of an orderly account of what is happening in the world requires that theology be used as an explanatory category. If those committed to methodological naturalism or to an Epicurean worldview choose to opt out of such a project, that is no cause for biblical scholars and theologians to lose their nerve. It simply confirms what we knew already: not all enquirers operate from the same worldview or share the same hermeneutical frameworks. Note well that this does not mean, as has sometimes been alleged, that those historians, theologians, and biblical scholars who consider theological explanation and theological modes of inquiry to be indispensable are retreating to some private enclave that permits no public scrutiny. It merely means that they are committed to some premises that others do not share. The same is true of the methodological naturalists, and indeed of all other methodological variants in the realm of historiography. As I have already pointed out, the legitimacy of such premises is not determined by the extent of public agreement but rather by their conformity to the reality under investigation.

I have attempted so far to outline the need for fresh thinking about how to conceive the relation between theology and history in our reading of the Bible. The predominance of a historical-critical method that has resisted the involvement of theology is fast losing its appeal, not, it must be noted, because of how little support it provides for Christian piety, but rather because it is grounded in a positivist account of history that is no longer compelling. We need to think afresh about how "the events that have been fulfilled among us" may be *rigorously* and *faithfully* investigated. To be rigorous in this context means to consider the available evidence as thoroughly and carefully as we can and with a readiness to have preconceived notions and interpretations challenged and perhaps overturned. To be faithful means to undertake this task in humble recognition that we stand in need of God's help to truly see and understand where and how he has been at work among us. It is to acknowledge that our apprehension of what is going on in the world is itself a theological task for which we need the tutoring of Christ himself, as once took place on the road to Emmaus (Luke 24:13–35), and the promised guidance of the Spirit (John 16:13).

The critiques I have previously offered of the positivistic assumptions of the historical-critical method and of its limitations are commonplace now. They have been thoroughly examined in a range of recent works.[16] They have been subjected to philosophical critique under the auspices of the Scripture and

16. See for example, Samuel V. Adams, *The Reality of God and Historical Method: Apocalyptic Theology in Conversation with N. T. Wright* (Downers Grove: IVP Academic, 2015); Seth Heringer, *Uniting History*

Hermeneutics Seminar by such figures as Alvin Plantinga, Peter van Inwagen, and William P. Alston.[17] They have led N. T. Wright to propose a critical realist approach to biblical scholarship that is aware of the impact of one's worldview upon what and how we see, and Wright encourages an "epistemology of love" in which we may enter sympathetically into the worldview of the biblical authors.[18] Focusing particularly upon the historical critics' reconstruction of the person and work of Jesus, these critiques have also prompted some biblical scholars to question the reliance that has been placed upon particular tools of historical inquiry.[19] Other scholars have observed that "historical research may illuminate a range of significant issues, but it will not tell us whether Jesus's person and mission are truly from God, definitively embodying the divine saving action on the world's behalf." Francis Watson, who makes this latter claim, goes on to say, "The Christian community has its own compelling reasons to resist and reject any limiting of Jesus's reality to what is historically verifiable."[20] This should not lead us, however, to abandon historical inquiry. History still matters for Christian faith, and so the Lukan goal of producing an orderly account of the events that have been fulfilled among us is essential if we are to know the truth. An orderly and truthful account, however, will be one which recognises where and how God is at work in history.

Clearly this will require, as I suggested earlier, a new historiography – a new account, that is, of what history is – and a new account of how those investigating history may go about their work. I use the term "new" here only in relation to the historiography that has developed in the Western world following the Enlightenment, which has driven a wedge between history and theology. It will not be new to those who have preferred to operate within a biblical view of the world. That biblical view, birthed through the story of Israel and brought into sharp focus in the New Testament, regards history as the unfolding of God's creative purposes for the world, of humanity's rebellion against those purposes and against God, and thus also of God's redemptive re-creation of all things through the person and work of Christ. It is important to note that we cannot arrive at

---

and Theology: A Theological Critique of the Historical Method (Lanham, MD: Lexington Books / Fortress Academic, 2018); and my own *History and Hermeneutics* (London: T&T Clark, 2005).

17. See their essays in Bartholomew et al., *"Behind" the Text.*

18. These proposals are repeated throughout Wright's corpus, but see, for example, the outline of critical realism offered in *The New Testament and the People of God*, ch. 2, and a recent account of the epistemology of love in *History and Eschatology*, ch. 5 and passim.

19. Dale Allison observes, for instance, that the conflicting results produced through application of the so-called criteria of authenticity suggest that "the criteria themselves are seriously defective" and that "they cannot do what is claimed for them." Dale C. Allison Jr., "The Historians' Jesus and the Church," in Gaventa and Hays, *Seeking the Identity of Jesus*, 79.

20. Watson, "*Veritas Christi*," 106.

this view of history other than by trusting in the testimony of the Bible itself.[21] Nor can we verify it independently, such as by seeking the counsel of historians. There is, as Samuel Adams has advised, no way out of this circularity. But, Adams continues, "there is a way *into* this circularity." The way in is what Adams calls the "apocalyptic event," although he concedes the ambiguity of this term. What he means by it, though, is an event that is revelatory of the true nature and meaning of history. This event is the incarnation, the "Father's action of sending the Son, becoming Jesus of Nazareth, living, bearing witness to the kingdom, dying, rising and ascending. This is the reality of God that is given in history but cannot be contained by any one prior telling of history . . ."[22] This revelatory event is the proper framework through which to consider all that has and is happening in the world, and indeed all that will happen, for the life, death, and resurrection of Jesus discloses the *telos* of all things in their final reconciliation to the Father. All of this is to say that the combined testimony of the biblical authors does establish "an orderly account of the events that have been fulfilled among us" and does enable us to "know the truth concerning the things about which [we] have been instructed."

It is quite true that this account of what history is cannot be confirmed by or accommodated within the hermeneutical framework commonly insisted upon by historians working in the Western academy. That is merely to say, however, that they prefer another story about the nature and meaning of history. While Christian historians ought, I suggest, to take their bearings from God's action among us in Jesus Christ, believing that the series of events constituting the career of Jesus reveals the true nature and purpose of what is happening in the world, secular historians will inevitably take their bearings from somewhere else and prefer to operate with a de facto atheism, to use Watson's phrase again. That is their prerogative, but there is no warrant at all for supposing that their framework should be privileged in the way that it has been, especially in the field of biblical studies.

What is proposed here is that it is through the story of Jesus, through his life, his proclamation of the coming kingdom of God, and his death, resurrection, and ascension that we truly learn what is going on through the course of human history. The coming of Jesus sheds a new and different light upon much of what we thought we knew about history. An important epistemological claim is necessary here, however: we need God's help to see what is really going on. As

21. In support of this point, Iain Provan makes the case that our "*knowledge of the past* is more accurately described as *faith in the testimony*, in the interpretations of the past, offered by others." Provan, "Knowing and Believing," 245 (Emphasis original).

22. Adams, *The Reality of God and Historical Method*, 271–72 (emphasis original).

hinted at earlier, we need the tutoring of Christ himself and the guidance of the Spirit in order to apprehend what God is doing among us. This is not a novel claim. It is what the biblical texts repeatedly stress. The conversation between Jesus and the two disciples on the road to Emmaus is paradigmatic: "Then [Jesus] said to them, 'Oh, how foolish you are, and how slow of heart to believe all that the prophets have declared! Was it not necessary that the Messiah should suffer these things and then enter into his glory?' Then beginning with Moses and all the prophets, he interpreted to them the things about himself in all the scriptures" (Luke 24:25–27). So too are Jesus's declaration to Peter that "flesh and blood has not revealed this to you, but my Father in heaven" (Matt 16:17), and his promise in John 16:13: "When the Spirit of truth comes, he will guide you into all the truth; for he will not speak on his own, but will speak whatever he hears, and he will declare to you the things that are to come."

The content of the biblical testimony renders unsustainable the bifurcation of historical and theological inquiry that has commonly been insisted upon in the Western academy. A reconciliation of the two disciplines is required. I conclude by citing Samuel Adams, who describes superbly well the outcome and the promise of this reconciliation:

> For the methodological question of the historian, this means that naturalistic accounts will never do. For the theologian, this means that theology is never finished, for theology is always engaged in thoughtful reflection on the continuation of a new history located in the continuing personal existence of Jesus, the risen and ascended Lord. For both, the reality of God means that doxology and prayer are the ground out of which each practice springs. Unsettled from their naturalistic soil, the historian and the theologian find themselves replanted in the living soil of the triune God's new creation, and therefore new history.[23]

23. Adams, *The Reality of God and Historical Method*, 273.

In the Church

CHAPTER 10

Toward a Practical Theology That Is Both Rooted and Relevant

Susan I. Bubbers

INTRODUCTION

This volume reflects on the work of the Scripture and Hermeneutics Seminar over the past twenty-five years. It also provides an opportunity to integrate that work with the newer Scripture and Church Seminar and to propose areas for future study. As a chapter in Part III, this essay contributes a perspective particularly from the point of view of the church. I suggest a way forward toward a synergy of academy and church along with a synergy of Scripture, pastoral care, and preaching. I propose a way to enhance our ongoing hermeneutics discussion and to develop an innovative type of seminary course: one that is rigorously academic while devoted to the needs of practitioners. I call this field of study "comparative hermeneutics." My thesis is that comparative hermeneutics can help us move toward a practical theology that is both rooted and relevant.

This chapter is not meant to critique the essays highlighted in Part II. Rather, some pertinent points will help me point us toward the development of a hermeneutical approach which will stay rooted in Scripture and also be relevant to the complex context of twenty-first century audiences. Several essays from the SAH Series trace the development of philosophical hermeneutics and theological hermeneutics in the eighteenth, nineteenth, and twentieth centuries, so I will leave it to the reader to review those discussions for that background. My own perspectives can be found in my *Scriptural Theology* book.[1]

In my career as a systems analyst before ordination, I learned skills to scrutinize the "raw materials," the "process," and the "desired product" of any given system, whether computer, social, or institutional. If our "desired product" is a generation of ministers who are better able to remain rooted in biblical truth while at the same time being relevant in the pulpit, counseling room, and culture, then to advance toward that end will require an analysis of the "process" and "raw materials" in use, such as seminary curriculum, textbooks, and training programs. Specifically, in this case, the system to be analyzed is how the field of hermeneutics is included in the equipping of practitioners.

An apt metaphor could be the importance of a supply line in war time. The World War II article "The Supply Front: The Allies' Key to Victory" begins with the declaration, "Of all the factors that helped the Allies win the war, none was more important than the unbroken flow of supplies to the front lines."[2] The World War I article "Transport and Supply During the First World War" details how crucial it was for troops in the trenches on the front lines to be properly equipped from the supply depots behind them. This was so critical that at times troops were relocated from fighting to provide necessary supplies. And strategies for supplying had to change to fit the need. For example, light rail had to be built because road vehicles were not always sufficient.[3] This chapter is "an appeal from the trenches" for the "supply lines" to retool as necessary in order to fit the need. My goal is to describe how the academic field of hermeneutics can be enhanced as part of the "supply line" that equips practitioners with a practical theology that will help them in the "trenches."

This chapter is divided into three parts. Part one, "Baptism as an Example of Practical Theology Shaped by Hermeneutics," will consider four views of baptism, each appealing to Scripture for their conclusions. This will provide a specific area of application for the hermeneutical concepts we will discuss. Part two, "Systems Analysis of the Need for Comparative Hermeneutics," will incorporate insights from the contributors' essays profiled in Part II of this volume and bring to the surface underlying hermeneutical dynamics which lead to differing views on baptism. This will highlight the need for an additional category of inquiry, namely comparative hermeneutics. Finally, part three, "Comparative

---

1. Susan Bubbers, *A Scriptural Theology of Eucharistic Blessings*, LNTS (London: T&T Clark, 2013), 1–44.

2. Glenn Barnett, "The Supply Front: The Allies' Key to Victory," *Warfare History Network*, 26 December 2018, https://warfarehistorynetwork.com/2018/12/26/the-supply-front-the-allies-key-to-victory.

3. "Transport and Supply During the First World War," Imperial War Museums, https://www.iwm.org.uk/history/transport-and-supply-during-the-first-world-war.

Hermeneutics Methods and Questions," will point forward to ways comparative hermeneutics could help the ongoing discussion to be more firmly rooted in Scripture and more effective in equipping practitioners for ministry.

1. BAPTISM AS AN EXAMPLE OF PRACTICAL THEOLOGY SHAPED BY HERMENEUTICS

At the beginning of the SAH Series, Craig Bartholomew makes an appeal for ". . . a depth diagnosis so that the solutions we propose contribute towards a genuine renewal of biblical interpretation."[4] His ensuing discussion shows how serious consideration of philosophy is a way to move into deeper hermeneutical waters. I want to build on those bases by pointing us in the direction of comparing how different streams of theology flow like undercurrents in these deep waters. As Bartholomew notes Francis Watson's work in this area, I too believe it is important for interpreters to keep in view how ". . . a theological position can itself function as a hermeneutic."[5] I propose that a careful comparison of deep-level hermeneutical theological and methodological streams will equip practitioners to remain more firmly rooted in Scripture while making them more able to reach diverse audiences.

We will proceed by considering four views of baptism, each appealing to Scripture for their conclusions. This will provide a specific area of application for the hermeneutical concepts we discuss. Then we will incorporate insights from the contributors in this SAH volume and bring to the surface underlying hermeneutical dynamics which lead to different views on baptism. This will highlight the need for an additional category of inquiry, namely comparative hermeneutics. Finally, we will point forward to ways comparative hermeneutics could help the ongoing discussion be more firmly rooted in Scripture and more effectively equip practitioners.

Four of Christendom's primary views of baptism are summarized in a book edited by John Armstrong.[6] Four views are followed by responding essays, all quite helpful and informative. Yet the conversation stays on the surface of comparing conclusions, with only a bit of "how we arrive at those conclusions" and almost no discussion of differing presuppositions or interpretive methodolo-

---

4. Craig Bartholomew, "Uncharted Waters: Philosophy, Theology and the Crisis in Biblical Interpretation," in *Renewing Biblical Interpretation*, SAH Series 1, ed. Craig Bartholomew, Colin Greene, and Karl Möller (Grand Rapids: Zondervan, 2000), 1.

5. Bartholomew, "Uncharted Waters," 28.

6. John Armstrong, ed., *Understanding Four Views on Baptism* (Grand Rapids: Zondervan, 2007).

gies. I agree with the editor's introductory goal, yet his book takes us only so far toward that goal. "And we should seek to understand why we disagree and thus learn how to face our disagreements with a better knowledge of real differences. All the while we must dig deep into Scripture and church tradition, seeking to understand why we believe what we do and what these beliefs mean for our own lives of faith."[7] He proceeds by asking his contributors the questions, "Who should be baptized? And how should baptism be administered?"[8] The book, when analyzed carefully, actually only addresses the "what is believed" and "what we do" questions, not the "why do we believe the way we do" question. This is an observation, not a criticism, since only so much can be covered in a small book of this type.

I agree with Armstrong's dream, "By working to understand our differences, we can demonstrate to the world that we love one another."[9] However, I would say that expounding on what our differences are only takes us partway to our goal of Christian cohesion and cooperation. Analyzing the unique currents beneath these differing theological streams will provide a way to have a conversation about these formative undercurrents rather than about the conflicting conclusions. This can show that differences may not be as stark as they appear and reveal how the currents could flow together in ways not previously recognized. This kind of analysis in the sphere of the seminary could produce practitioners better able to address questions, comfort confusions, and nurture growth in their audiences. Let us meet our first four conversation partners, each presenting a view of baptism. In Part two, we will add several of the contributors from this SAH volume to this Caird-type round table discussion.[10] In part three, we will complete our discussion group by adding practitioners. All these voices together can produce a more synthetic understanding of Scripture and the resulting practice of baptism.

The first of the four views is the Baptist view, presented by Thomas Nettles.[11] The Baptist view emphasizes an individual's choice to demonstrate to a local congregation that he or she does in fact have faith in the gospel. Nettles's primary appeal is to the New Testament era's practice, especially John the Baptist and the book of Acts. The unspoken underlying currents which steer the

7. Armstrong, *Understanding Four Views*," 12.

8. Armstrong, *Understanding Four Views*," 15.

9. Armstrong, *Understanding Four Views*," 21.

10. George B. Caird was a mid–twentieth-century New Testament scholar and minister who is known for his approach to New Testament theology which gave each biblical author a voice heard as distinct and yet also in-concert with the others. This led to an overall New Testament theology which was more of a synthesis, advancing this discipline beyond previous approaches which favored one particular voice over another.

11. Thomas Nettles, "Baptist View: Baptism as a Symbol of Christ's Saving Work," in Armstrong, *Understanding Four Views*, 25–41.

direction of his biblical interpretation include the starting points of ecclesiology and anthropology along with a more narrow and literal approach to the use of biblical terms rather than consideration of semantic ranges and concepts.

The second view of baptism is presented by Richard Pratt.[12] The Reformed view emphasizes the incorporation of an infant into the visible covenant community. His primary appeal is to the theological stream of the Westminster Confession, and this serves as the lens through which he reads and interprets Scripture. Pratt is clear about his view that baptism fits into the pre-established grid of a "covenant of grace" and an ecclesiology that emphasizes a distinction between the invisible church and the visible church, both of which are part of a "covenant community." He is also clear about his view that there is great continuity between the Old Covenant and the New Covenant, and that baptism is directly related to circumcision. The scope of a book such as this is not meant to address the underlying currents of the Reformed theological stream. Therefore, Pratt's biblical interpretations and theological conclusions are based upon Calvinistic concepts which are presumed as fact and not defended through biblical analysis.

The third view of baptism is presented by Robert Kolb.[13] The Lutheran view emphasizes God's gracious initiative and the sovereign power of God's word to create and to re-create. His primary appeal is to Genesis, Noah, the power of God's word in verbal, written, and incarnational/sacramental forms, and New Testament texts related to adoption and salvation. Kolb is more explicit about his presuppositions than are the other contributors, devoting five pages of his essay to describing his starting points. They include Martin Luther's views, the unity of the canon, God's creative Word in three forms, the fallen nature of humans including infants, and repentance not as a one-time event but as a lifetime journey (e.g., salvation can be lost). Again, the biblical basis for these presuppositions is outside the scope of a book like this.

The fourth view of baptism is presented by John Castelein.[14] The Christian Churches/Churches of Christ view emphasizes the original events of baptism in the New Testament, which were not actually "believer's" baptism but "convert's" baptism. Baptism happened at the same point when a person came to faith in the gospel. Castelein's interpretive starting point is the goal of returning to a "pure" New Testament-era church. The Restoration Movement calls this "patternism,"

---

12. Richard L. Pratt, Jr., "Reformed View: Baptism as a Sacrament of the Covenant," in Armstrong, *Understanding Four Views*, 59–72.

13. Robert Kolb, "Lutheran View: God's Baptismal Act as Regenerative," in Armstrong, *Understanding Four Views*, 91–109.

14. John Castelein, "Christian Churches/Churches of Christ View: Believers' Baptism as the Biblical Occasion of Salvation," in Armstrong, *Understanding Four Views*, 129–44.

which seeks to pattern current belief and practice on only the original thoughts and actions of the New Testament narratives. The unspoken underlying currents include a rejection of historical evidence outside of the text of the New Testament itself. For example, if the New Testament does not explicitly mention infants being baptized then this silence is interpreted as an absence, or at least a disapproval, of the practice.

The hermeneutical starting points and theological presuppositions which have led to such different beliefs and practices about baptism can be analyzed in greater detail, leading to more helpful dialogue. An analysis of the hermeneutical systems of the predecessors of these four views would help take the conversation to the point where the divides begin to occur. Nettles explains a traditional post-Reformation Baptist view, from a perspective which limits the meaning of the term "baptism" to what the Greek term normally denotes in New Testament narratives – that is, immersion. Pratt explains John Calvin's view. Kolb explains Luther's view. Castelein explains Barton Stone's and Thomas and Alexander Campbell's view, the American Restoration Movement view. For the most part, they are still simply articulating their different inherited conclusions, and so the "I'm right and you're wrong" ethos continues.

To help the global church toward greater cohesion and cooperation, and to help practitioners minister more effectively to people from all these (and more) backgrounds, an academic conversation about the biblical interpretive methodologies underlying these theological streams is needed. In Armstrong's book, each of the four essays are followed by a few pages of response by the others. Sprinkled sparingly amidst these few pages are observations along the lines of what I am suggesting, perhaps a sentence or two, or at most a paragraph or two, analyzing the underlying hermeneutical differences which are giving rise to the disparate conclusions about baptism. It is at this deeper level that we need to develop complete monographs and dedicate complete semesters of study to comparative hermeneutics.

2. SYSTEMS ANALYSIS OF THE NEED FOR COMPARATIVE HERMENEUTICS

Having heard four different baptismal views from four presenters, we will now add to the round table discussion the contributors profiled in the current SAH volume, so that we can incorporate insights from the advancing field of hermeneutics. The four presenters in Armstrong's book were often talking past each other on the level of conflicting conclusions rather than engaging at the level of the impetus of those diversions. The work done by the SAHS can be brought to bear on this conversation, and it can bring to the surface some underlying hermeneutical dynamics which lead to differing views on baptism. This can take the conversation to the level of actual points of departure. As we identify various formative undercurrents, this will highlight the need for more intentional study in the area of comparative hermeneutics.

The approach of Views books comparing conclusions about biblical topics is typically: "This is what we believe. That is what they believe. We understand so-and-so text to mean this, while they mean that. We are guided by the theological teachings of So-and-So; they, of someone else. We basically agree on points 1 2 3; we disagree on points 4 5 6." To move toward a conversation at a deeper level, brief comments that have been largely in the background need to be brought to the fore through comparative hermeneutics. More specifically, "comparative hermeneutics" is the term I use to refer to a discipline of study which analyzes the underlying biblical interpretive methods and presuppositions that shape understandings of the meaning of a Scriptural text and resulting theological conclusions. In this discipline, there is no need to sacrifice loyalty to a chosen theological stream. There need be no watering down of any given doctrinal system. However, we do need to learn how to move toward a way of interpreting Scripture and a way of pursuing theological studies which will better equip practitioners to teach, preach, and pastorally care for increasingly diverse audiences. Practitioners have audiences with an ever-broadening collection of worldviews and backgrounds. To care for these people, practitioners need to be better equipped to understand and relate to those from outside their own theological stream. A first step in analyzing a hermeneutical system is to identify the interpreter's presuppositions about the ontology of the Bible itself. This clarification of the "headwaters of a theological thought world" is crucial to advancing the conversation and to equipping practitioners.

This is a good place in our round table discussion to listen to our contributors Alvin Plantinga and Al Wolters. It is important to train seminarians how to recognize if interpreters are located at the headwaters Plantinga and Wolters describe. All four of the baptism presenters would be located here, but not every interpreter is. Plantinga[15] highlights one of the most basic underlying hermeneutical questions. Is interpretation happening from the viewpoint of the Bible as Scripture, the divinely inspired Word of God, or from the viewpoint of the Bible as human literature, which can be fully understood through belief-less inquiry?

15. Alvin Plantinga, "Two (or More) Kinds of Scripture Scholarship," in *"Behind" the Text: History and Biblical Interpretation*, SAH Series 4, ed. Craig Bartholomew et al. (Grand Rapids: Zondervan, 2003), 19–57.

He goes on to present a well-argued defense for interpreting the Bible as Scripture, and suggests ways for a Christian to respond to secular biblical readings.

Wolters makes explicit the headwaters of interpreting from a vantage point of faith. He chooses an excellent term, "confessional criticism," to describe scholarly interpretation ". . . rooted in the classical Christian confession of Scripture as the Word of God."[16] He addresses the chasm between academy and church, the ". . . split between 'knowledge' and 'belief.'" He presents an interpretive method, very much like Robert Traina's, involving nine areas of analysis, bringing together careful criticism and confessional faith.[17] What a text meant and what it means are distinguishable, but closely connected.[18] Just so, academy and church are still distinguishable, but via comparative hermeneutics can be more closely connected.

Wolters affirms, "It is clear that ideological readings of the biblical text depend on basic assumptions which may themselves be called ideological, and are likely to be vigorously contested."[19] But, currently there is no systemic attention given to identifying and comparing these basic assumptions. Wolters goes on to say, "As a responsible human act, interpretation is therefore always enmeshed in a whole range of interpretive 'judgment calls.'"[20] I am proposing to improve "the supply line" by including in the system of practitioner training a much more specific study of these "judgment calls."

Regarding the practical theology of baptism, our four presenters would all meet at the headwaters of seeing the Bible as Scripture and employing confessional criticism. However, they each make "judgment calls" which then point them in different directions. This is the level which needs more attention. For example, how would each presenter address the underlying hermeneutical issue about how to interpret biblical silence regarding infant baptisms? This needs to be made explicit before other resulting conclusions are considered.

Judgment calls are made by interpreters, and here we can add the voices of Anthony Thiselton[21] and William Olhausen.[22] Thiselton engages with phil-

16. Al Wolters, "Confessional Criticism and the Night Visions of Zechariah," in *Renewing Biblical Interpretation*, SAH Series 1, ed. Craig Bartholomew, Colin Greene, and Karl Möller (Grand Rapids: Zondervan, 2000), 91.

17. Wolters, "Confessional Criticism," 92–104.

18. Wolters, "Confessional Criticism," 103.

19. Wolters, "Confessional Criticism," 102.

20. Wolters, "Confessional Criticism," 104.

21. Anthony Thiselton, "'Behind' and 'In Front Of' the Text: Language, Reference, and Indeterminacy," in *After Pentecost: Language and Biblical Interpretation*, SAH Series 2, ed. Craig G. Bartholomew, Colin Greene, and Karl Möller (Grand Rapids: Zondervan, 2001), 91–120.

22. William Olhausen, "A 'Polite' Response to Anthony Thiselton," in Bartholomew, Greene, and Möller, *After Pentecost*, 121–30.

osophical hermeneutics and theological hermeneutics. Since the eighteenth century, it has been recognized that behind the text is an author who was writing from a particular viewpoint and motivation.[23] As "facilitator" of the round table discussion, I would agree that much attention has been given to the attempt to stand in the place of human authors and objectively identify their intended meaning of the text. I would add here that it is just as important for interpreters to explicate their own viewpoint and motivation deliberately. What is directing their judgment calls? Often, this step is abbreviated or absent, perhaps because there is an assumption that their audience already shares the same starting point. For example, the four presenters' conclusions are each based on inherited theological thought worlds. Those worlds are not explained, defended, or compared. The result "in the trenches" is the unfortunate reality that baptism divides Christendom rather than building cohesion. In actuality, it is not baptism that is divisive; it is conflicting underlying hermeneutical currents which are not being directly analyzed.

Thiselton goes on to discuss the concept of the impact of the text, the effects "in front of" the text. There is a wide range to consider here, from reader-response theory to the goal of canonical Scripture to be formational. This points to the link between hermeneutics and practical theology. Applied to the baptism conversation, each view has a different practice of baptism "in front of" the text, and each difference arises from a set of hermeneutical issues. For example, baptismal practices are shaped by the interpretive questions "To what extent is a narrative about baptism in the book of Acts meant to be patternistic?" and "Does the biblical text provide trajectories which support the development of ecclesiological practices beyond what was explicitly done in the New Testament era?" Nettles and Castelein would probably say "yes" to the first question and "no" to the second question, but to differing degrees. Pratt and Kolb would probably hesitate to answer the first question definitively either way, and say "yes" to the second question, but for different reasons.

Olhausen helpfully summarizes Thiselton's chapter, "The chapter steers a *via media* between, on the one hand, simplistic and deterministic approaches to meaning and reference for all texts and, on the other, interpretative strategies that prioritize pragmatic or 'local' considerations at the expense of tradition and/or the extralinguistic world."[24] Navigating this *via media* course is not plain sailing. More cross-stream discussion would help provide guidance, as well as a renewed emphasis on the role of spiritual discernment in the interpretive process,

23. Thiselton, "'Behind' and 'In Front Of' the Text," 98.
24. Olhausen, "A 'Polite' Response," 121.

as Richard Hooker would prioritize.[25] Olhausen asks the exact kind of question I am promoting. "What difference has Pentecost made to the ability of human beings to interpret the Bible?"[26] While it is likely all four presenters would say their baptismal views are of the Spirit, the conversation is lacking the important theological stream of Pentecostal theology. All of the presenters overlook hermeneutical questions such as "What is the meaning of baptism in the context of phrases referring to the Spirit and to *glossolalia*?" Hermeneutical undercurrent questions here are "What role did the Holy Spirit play in the inscripturation of the text?," "What role does the Holy Spirit play in interpretation and effects?," and "To what extent do activities of the Holy Spirit seen in the New Testament era continue throughout the church era?"

Mary Healy[27] and Joel Green[28] discuss something similar when they explore not the activity of the Holy Spirit per se, but the activity of God in history. Healy presents an analogy to help identify how God is at work in history and through the text of Scripture.[29] I summarize it by saying that as the incarnation manifests the Word of God in human form, so Scripture manifests the Word of God in written form, embodying both divine and human characteristics. God's actions in history, as narrated in Scripture, are revelatory. "For the biblical authors, every event is a mystery whose inner depths reveal something of God and his gracious dealings with humanity."[30] Kolb would make the most of this hermeneutical principle, as seen in the Lutheran focus on God's acts in creation and with Noah as a lens through which to understand baptismal texts. Nettles and Castelein would struggle with this principle, and Pratt would probably be in the middle of that spectrum. Healy recognizes that "unexamined philosophical presuppositions" and "hidden epistemological premises" shape interpretation.[31] Where and how are our seminarians taught to examine and uncover these? Rather than looking across at other streams and feeling separated by disagreements over matters such as baptism, it would be possible to build bridges of understanding and cooperation if conversations were held over deeper-level questions.

Flowing in the same direction as Healy's thoughts about God at work in history, Green explores how theology need not be seen as so separated from

25. Cf. Bubbers, *Scriptural Theology*, 16–21.

26. Olhausen, "A 'Polite' Response," 127.

27. Mary Healy, "Behind, in Front of . . . or Through the Text? The Christological Analogy and the Lost World of Biblical Truth," in *"Behind" the Text*, ed. Bartholomew et al., 181–95.

28. Joel Green, "Learning Theological Interpretation from Luke," in *Reading Luke: Interpretation, Reflection, Formation*, SAH Series 6, ed. Craig Bartholomew, Joel Green, and Anthony Thiselton (Grand Rapids: Zondervan, 2005), 55–178.

29. Healy, "Behind, in Front of . . . or Through the Text?," 191.

30. Healy, "Behind, in Front of . . . or Through the Text?," 187.

31. Healy, "Behind, in Front of . . . or Through the Text?," 181.

history.[32] Green views the gospeler Luke as presenting a narrative which is meant to form Christians, which he understands as an ecclesiological aim.[33] This ecclesiological approach opens a way to read Scripture in a way that need not drastically separate what the text meant and what the text means, because ". . . the chasm that separates the contemporary reader and the Lukan narrative is, in theological interpretation, defined theologically rather than historically."[34] This ecclesiological starting point shapes Green's interpretation of Luke, and there are parallels with Nettles's ecclesiological starting point. Thus, these interpreters from two different theological streams may have more to talk about than they previously assumed if they would move their conversation to hermeneutical issues such as starting points. Having an ecclesiological starting point for interpretation makes a significant difference in the discussion about baptism, as compared, for example, with a Calvinistic covenant of grace starting point.

Christopher Wright moves the conversation from looking at the disconnect between academy and church to the disconnect between theology and mission. In this more specific look at a starting point for scriptural interpretation, he puts forth the purposes of God as a "matrix for hermeneutics and biblical theology."[35] This is a wonderful step in the direction I am urging, both in terms of hermeneutical work done with practitioners in mind and the way in which he writes clearly about his presuppositions. Wright is transparent about his starting point and the undercurrents which will direct his Scriptural interpretations. "The writings that now comprise our Bible are themselves the product of, and witness to, the ultimate mission of God."[36] Therefore, when others compare their conclusions about the meaning of biblical passages with Wright's, they can immediately incorporate into the discussion how his matrix of mission shapes his conclusions. Wright takes the time to carefully define his terminology. So, for example, I can understand that he is using the term "missional" more broadly to refer to God's overarching and sovereign purposes and all their corollary purposes as they are worked out in the created order, rather than the more limited use of the term "missional" referring to only social justice issues. None of the four presenters about baptism pursue their interpretive task from a missional starting point. Adding a missional lens interpretation of baptismal texts to the

---

32. Green, "Learning Theological Interpretation from Luke," 56.
33. Green, "Learning Theological Interpretation from Luke," 57.
34. Green, "Learning Theological Interpretation from Luke," 57.
35. Christopher J. H. Wright, "Mission as a Matrix for Hermeneutics and Biblical Theology," in *Out of Egypt: Biblical Theology and Biblical Interpretation*, SAH Series 5, ed. Craig Bartholomew et al. (Grand Rapids: Zondervan, 2004), 102–43.
36. Wright, "Mission as a Matrix," 103.

round table would enhance the discussion of how hermeneutics shape baptismal belief and practice.

Another contribution to the round table discussion provided by Wright is his attention to perspectives. Just as different perspectives of the original authors need to be carefully considered, so Wright highlights how missional interpretation will carefully consider the different perspectives of readers. "So a missional hermeneutic must include or at least recognize the multiplicity of perspectives and contexts from which, and within which, people read the biblical texts."[37] This is a specific hermeneutical implementation of the case I am making to equip practitioners for diverse audiences. Teaching seminarians about hermeneutical systems other than their own, along with the resulting views of baptism, will help them speak to a multiplicity of situations involving baptism.

Wright expounds on this multicultural community of interpretation, warning against the results of, in my words, syncretism and pluralism. "Are we consigned to a relativism that declines any evaluation? Are there any boundaries as to readings of biblical texts that are 'right' or 'wrong' – or even just 'better' or 'worse'? And how are those boundaries or criteria to be defined?"[38] The community of interpretation is not just a context of multiple cultures; ideally, it will be conducted by a conversation of multiple theological streams. My purpose here is not to offer a "final answer" to "the best starting point for interpretation" (although I do offer a defense of my preferred starting point elsewhere).[39] My purpose here is to point the way forward toward a way the academy can serve the church to better prepare practitioners to root their ministries in Scripture while at the same time offering sermons and pastoral care which are relevant to an ever more heterogeneous audience.

Nicholas Wolterstorff[40] touches on a principle related to the point made by Healy's incarnation analogy. Wolterstorff mentions approaching interpretation with an openness to "double-agency discourse," that is, that Scripture is ". . . the manifestation of God speaking by way of human beings speaking."[41] He concludes with a question that is a primary undercurrent. "The fundamental question before us, then, is whether we should practice divine-discourse interpretation in our interpretation of Scripture."[42] In the case of baptism, for example, is the divine voice speaking about something baptismal through the

37. Wright, "Mission as a Matrix," 114.

38. Wright, "Mission as a Matrix," 114.

39. Cf. Bubbers, *Scriptural Theology*, 1–25.

40. Nicholas Wolterstorff, "The Promise of Speech-act Theory for Biblical Interpretation," in Bartholomew, Greene, and Möller, *After Pentecost*, 73–90.

41. Wolterstorff, "The Promise of Speech-act Theory," 83.

42. Wolterstorff, "The Promise of Speech-act Theory," 89.

term "water" (John 3:5; 13:5; Eph 5:26; Heb 10:22; 1 Peter 3:20; 1 John 5:6, 8)? The four presenters do not directly address this fundamental question. They write as if the answer is self-evidently "no" (Nettles and Castelein) or self-evidently "yes" (Pratt and Kolb). The answer to this underlying question directs the flow of theological conclusions.

Scott Hahn[43] takes us another step closer to the kind of conversation I am advocating. He adds an additional category of hermeneutics to the conversation: "liturgical hermeneutics." Hahn's preferred starting point for interpretation is from the viewpoint of the liturgical community. He sees the liturgy as ". . . the original and privileged locus of biblical interpretation."[44] And, ". . . the church's early cult and worship were decisive in the composition, content, and use of the scriptural texts."[45] "The liturgy emerges as the proper – though not exclusive – setting for reading and interpreting Scripture, and for actualizing its saving truths."[46]

Hahn's liturgical focus impacts how, as an interpreter, he will define and identify such exegetical tools as trajectories and typology. These are significant, particularly in studies involving sacramental topics such as baptism and the Eucharist.[47] Hahn clearly articulates two of his most determinative underlying currents. "First, the recognition that Scripture's final canonical shape is essential for determining the meaning and purpose of individual passages and books; and secondly, the identification of covenant as Scripture's keynote narrative theme."[48] Applying Hahn's thoughts to the comparative hermeneutics of baptism, we would ask questions such as "How does the starting point of covenant (Hahn, Pratt) compare with the starting point of patternism (Nettles, Castelein) and lead to different understandings of biblical texts?" Baptism is just the "fruit on the tree" that is rooted in hermeneutical issues such as "Which theme is the starting point for interpretation? Mission? Covenant? God's nature and character?"

Our presenters of views of baptism and our contributors of SAH essays have provided us with a discussion of a practical theology issue, baptism, and the ways that underlying hermeneutical considerations significantly shape interpretations and resulting beliefs and practices. Such an influential area of study deserves an increase in resources, research, and curriculum space in the system used to prepare practitioners.

---

43. Scott W. Hahn, "Canon, Cult and Covenant: The Promise of Liturgical Hermeneutics," in *Canon and Biblical Interpretation*, SAH Series 7, ed. Craig Bartholomew et al. (Grand Rapids: Zondervan, 2006), 207–35.

44. Hahn, "Canon, Cult and Covenant," 207.

45. Hahn, "Canon, Cult and Covenant," 207.

46. Hahn, "Canon, Cult and Covenant," 208.

47. cf. definitions and use of trajectories and typology in Bubbers, *Scriptural Theology*, 25–29, 41–44.

48. Hahn, "Canon, Cult and Covenant," 209.

3. COMPARATIVE HERMENEUTICS: METHODS AND QUESTIONS

So, we will now add the perspective of practitioners to the round table discussion. I will function as a facilitator and introduce other methods and questions from the field of comparative hermeneutics. These are inquiries which the other conversation partners may not have identified from their particular vantage points. Biblical interpretation needs to be informed by dialogues not only with other fields of study but also with practitioners. This is complex because practitioners are operating on many different "fronts" (denominations, cultural contexts). From a systems analyst perspective, the system of connecting academy and church in the field of hermeneutics needs to be enhanced in a way that does not diminish doctrinal purity and loyalty while at the same time promoting cohesion and cooperation across Christendom.

The academy's role in this system is crucial. Dallas Willard[49] does not specifically address the role of seminaries, but his more general discussion of universities is applicable to the process of training practitioners. Willard sees the university as a source of knowledge and wisdom, and goes on to say that the nature of knowledge includes power: "This leads to struggles between individuals and groups to *control* knowledge . . . to defend its status as knowledge and to attack the claims of others who advocate alternative sources of knowledge."[50] This is also true of theological streams, which each seek to defend their status and gain influence, orienting seminary curriculum and other theological training to those ends. In this way, institutional and personal agendas seek to maintain power and influence. These agendas work against investing in understanding the theological streams of others. However, I believe it is a realistic goal to prioritize a kingdom agenda of a more cohesive Christendom, and we can make room for comparative hermeneutics.

I contend that the decrease of the Bible's influence in university settings happened not only because of Renaissance and Enlightenment philosophies but also because the global church was losing a corporate voice. The proliferation of denominations has left a collection of whispers instead of a piercing proclamation as to what true knowledge and wisdom are. With no consonant message coming from Christendom to the surrounding secular world, our influence has been greatly diminished. For example, if Christians cannot articulate a

49. Dallas Willard, "The Bible, the University, and the God Who Hides," in *The Bible and the University*, SAH Series 8, ed. David Lyle Jeffrey and C. Stephen Evans (Grand Rapids: Zondervan, 2007), 17–39.

50. Willard, "The Bible, the University, and the God Who Hides," 17 (emphasis original).

harmonious message about their most basic practice of baptism, then how valid can an appeal to be baptized really be? What trustworthy "knowledge" can one expect to find from a Christendom that has not found a way to express itself as a more harmonious, knowledgeably trustworthy entity?

The way forward is for us to create a new paradigm of learning and discussion that will bridge streams, a course that will be the context for an equanimous and equitable discussion of not only the theological stream of a given institution but also of other theological streams. Such a comparative discussion can equip practitioners to better engage with their audience, including those who have been harmed by other streams and those who have rejected Christianity because of a perception of untrustworthiness due to multiformity. This Comparative Hermeneutics course can address questions which bridge gaps between hermeneutics and theology and practical ministry.

I am indebted to Dr Don Tinder, who pointed me toward creating a curriculum for this kind of course. He asked me to develop and teach a new THEO 810 Advanced Biblical Hermeneutics course in Olivet Seminary's DMin program in November 2017. We spent quite a bit of time walking throughout the SBL Exhibit Hall the year prior to that, talking with every publisher we could find and seeking a textbook for such a course. Unfortunately, we could not find one that was suited to our needs and goals. So I designed the readings, lesson plans, and lectures from scratch. Since that time, I have begun work on a textbook for a "Comparative Hermeneutics Course" that could be used in multiple denominational settings.

At Olivet the students had all been educated through MDiv programs, and the goal of our course was not to challenge what they had been taught nor dilute the theological stream they brought with them. For the sake of effectiveness in the pulpit, classroom, counseling room, and public sphere, a consideration of comparative hermeneutics was meant to equip the students to engage other views with equanimity. These students needed to interact with other theological streams with calm, confident, pastoral care. This course was the "supply line" to equip these practitioners for their time in "the trenches." For example, many of these students came from backgrounds, theologically and culturally, which had no exposure to the idea that women could not or should not be ordained. However, they were likely to find themselves soon sin ministry situations where the ordination of women was disliked or disallowed. They needed to be equipped not just with knowledge that different conclusions were reached for Scriptural reasons, but they also needed to be equipped to understand how Christians of sincere faith could arrive at such different conclusions using various hermeneutical methodologies. The same can be said for core topics such as baptism and the Eucharist along with other hot topics such as divorce, remarriage, *glossolalia*, cremation, vegetarianism, abortion, pacifism, etc. Deep-level hermeneutical analysis includes defining how the following shape interpretive methods: starting point, primary biblical book, primary dogmatic language (e.g., Latin), worldview (including culture and philosophy), context of interpreter, influence of predecessor theologians, and definition of exegetical tools.

In this brief chapter, our discussion has centered on the first issue, an interpreter's starting point. This is the lens through which biblical texts and other sources are seen. The presenters of four views of baptism each had a different hermeneutical starting point. The SAHS contributors profiled in this volume, if they actually were to participate in a round table discussion comparing hermeneutical approaches to baptism, would likely bring another collection of starting points. The spectrum of this list of hermeneutical starting points would then be quite diverse: Nettles – ecclesiology and anthropology; Pratt – Westminster Confession; Kolb – God's Word in three forms; Castelein – patternism; Plantinga – Bible as Scripture; Wolters – confessional criticism; Thiselton – speech acts; Olhausen – pneumatology; Healy – incarnational Word; Green – ecclesiological formation; Wright – God's mission; Wolterstorff – double-agency discourse; Hahn – liturgics; and, I would add, Bubbers – God's nature and character. A course in the comparative hermeneutics of baptism would include a careful definition, comparison, and contrast of how the different starting points shape interpretation.

In addition to the issues mentioned earlier, a comparative hermeneutics course also considers undercurrent questions such as: Can salvation be lost? Is "salvation" distinct from "justification"? In what ways are the Old Covenant and the New Covenant in continuity? In discontinuity? Does a Greek term in the New Testament warrant a meaning beyond a literal denotation (e.g., typology, symbolism, semantic ranges, connotations)? What qualifies as an Old Testament type? How is its antitype to be identified? Which biblical metaphor is being used as the primary interpretive lens (adoption, new birth, ark of salvation, exodus, circumcision)? What is "original sin"? What is "original guilt"? What is the purpose of an "infant dedication," and what forms does it take in different theological streams? What is the purpose of an "adult profession of faith," and what forms does it take in different theological streams? When a credobaptist attempts to understand a paedobaptist, is a consideration of confirmation included? When a paedobaptist attempts to understand a credobaptist, is a consideration of dedication included? To what extent is "development" valid after the New Testament era itself, in terms of ecclesiastical, doxological, and theological steps taken based upon apostolic foundations (e.g., the Trinity, believer's or infant's baptism rather than convert's baptism, music in worship services, large-sized congregations, women in leadership, ordained clergy, etc.)?

Asking questions directed not only to the biblical text but also to interpreters from various theological traditions will distill the issues that are actually in opposition. This line of inquiry will also identify areas of more agreement. For example, in the Views book the topics of dedication and confirmation are not considered. When these are included in the analysis, beliefs and practices are not as different as usually thought. The question becomes more about the "placement and purpose of water," not the genuineness of faith.

As I elaborated in a previous IBR paper presentation, the interpretation of Scripture will be aided by adding new kinds of questions.[51] As we see in our case study of baptism, different answers to underlying hermeneutical questions will direct interpreters to different conclusions about the meaning and practice of baptism. However, neither academics' nor practitioners' discussions of baptism typically make the effort to step back and consider these deeper-level issues before proceeding to compare their conclusions. The field of comparative hermeneutics is a place for these discussions.

CONCLUSION

The discussion in this chapter integrating four views of baptism with the essays profiled in Part II of this volume has served as a way to illustrate the need to enhance "the process" of training practitioners. More work is needed in the academic area of clarifying and comparing hermeneutical issues influencing practical theology topics such as baptism. This need can be addressed by adding a category of inquiry devoted to analyzing the underlying biblical interpretive methods and presuppositions that shape understandings of the meaning of a Scriptural text and resulting theological conclusions. This discipline of study that I call "comparative hermeneutics" can help the ongoing hermeneutical discussion be more firmly rooted in Scripture and be more effective in equipping practitioners for relevant ministry.

---

51. Susan Bubbers, "A Guiding Principle and a Question-based Strategy for Integrating Biblical, Systematic, and Practical Disciplines," in *Explorations in Interdisciplinary Reading*, ed. Robbie Castleman, Darian Lockett, and Stephen Presley (Eugene, OR: Pickwick, 2017), 168–85.

With the South

CHAPTER 11

Reading the Bible with the Global South

Havilah Dharamraj

In India, the Christian canon has always had to compete with texts that also claim to be divine revelation(s). When the Bible first entered through the trading routes, perhaps in the first century, the sacred texts of Hinduism had been around for a couple of millennia.[1] When the Bible came again, this time through the gateways of colonial rule and more forcefully than before,[2] it was preceded by another scripture. The Quran had already been around in India for almost a millennium, as the sacred text of the Muslim rulers.[3] There is no other environment as competitive for a sacred text as India. The canons of major world religions jostle for space, while the demographically lesser rivals of the Parsi *Zendavesta* and the sacred writings of the reform movements within Hinduism – Buddhism, Jainism, and Sikhism – are acknowledged.

This is the environment in which I was raised: a third-generation Christian, speaking multiple Indian languages, with Hindus as neighbours and a Muslim friend or two at school. The dawn would be greeted with the *azaan*, the call

1. The entry of the Aryans into the Indian subcontinent may be dated between 1500 and 1300 BC. John Keay, *India: A History* (London: Harper, 2010), 27.

2. The first European Protestant missionaries were the Pietists Bartholomew Ziegenbalg and Heinrich Plütschau (1706). The century following saw a tremendous burst of missionary activity in India as well as across the rest of the "pagan" world. See a global overview in Paul E. Pierson, "Why Did the 1800s Explode with Missions?," *Christianity Today* 36 (1992), http://www.christianitytoday.com/history/issues/issue-36/why-did-1800s-explode-with-missions.html.

3. Muslim entry into India began c. 663 AD. Keay, *India: A History*, 181.

to prayer, sounding out from the local mosque. By the time the sun rose, the small temple around the corner would commence the invocation that would rouse its deity from the slumber of the night: "*Wake up, O Manjunatha!*" (What was missing were church bells.) In Scripture lessons in my Church of England missionary all-girls school, we learned the Bible. During library hours I read, among others, stories from the *Ramayana* and the *Mahabharata*, the sacred epic poems of Hinduism. I think my parents would have disapproved if this literature had been in anything more serious than comic book form. For conservative Christians such as us, the sacred books of the East had neither place nor purpose. Meanwhile, subconsciously, I ended up reading my Bible through the *Ramayana* and the *Ramayana* through the Bible.

THE BIBLE VIS-À-VIS NON-CHRISTIAN SACRED TEXTS

This general reluctance of Indian Christians to engage with other sacred scriptures is often a reflection of the polarizing mindset of the European missionaries from the eighteenth century downwards: "Hindu scriptures were compared to a forest in which one could get lost, to poison, to a disease and a false light; in contrast, Christian scriptures pointing the way to human salvation, were a life-giving potion, a medicine, and compared to the welcoming light of a home. Such contrasts were not just confined to tracts but were also elaborated in book-length works."[4] Certain groups of missionaries, for example the Scottish group in Bombay (now Mumbai), poured effort into getting the "native" population to read their own sacred texts with the hope that comparing those texts with the Christian Scriptures would compel them to abandon the former in favour of the latter.[5]

Against this backdrop, a new approach sprang from the seedbed prepared by Indologists such as Max Müller (1823–1900). His endeavours (the fifty-volume *Sacred Books of the East*, published between 1879 and 1910) were motivated by a certain openness and sympathy towards the sacred texts of other religions. Building on this, William Temple Gairdner produced *The Rebuke of Islam* (1920) from his experience of missions in Egypt, and John Nichol

---

4. Hephzibah Israel, *Religious Transactions in Colonial South India: Language, Translation and the Making of Protestant Identity*, Palgrave Studies in Cultural and Intellectual History (New York: Palgrave Macmillan, 2011), 45.

5. Mitch Numark, "Translating *Dharma*: Scottish Missionary-Orientalists and the Politics of Religious Understanding in Nineteenth-Century Bombay," *Journal of Asian Studies* 70, no. 2 (2011): 471–500 [489–93].

Farquhar published *The Crown of Hinduism* (1913) out of his missionary encounters in India.

Farquhar posits that "Christianity is the fulfilment and crown of each" of the Indian subcontinent's many religions. "[I]t is our privilege and duty to trace the lines of connection and lead the peoples up to the Christ."[6] This view – that there can be continuities between the sacred texts of other religions and the Christ event – began to dominate the British missionary approach to Hinduism and other religions in the 1920s and early 1930s. Interestingly, earlier expositions of this approach were indigenous, going back to the mid-nineteenth century when Indian Christian theologians attempted to show Jesus as the fulfilment of the close parallels they saw between the Vedas – the earliest sacred texts of Hinduism – and the Old Testament.[7]

The discipline of intercultural theology continues to debate – often bitterly – whether there can be continuities between the sacred texts of other faiths and Jesus; whether there is indeed such a thing as *praeparatio evangelica*, a "preparation for the Gospel," in their texts and practices and worldviews.[8] Meanwhile, mission strategy continues to include looking for "bridges" that can introduce Jesus to people of non-Judeo-Christian faiths.

Against this historical backdrop, I submit these two proposals. One: with the tectonic shift of the locus of the church to the Global South, the South needs to discover how to read the Bible in conversation with the sacred literature of other faiths. These readings need to be sympathetic rather than adversarial, yet without compromising the orthodox faith and practice of the Christian reader.[9] Two: the West, meanwhile, needs to appreciate that such reading is not to be limited to the Global South, but is a new skill to be learned as cities and neighbourhoods become increasingly plural in culture and faith. Even as I write, thousands of Afghans fleeing the political situation in their home country are being airlifted to the West. In the decades ahead, migration – by way of economic migration, political asylum, and climate change refugees – will only increase.

---

6. Geomon K. George, "Early 20th Century British Missionaries and Fulfilment Theology: Comparison of the Approaches of William Temple Gairdner to Islam in Egypt and John Nicol Farquhar to Hinduism in India," in *Christian Witness Between Continuity and New Beginnings: Modern Historical Missions in the Middle East*, Studien zur Orientalischen Kirchengeschichte 39, ed. Martin Tamcke and Michael Marten (Berlin: LIT Verlag, 2006), 18.

7. K. M. Banerjea, *The Arian Witness: Or the Testimony of Arian Scriptures in Corroboration of Biblical History and the Rudiments of Christian Doctrine* (Calcutta: Thacker, Spink and Co., 1875), 10.

8. See Leonard N. Bartlotti, "Seeing Inside Insider Missiology: Exploring Our Theological Lenses and Presuppositions," *International Journal of Frontier Missiology* 30, no. 4 (2013): 137–53, [145].

9. See Havilah Dharamraj, "The Curious Case of Hagar: Biblical Studies and the Interdisciplinary Approach of Comparative Literature," *Journal of Asian Evangelical Theology* 23, no. 2 (2019): 49–71.

Whether in the East or West, comparative reading needs to be seen as something more than "contextualization" – a term that could mean exotic, esoteric, or idiosyncratic readings, each with relevance only to its own little province in the kingdom of God. Comparative reading needs to be recognized as a method of handling the Christian Scripture that seminarians worldwide learn alongside other methods. For both the majority and the developed world, the writing on the wall declares the end of the era of reading the Bible in "splendid isolation."

BIBLICAL STUDIES, INTERTEXTUALITY, AND THE DISCIPLINE OF COMPARATIVE LITERATURE

So, setting aside the debates that polarize the discipline of intercultural theology, I propose that there is another way to place the Bible in conversation with the sacred literature of other faiths. This is through the method already in use in biblical studies, namely, intertextuality, and leading on through intertextuality to the secular discipline of comparative literature.

Traditionally, the intertextual method of reading texts side by side has been largely *production-centered*, seeking to establish how an older work historically influenced and shaped the writing of a later one – technically called *causality*. The goal is to discover the *purpose* of the intertextual relationship. An example of reading a text intertextually, with *causality* in mind, would be setting the story of the Levite's concubine (Judg 19:22–26) alongside the story of Lot's last night in Sodom (Gen 19:4–8). The events of the two fateful nights are unmistakably in parallel. In Hebrew, sixteen words – almost one-fourth of the vocabulary – are identical. Another twenty-four expressions are in close parallel. Even the length of the text is identical: sixty-nine words in each account. The narrator of the Judges story is intentionally evoking the Sodom account. His point couldn't be clearer: the Levite thought he had found a secure halting place among his own countrymen. Yet he had arrived in what was virtually Sodom. It could be argued that the chronologically later text (Judges) is *caused* by the earlier text (Genesis). The *purpose* is to show that Israel at this stage is so Canaanized that it is indistinguishable from Sodom, a byword for wickedness and perversity. *Causality* and *purpose* mark production-centered intertextuality, which is a largely author-centered, historical endeavor.

When intertextuality, as just deployed, is applied to reading the Bible alongside a non-Christian sacred text, what we have is an investigation in comparative literature. Here, the purpose of the comparatist is to establish a vector of influence pointing from an older work to a later one, showing how the production of the latter was shaped. This is what we might do in Islamic studies when we compare, say, the Quranic account of the "son of the sacrifice" with Genesis 22, the account of the ordeal of Isaac. If it is assumed that the direction of influence is from the Hebrew Bible to the Quran, the comparatist takes the Hebrew text as the norm against which to examine the continuities and discontinuities of the younger version. Beyond this, the comparatist may wish to investigate the historical route of influence; and, being a theologian, (s)he will be intrigued by the theological import of the continuities and discontinuities. Again, *causality* and *purpose* mark this production-centered study, which is a largely author-centered, historical endeavor.

What we are considering in this proposal to read the Bible with the Global South is *reception-centered* intertextuality/comparative literature.[10] These methods intentionally resist investigation of how one text might be dependent on another. Instead, the comparatist simply reads a pair of texts side by side, one a biblical text and the other a non-Christian sacred text. The pairing is directed by a dominant theme shared by the texts, technically called an *icon*. When one text (T1) is paired with and engaged with another (T2), the transcript of the conversation between the two becomes a third text (T3). Discovering the *effect* of this intertextual conversation is the purpose of this method. In sum, *iconicity* and *effect* are the unique identifiers of the reception-centered intertextual/comparative literary method, which is a largely reader-centered, literary investigation.

Let us look at two examples in which a poem from the Song of Songs (T1) is read alongside a parallel poem from a non-Christian sacred text (T2).

SOS AND ANDAL (C. EIGHTH/NINTH CENTURY CE)

One way to read the Song of Songs is as allegory, as expressions of the ideal relationship between deity and devotee.[11] It is a reading that finds resonance in the sacred love poetry that belongs to the wave of spirituality called the Bhakti movement, which spread across the Indian subcontinent over the period

10. For a helpful tabulation comparing production-centered and reception-centered intertextuality, see Ellen van Wolde. "Texts in Dialogue with Texts: Intertextuality in the Ruth and Tamar Narratives," *BibInt* 5 (1997): 5–7. For a survey of methods in use, see B. J. Oropeza, "Intertextuality," in *The Oxford Encyclopedia of Biblical Interpretation*, ed. Steven L. McKenzie (Oxford: Oxford University Press, 2013), 1:453–63. For a comprehensive bibliography of reading on intertextuality, see B. J. Oropeza and Steve Moyise, eds., *Exploring Intertextuality: Diverse Strategies for New Testament Interpretation of Texts* (Eugene, OR: Cascade, 2016), xviii–xix.

11. I have summarized here from my detailed treatment of poems from the Song of Songs in Havilah Dharamraj, *Altogether Lovely: A Thematic Intertextual Reading of the Song of Songs* (Minneapolis: Fortress, 2018).

800–1700 CE. The movement burst through the barriers of caste and clergy to promote individualized and deeply personal devotion to the deity. In fact, the term *bhakti* means "devotion." In Hinduism, the Bhakti movement gathered itself around the worship of Shiva – more particularly, around Shiva's human incarnation, Krishna. Poems from this corpus of sacred love songs make excellent conversation partners with poems from the Song of Songs.

A theme common to any anthology of love poems, whether sacred or secular, is the theme of love in separation. Two poems in the Song express this with exquisite intensity: Song 3:1–4 and 5:2–8. Both are spoken by the woman. The woman *feels* separated from her beloved, and the poems dramatize that mood. What is of interest is that each poem plays out a distinctly different aspect of love in separation. But, let us begin with the first poem, Song 3:1–4 (our T1):

> All night long on my bed
> I looked for the one my heart loves;
> I looked for him but did not find him.
> I will get up now and go about the city,
> through its streets and squares;
> I will search for the one my heart loves.
> So I looked for him but did not find him. . . .
> I found the one my heart loves.
> I held him and would not let him go
> till I had brought him to my mother's house,
> to the room of the one who conceived me.

Let us agree that the dominant icon of the poem is *yearning*, the yearning for the cessation of the separation. For a conversation partner with a matching icon, we select a sacred love poem from the anthology of the eighth or ninth century CE poet Andal (T2). She lived out her short life of sixteen years in utter dedication to the deity Vishnu, in his human incarnation as Krishna. One version of the legend of her end is that she persuaded her foster father to present her to the idol of Vishnu at Srirangam in South India, clothed in full wedding dress. At the shrine, the idol stretched out his hands to embrace her, and she disappeared.[12] Her devotion had supposedly caused her apotheosis – her crossing over into divinity by merger with the deity. Be this as it may, what interests us are the intensely emotional songs left behind by this girl-poet.

The poem that follows is set against the backdrop of an episode in the

12. Charlotte Vaudeville, "Evolution of Love-Symbolism in Bhagavatism," *Journal of the American Oriental Society* 82 (1962): 31–40, [37].

Krishna cycle of stories. One year, the forest village in which Krishna was growing up as a child had such heavy rains that the people feared they would be washed away in the rising water. The child Krishna came to their aid by lifting the nearby Mount Govardhan with his finger, allowing the villagers and their cattle to take shelter under it till the fury of the rains subsided. This is Andal's poem:

> Anguish floods my body and will sweep
> it away unlike the land he rescued by yanking
> the mountain from earth's bosom to hold
> as umbrella over devotees. Yet for me, no glance.
> If I see that thief who's savaged me I'll savage
> my breasts. Uproot their round mounds from
> my body's earth, uproot my love to throw at him.
> If he won't caress me, what use is this howling tenderness?[13]

Here is T3, the transcript of a possible conversation between the two poems.

The pair of poems is a study in contrast: the Song is a blur of changing locations, while in Andal the protagonist is static. The Song's poem opens sedately enough, but soon we find ourselves hastening our steps to keep up with it. Night after night, on her bed, the woman has "looked for" her beloved, but he has failed to come. And so, in bed, in a place normally associated with rest and inactivity, the woman's thoughts allow her neither. "I looked for the one my heart loves," she says. "I looked for him . . ." The repetition signals the seriousness of the initiative and, simultaneously, the disappointment at the outcome: "I did not find." The yearning has met with non-fulfilment, and the waiting has exceeded the tolerable. She makes up her mind to resolve this debilitating impasse of uncertainty.

The search moves out of the bedchamber into the streets, and the streets flow into squares. We are by her side as she hurries along this street, turns into that one, then darts across the square and into yet another street. She is searching as widely and thoroughly as she can. She is also traversing dangerous places. City squares are where prostitutes entice potential clients.

Meanwhile, we assume the search is random, for she has not told us she has any idea of where the man may be. If so, the enterprise is fueled by desperation and is unlikely to succeed. It is not long before our misgivings are confirmed.

---

13. Andal, "Kannan, My Lord, My Love," verse 8 from "Nacciyar Thirumoli," trans. Priya Sarukkai Chabria in *Andal: The Autobiography of a Goddess*, trans. and ed. Priya Sarukkai Chabria and Ravi Shankar (New Delhi: Zubaan, 2015 / Chicago: University of Chicago Press, 2016), 41.

The search in the city ends as did the one in her bedroom: "I looked for him but did not find him."

Suddenly, just like that, just a little farther down the street, or perhaps just around the next corner, the man materializes out of the night. She seems to know him right away, even in the dark streets of the city, even at a time when she was more likely to bump into some undesirable element prowling the city: "I found the one my heart loves." Twice she "did not find"; and now, finally, the seeking meets with finding that which is sought for.

Now the movement reverses itself. She returns by all those streets and squares she has travelled, reaching home again, and bringing her beloved with her. The narrative cycles from her bedchamber to the city to back into the house and then deeper into it, back into a bedchamber. The poem has adeptly deployed the protagonist's movement to convey the intensity of the yearning, the desire for separation to be ended.

Andal's poem, instead, keeps its protagonist standing still. Other things move, though. In her recollections, a mountain moves and changes location. It is pulled up, torn clean from the earth out of which it has grown, and is suspended above the ground, lashed by torrents of rain. That memory speaks of her beloved's love – but it is love directed at his other devotees, not at her. She experiences only his absence. As she grapples with her separation from him, a flood rises through her body, a flood of anguish that threatens to overwhelm her and sweep her life away in its swollen waters. The movement of the mountain and the movement of the flood are related by contrast. The former is caused by her beloved's concern for those who love him; the latter is caused by the same beloved's seeming indifference to the protagonist: he does not even cast a glance at her.

This indifference brings about the reciprocal construction in the second half of the poem. The devotee will mimic her beloved. She will uproot the "round mounds" of her breasts from "[her] body's earth" in demonstration of her love for him. Indeed, these "mounds" are love itself, for she will "uproot [her] love." She imagines that if she mimicks the beloved's action, but with an intensity that well exceeds his, this might end the separation. Unlike the mountain Govardhan that was balanced on the beloved's finger, these mountains will be flung. Here is a bloody arc of motion carrying the devotee's ferocious offering. At least, this should get the attention of the beloved who will not spare even a look. At last, he may realize that he has not only savaged a mountain but savaged this bereft devotee into savaging herself.

The two poems use movement to mediate the mood of yearning, but portray it very differently. In the Song's poem, the mood changes as the narrative circles round on itself. Indeed, as the narrative swiftly spirals inward through the concentric circles of city, mother's house, and bedchamber, the bizarre and dangerous is replaced by the normal and safe. The poem has moved from yearning *to* an irrational fear of abandonment *to* panic-driven action *to* a rush of relief.

Andal's poem balances its two halves with matching descriptions of mounds uprooted, both times as an extraordinary show of affection. The second half, however, leaps off the first half in a searing intensification. The poem moves from anguished yearning for the absent one *to* envious dissatisfaction *to* construction of a (supposed) fitting future response *to* a plaintive wail. The end circles back to the beginning, for the state of separation remains unchanged. Wordless "anguish" finds articulation: ". . . what use is this howling tenderness" if it goes unreciprocated?

As much as the Song ends with the seeking finding satisfaction, Andal ends with seeking unresolved. Any hope of finding is predicated with "if": "If I see that thief . . ." In the Song separation is replaced by reunion, in the dark street and then in the intimacy of the bedchamber. In Andal, separation is replaced by the thought of further separation. The devotee will attempt the impossible in separating herself from her love for the beloved – "I'll uproot my love" – but, ironically, this act might be an extreme and desperate attempt to prove her love and to end the separation. In the Song, the devotee gladly seizes her beloved and will not let him go. In Andal, the devotee is driven to thoughts of seizing herself in an attempt to let go of her beloved. As much as certain (re)possession of the beloved concludes the Song, uncertainty leaves Andal hanging and incomplete; despairing, yet hopeful of a caress.

Taken together, the *effect* of the sacred love songs is to describe the full range of emotions that characterize love for a God who appears absent. If one poem foregrounds yearning as desperate seeking which will not give up till the seeking finds God, the other foregrounds yearning as rage at perceiving oneself as abandoned by God. The Christian canon does not withhold reporting the latter, though in a different genre (Ps 83:1; Job 23:8–9). The poems together offer both endings, one in which the waiting ends and one in which the waiting continues on. We know from experience the agony and the ecstasy of each.

SOS AND VIDYAPATI (C. 1352–1448)

A second pair of poems looks at a very different, and rather startling, aspect of love in separation. Here is the excerpt from the poem in Song 5:2–6 (T1):

I slept but my heart was awake.
    Listen! My beloved is knocking:
"Open to me, my sister, my darling,
    my dove, my flawless one.
My head is drenched with dew,
    my hair with the dampness of the night."
I have taken off my robe –
    must I put it on again?
I have washed my feet –
    must I soil them again?
My beloved thrust his hand through the latch-opening;
    my heart began to pound for him.
I arose to open for my beloved,
    and my hands dripped with myrrh,
my fingers with flowing myrrh,
    on the handles of the bolt.
I opened for my beloved,
    but my beloved had left; he was gone.
    My heart sank at his departure.
I looked for him but did not find him.
    I called him but he did not answer.

The unique icon that emerges is that of *withholding*. The woman is dozing lightly, both asleep and awake at once. It appears that she is listening for the beloved to knock, for she springs alert at the sound. She hears his words, his entreaty to let him in. But here is the conundrum: she is reluctant. To whom are the words addressed? We are not sure. Either she addresses the beloved on the other side of the bolted door, or she thinks her thoughts aloud to us:

I have taken off	my robe	must I put it on again?
I have washed	my feet	must I soil them again? (5:3)

If this is bantering with her beloved, we are not overly surprised. Such teasing is not unexpected between lovers. But if this is an aside to the reader, then it is reason for some disquiet. Either the woman has made up her mind not to attend to the door, making the questions entirely rhetorical, or she is in two minds and is talking herself through to a decision. As much as she loves the beloved, the woman is not always pining for his company. That other night (3:1–4), it was intolerable that she should be separated from him. This night, she is not so sure she wants him with her – even though she may well have prepared for his arrival by perfuming herself and her bed with myrrh (5:5).

Meanwhile, either in response to her teasing or anxious about her silence, the beloved redoubles his effort. Suddenly, there is a rush of the visual, the auditory, and the tactile. All at once, she can see and hear him. His fingers, trying to work the bolt open, stimulate her sense of touch. The door is still shut, but he has invaded the room! The sensory overload shoots a frisson through her. Spontaneously, she gets up.

Attention now shifts from his hand to her hands, which are described as if in slow motion and with increasing detail. The liquid myrrh of her fingers smears the handles of the lock. Her grip slips, and she must try again and again till the door unbolts. The aggregation of sensory stimuli is directed at the reader this time – the sight of the woman's hands clumsily at work, the sound of the bolt being worked, and the feel of oiled fingers against the door's lock. The slickly perfumed fingers are willing, but they themselves become the hindrance.

In all, there have been two pauses so far: once when the woman deliberated on getting out of bed, and next with the slippery bolt. Paronomasia links the two pauses: she had hesitated to soil her freshly washed feet, and her hands drip with liquid myrrh. Both hands and feet are unwilling participants, and there will be a price to pay. The lapse between his request "Open . . ." (5:2) and the actual opening of the door is considerable. Half the poem (5:2–8) has gone by before the door finally swings open. Even as she was struggling with the bolt, the beloved has made an exit from the narrative.

As a companion poem (T2), we have a composition of Vidyapati Thakur (c.1352–1448),[14] born in what is now eastern Bihar, in North India. Commissioned as a court poet, Vidyapati created an anthology of love songs articulating the courtship between the deity, Krishna, and the human soul, typified by Radha, a cowherdess. Vidyapati's love songs interlace folk themes with court traditions, and, perhaps for that reason, to this day these compositions remain household poetry across the eastern states of Bihar and West Bengal.

While Vidyapati's songs could well pass for an interchange between a pair of human lovers, "[i]t is quite certain that many poems of Vidyāpati have an almost wholly spiritual significance."[15] Love directed at a human object of adoration is hardly mutually exclusive from that directed towards deity. Indeed, the evolving cult of Krishna in Bengal picked up and popularized Vidyapati's compositions, directing them firmly towards deity.

---

14. Ananda Coomaraswamy, "Introduction," in *Vidyāpati: Bangīya Padābali*, trans. Ananda Coomaraswamy and Arun Sen (London: Old Bourne Press, 1915).

15. Coomaraswamy, "Introduction," *Vidyāpati*, 4.

Vidyapati's songs are largely directly spoken to the audience, and in this poem the devotee Radha speaks. The poet closes the poem with a summarizing observation.

> I had desired to look on Kānu [Krishna],
> But when I saw him I was filled with fear:
> Ever since then I am both fond and foolish,
> I have no knowledge at all what I say or do.
> My twin eyes wept like dripping rain,
> Unceasingly my heart went pit-a-pat:
> I cannot think what made me look on him, my dear.
> Just for that whim, I lent my life into another's hand!
> I cannot tell what that dear thief has done to me, –
> When I beheld him, he did steal my heart, and went away,
> And as he went he showed so many signs of love,
> The more I would forget, the less I may!
>
> Hearken, fair maid, says Vidyāpati:
> *Have patience in your heart, for you shall meet Murāri [Krishna].*[16]

While the Song conveys the devotee's mood through both "showing" and "telling," Vidyapati's mode is "telling," using a monologue directly addressing us, the audience. The devotee confides to us her dilemma. She loves him, but she wishes she did not love him. She desires to see her beloved, but fearfully withdraws when she does see him. Her heart says one thing, but her eyes say another; one beats faster at the memory of the encounter, while the other sheds regretful tears that the meeting transpired at all. It was merely a whim that set the sequence rolling, but now she is in a situation that cannot be reversed. He is a thief, but a dear thief. She is caught between remembering and resisting remembering. She swings between wanting and withdrawing. She does not know what she says or does, confusedly inhabiting this liminality between ebb and surge.

The transcript (T3) of the interaction of the two poems (T1 and T2) could read as follows.

The protagonists of both poems are sure of this: the beloved loves them deeply. In the Song, the beloved has travelled a distance to reach the woman's door. He says his hair is wet with night dew, a declaration of his eagerness to be with her. His affection tumbles out in a string of endearments: she is his "own"

16. Coomaraswamy, *Vidyāpati*, 16-17.

(so JPS), his loved one, his dove, his flawless one – making this the longest string of consecutive endearments in the Song's anthology. Vidyapati's protagonist is similarly in no doubt: "he showed so many signs of love."

Despite having a beloved who loves truly and deeply, both poems are agreed that he is not predictable. He comes and goes at will. In Vidyapati, the beloved "did steal my heart, and went away . . ." In the Song, the devotee opens the door to find the threshold empty. Thus, both poems also conclude similarly: the protagonist returns to the other mood that characterizes love in separation, namely, yearning. In the Song, her "heart sank at his departure." She looks up and down the street, and she calls him. And the cycle of seeking and finding (or not finding) starts up again. Similarly, at the end of the Vidyapati poem desire for the beloved wins over fearful regret: "The more I would forget, the less I may!" Reading her mind, the poet consoles the protagonist. "Have patience in your heart," he advises. "You shall meet [him again]."

The *effect* of reading the two compositions side by side is that it reminds us that our love for God is more complex than we like to admit (cf. Job 23). Rabbi Soloveitchik's discourse on Song 5:2–3, titled "The Voice of My Beloved Knocking," sets out the dilemma: "Why should she refuse to undo the latch and open the door to her lover?" Why, especially if shortly thereafter she will begin "pursuing him, . . . suffering insults, blows, and spiritual torment on his behalf"?[17] We are bemused by the Song's devotee till we recognize ourselves in the mirror Vidyapati holds up, all the more because his Radha confides in us, laying bare her conflicted heart. Like Vidyapati's protagonist, we slide between wanting God and withholding ourselves from him, between adoring and fearfully withdrawing.

CONCLUSION

The secular interdisciplinary method of comparative literature defines the cognitive exercise of literary comparison as "reading a work through other works."[18] I prefer a different preposition: we read the Bible *alongside* non-Christian texts. Such comparative reading is not new to biblical studies. There is not a literary genre that we do not compare with its contemporaneous counterparts: the Genesis creation narratives with the epic poems of ancient West

17. Rabbi Soloveitchik in Shalom Carmy, "Perfect Harmony," *First Things* (2010), https://www.firstthings.com/article/2010/12/perfect-harmony.

18. César Domínguez, Haun Saussy, and Darío Villanueva, "Preface," in *Introducing Comparative Literature: New Trends and Applications* (London: Routledge, 2016), xi.

Asian cosmogonies; the Mosaic law codes with those of Hammurabi; proverbial wisdom with the Instruction of Amenemope; and the Song of Songs with Egyptian anthologies of love songs. Sometimes these readings are competitive, and such readings have their place and value. At other times we read comparatively in order to understand, appreciate, and appropriate the Bible better. In biblical studies, comparative reading has stayed too long in the echo chambers of the then and there. It is time to let it (also) step out into the here and now.

A caveat here: As I read these compositions, whether biblical or nonbiblical, I confess the object of my affection to be a unique particularity – Jesus Christ. That the "other" poem in each pair is directed at another particularity – with its own infrastructure of deities and beliefs and practices and worldview – is a (sometimes uncomfortable) reality that I must learn to navigate with both eagerness and caution. My students have essayed dissertations in which they have comparatively investigated the concept of fate or determinism in the narratives of Pharaoh and Saul alongside narratives in the *Mahabharata*; the legal options for women in distress (rape; barrenness; widowhood) in the Mosaic canon and in the *Manusmriti*; and the idea of the "good life" in Proverbs and in the *Thirukkural*. Sometimes the students have been adversarial, but more often they have been happily surprised by the richness of the intertextual conversations that result. The older series from Peeters, *Christian Commentaries on Non-Christian Sacred Texts*, the new Langham series *Bible Commentaries from Muslim Contexts*, and Routledge's new series *Biblical Interpretation in Islamic Context* are some of the emerging spaces in which one may overhear such conversations.

This essay has proposed that one way of reading the Bible with the Global South is to read intertextually, that is, read the Bible alongside other parallel texts. In Asia these texts might be the sacred texts of Hinduism and Buddhism, or of Islam and Zoroastrianism. In other continents, these texts might voice worldviews or philosophies. As we put the Bible into conversation with these expressions of human longing for understanding, we do so with the conviction that the Bible is to be uniquely privileged. It is God-breathed and infallible. It is the full and final witness to Jesus Christ as the only means by which sins can be forgiven, allowing humankind to inherit life everlasting. The Bible is eminently incomparable. However, reading these luminous, living words alongside those that our neighbours deem sacred can layer and nuance our (perhaps tired-ly traditional) reading of the Bible. We might find ourselves surprised by the God of the Bible in ways we might not have thought of before. We might understand him, ourselves, and the world in ways that are more intimate, more urgent, and more present.

In the University

CHAPTER 12

Cultivating a Biblical Intellect: The Bible in the University

David J. H. Beldman

INTRODUCTION

> And when he sits on the throne of his kingdom, he shall write for himself in a book a copy of this law . . . and he shall read in it all the days of his life, that he may learn to fear the LORD his God, by keeping all the words of this law and these statutes, and doing them; that his heart may not be lifted up above his brethren, and that he may not turn aside from the commandment, either to the right hand or to the left; so that he may continue long in his kingdom, he and his children, in Israel. (Deut 17:18–20 RSV)

These are the instructions that Deuteronomy provides for future kings of Israel. Demonstrated here is a key insight: success in the realm of royal rule will depend on the extent to which the king finds his anchor and orientation in the expressed revelation of God. It is important to note that "the law" that the king would copy is not a comprehensive code of all things pertinent to kingly rule that the king should memorize and execute. Rather, "the law" is an orientation to God's comprehensive way of righteousness and holiness and would guide the king in wise ruling and prudent arbitration (see Prov 8:15–16). As the king navigated the challenges of day-to-day rule, the Word of God would not provide every proviso for every circumstance but would be for the king a lamp to his feet and a light to his path (Ps 119:105). In this way, the king was summoned to be thoroughly "biblical," though perhaps not in the ways that we often conceive of the word.

Christianity, as the historian Robert Louis Wilken notes, "is more than a set of devotional practices and a moral code: it is also a way of thinking about God, about human beings, about the world and history."[1] He states that the purpose of his book *The Spirit of Early Christian Thought: Seeking the Face of God* is "to depict the pattern of Christian thinking as it took shape in the formative centuries of the church's history."[2] Over the course of his research, what impressed him the most "is the omnipresence of the Bible in early Christian writings. Early Christian thought is biblical, and one of the lasting accomplishments of the patristic period was to forge a way of thinking, scriptural in language and inspiration, that gave to the church and to Western civilization a unified and coherent interpretation of the Bible as a whole."[3] In the early church's endeavour to capture the hearts and minds of their contemporaries and to transform their lives, the Bible was central:

> It narrated a history that reached back into antiquity even to the beginning of the world, it was filled with stories of unforgettable men and women (not all admirable) . . . and it poured forth a thesaurus of words that created a new religious vocabulary and a cornucopia of scenes and images that stirred literary and artistic imagination as well as theological thought. God, the self, human community, the beginning and ending of things became interwoven with biblical history, biblical language, and biblical imagery.[4]

It should go without saying that Scripture stirred the intellectual imagination of early Christian thinkers, even as they engaged deeply with Greco-Roman ideas.

There is no shortage of Christian scholars today who have achieved the highest levels of expertise in their academic fields and are contributing in meaningful ways to their disciplines. However, to what extent are Christian scholars and Christian communities (academic and otherwise) cultivating and forming minds that, to borrow Wilken's language, are "thoroughly biblical?" How can (or should) the Bible shape and contribute to Christian scholarship? The use of the Bible in scholarship is a long-standing problem that, to the best of my

---

1. Robert Louis Wilken, *The Spirit of Early Christian Thought: Seeking the Face of God* (New Haven: Yale University Press, 2003), xiii.
2. Wilken, *The Spirit of Early Christian Thought*, xiv.
3. Wilken, *The Spirit of Early Christian Thought*, xvii.
4. Wilken, *The Spirit of Early Christian Thought*, xiv–xv.

knowledge, has yet to be resolved. That said, I am aware of some creative and fruitful examples of Scripture use in scholarship in various disciplines, and readers from various disciplines are undoubtedly aware too. A key agenda item for the future of Scripture use in Christian scholarship should be to examine some of the best examples and to discern what makes these uses of the Bible in scholarship so helpful.[5]

This essay aims to shed light on the challenge of Scripture use in Christian scholarship. It will do so by identifying the problem, highlighting some fruitful examples of biblical interpretation from the perspective of multi-disciplinary expertise, and providing some orientation points for a pathway forward.

THE PROBLEM: LACK OF BIBLICAL LITERACY, BIBLICAL FLUENCY, AND BIBLICAL HERMENEUTICS

It probably can go without saying that rampant biblical illiteracy is plaguing Christians today (this is certainly true in the West). More and more Christians simply do not know the contents of the Bible. While it would be nice to assume that Christian scholars are the exception, I fear they are not immune to this lack of knowledge of the Bible. Simply put, if we do not have an awareness of the Old and New Testaments and of the vast array of topics and subjects the Bible addresses, we cannot hope to allow Scripture to come to bear on and be used meaningfully in our scholarship. But biblical literacy is not the only problem facing Christian scholars, and becoming biblically literate, though a necessary first step, is not the full solution.

Compare knowing the Bible with learning a second language. Becoming conversant with the contents of the Bible is vital and will provide something of the vocabulary of the Bible. However, anyone who has learned a second language knows that learning vocabulary, although essential, is not sufficient for becoming a native speaker. The goal is not learning a comprehensive list of foreign words but understanding thought patterns of the language such that we get to the point where we formulate thought. Then, on that basis and over time, we seek to communicate effortlessly in the foreign language. The goal, in short, is fluency.

---

5. The Scripture and Hermeneutics Seminar volumes are worthy of special mention, as they fruitfully address topics like history, ethics, philosophy of language, and so on. Readers interested in the topic of this essay should especially consult the volume *The Bible and the University*, edited by D. L. Jeffrey and C. S. Evans (Grand Rapids: Zondervan, 2007) and keep up to date with the Scripture and the University Seminar (part of the Kirby Laing Centre Scripture Collective).

For some time, the Center for Hebraic Thought has been advocating for what it calls "biblical fluency," which helpfully captures what is lacking but vital in Christian scholarship (not to mention the church broadly). The assumption here is that the Bible speaks and thinks in distinctive ways about reality and invites readers to develop a biblically formed mind for navigating the world we inhabit on the basis of the deep structures of the Bible's thought world.[6] The problem facing Christian scholars is not just a lack of biblical literacy but, more foundationally, a lack of biblical fluency. The result is that Christian scholars across the disciplines are ill-equipped to deal meaningfully with Scripture.

Some of the blame does fall to scholars of the Bible and departments of biblical studies in Christian colleges. The latter should be places where Bible scholars and theologians regularly open up the Bible in ways that are helpful for other disciplines. The kind of scholarly biblical interpretation on display in the next section of this essay is sadly all too rare in biblical scholarship, which has its own idiosyncrasies and preoccupations that prevent the riches of Scripture from being brought to bear on other academic disciplines. However, scholars outside the theological disciplines must also bear some of the blame. How many scholars of other disciplines have engaged seriously with the Bible and have done any work at all in the area of healthy biblical scholarship? An audit of this along with how professors at Christian colleges are using the Bible in their disciplines (teaching and scholarship) would be fascinating and telling. My suspicion is that the kind of biblical fluency that opens up into disciplinary specialty is rare today.

I will explore solutions for these problems facing Christian scholars, but before doing so I want to briefly indicate why the situation is so problematic. First, and by far the most insidious, is the influence of competing stories that shape the way each person experiences and interprets reality. Brandon O'Brien maintains that everyone sees and reads (and consequently responds to) the world through four "myths": the personal myth, the communal myth, the national myth, and the religious/philosophical myth.[7] O'Brien makes an important observation that has a bearing on the use of Scripture in Christian scholarship. He notes that the personal myth dominates Western society and Christian discipleship. In other words, Western Christians tend to see the power of worldviews and ideologies as influencing *the individual*. Thus, a Christian worldview tends to focus on the individual, leaving the realms of the other myths largely unscathed and hence unexamined (but no less operable). The result is that

---

6. I am deliberately utilizing language derived specifically from the Center for Hebraic Thought. See www.hebraicthought.org.

7. I am indebted to Brandon O'Brien's four-fold myth categories in his unpublished paper "The Myths that Make Us."

one's communal and national stories are not made subservient to the story of Scripture, and yet they still profoundly influence the way one experiences and interprets reality. (A corollary is that the influence of the biblical story even on the personal myth becomes truncated and/or distorted.)[8]

Of course, there may be many Christian scholars who understand that Scripture should speak to public matters – to politics, the economy, art, and so on; however, many seem to struggle to know *how* it comes to bear, because this is not something we have typically done well in the West.[9] Moreover, a casualty of the triumph of modern secular ideology is that there are Christian scholars who seem unaware that the biblical story might transform the way they understand and interpret their discipline, not to mention that biblical teaching might have something specific to say about particularities of their discipline. In short, the competing stories of our cultures are dominating Christian scholarship, and we need ways of living more consistently into the biblical story and bringing that to bear in the academic realm.

Second, Christians (including many Christian scholars) tend to work with distorted views of the Bible and especially the Old Testament, thereby ignoring Scripture as a resource for Christian scholarship. The distortions range from seeing a (sometimes irreparable) distinction between the OT and NT, including the operation and even the nature of God in the Testaments, to a twisted Christocentrism that finds Jesus in the most bizarre and unlikely places, objects, and actions (an approach a colleague comically termed the "Where's Waldo" approach to finding Jesus in the OT). Christopher Wright tells a story of an Indian man who was converted to Christianity by reading the OT, particularly OT law. The man was overwhelmed by the enormous scope of God's interest demonstrated in the *Torah* and expressed with wonder: "Your God thinks of everything!" However, Christians have inherited a tradition of either regarding the OT as so foreign that it has no public relevance today or domesticating the OT (i.e., as a simplistic preview of Jesus) and thereby muting its public relevance. Once we recover the public and all-encompassing scope of the teaching of the OT and its continuity with the NT as the true story of all of history and the whole of reality, not only will we regain Christian faith and teaching as public

8. On the importance of the Bible as a narrative, see Craig G. Bartholomew, "Story and Biblical Theology," in *Out of Egypt: Biblical Theology and Biblical Interpretation*, SAH Series 5, ed. Craig Bartholomew et al. (Grand Rapids: Zondervan, 2004), 144–72.

9. It is easy to overgeneralize here. What Esau McCaulley calls "Black ecclesial interpretation of the Bible," for example, has always been interested in how the texts of the Bible speak directly to issues that Black Christians face and, therefore, is particularly attuned to the public, social, and political nature of the Bible's teaching. See Esau McCaulley, *Reading While Black: African American Biblical Interpretation as an Exercise in Hope* (Downers Grove: IVP Academic, 2020).

truth, but we will also find Scripture as a significant source for Christian scholarship across the disciplines.

Third, sometimes content from the Bible appears in academic work by means of a prooftext. A prooftext is a verse or two that Christians may quote to prove a particular point or support some claim or other. There may be a case for legitimate prooftexting, but the danger of prooftexting is that biblical statements are too often divorced from their literary and historical contexts and assigned meaning that they were never intended to communicate. An extreme example of this was recently captured on video and went viral. At the Texas State Senate Committee on State Affairs, a witness (who has a PhD in physical chemistry from the University of Texas at Austin) was testifying on election fraud. Speaking of the function of "poll watchers" (those who help ensure votes are properly counted and report on irregularities) in the 2020 US presidential election, the witness started her testimony with these words:

> I believe this is God's work, and there's a wonderful scripture about the security of elections that I wanna read, and that maybe some of us may have never heard before. It's 2 Peter 1:10. "Brethren, give diligence to make your calling and election sure, for if ye do these things ye shall never fall." I love that scripture because this is what our watchers do.[10]

The problem with this instance of prooftexting is plain, as a subsequent witness rightly exposed: "With all due respect . . . I do believe Saint Peter was referring to the election of the saints not the election of Texas State Senators." Hopefully such blatant twisting of Scripture does not appear in Christian scholarship and teaching, but this extreme example should warn us of the danger of naive understandings and readings of the Bible and shows how we might avoid the *mis*use of Scripture in academic work (and other places).

At the root of these problems is a truncated view of the Bible and what kind of instruction it has to offer, along with an insufficient way of reading the Bible (i.e., biblical hermeneutics) that leaves so much of life, including the realm of scholarship, untouched by the claims of Scripture. Craig Bartholomew and Matthew Emerson write, "[E]ven amid the welcome renaissance of theological interpretation, it is common to read the Bible for the institutional church or for Christian doctrine, but often without opening up the comprehensive range of Scripture's witness . . . [This] is a critique that can be leveled against large swaths of academic biblical interpretation on both the liberal left and the conservative

10. Texas State Senate Committee on State Affairs, July 10, 2021, 12:28:20–12:32:44, https://tlcsenate.granicus.com/MediaPlayer.php?view_id=49&clip_id=16333.

right."[11] The problem of the use or misuse of Scripture in Christian scholarship is deeply and intricately bound up with the problem of reading Scripture in general. A recovery of Scripture as the true story of everything is essential. The Bible is not just a collection of moral stories or spiritual nuggets or answers to this or that question we are facing; it offers wisdom and instruction for all of life because the story of the kingdom of God is about all of life. What we need for life and for scholarship is reading strategies that draw out the public nature of Scripture's instruction. The next section will present three examples that deal specifically with the book of Exodus, demonstrating a sense of this big picture of the Bible and what it might offer Christian scholarship. Following that, I will offer some reflections and avenues forward in the project of using Scripture in Christian scholarship.

BRINGING DISCIPLINE-SPECIFIC EXPERTISE TO THE BIBLE

What might happen when we bring disciplinary expertise and discipline-specific questions to the Bible? As a professor at a Christian undergraduate institution, I often encounter students seeking simplistic answers from particular passages of the Bible to questions the passages were never meant to address.[12] This is baffling, and exposes a naïve understanding of what the Bible is and what it is doing. Equally baffling, however, is that good and thoughtful scholars with profound expertise in an area of study rarely bring their academic expertise to bear on their reading of Scripture! What would it look like if English literature specialists read narratives or poetry of the Bible utilizing the very best theories from their field, if anthropologists explored the models of anthropology at work in the societies of ancient Israel or first-century Judaism, or if international relations scholars explored the Bible from the perspective of their field of expertise?

Consider the examples provided by three scholars centred around the book of Exodus: Leon Kass, Ellen Davis, and William Abraham. First, Leon Kass is a world-renowned bioethicist. For decades he taught courses on the history/foundation of ethics, in which students read primary sources from the Western tradition (the usual suspects from Plato and Aristotle to Hobbes, Locke, and Rousseau). At one point he decided to assign readings from the Torah (the

11. Craig G. Bartholomew and Matthew Y. Emerson, "Theological Interpretation for All of Life," in *A Manifesto for Theological Interpretation*, ed. Craig G. Bartholomew and Heath A. Thomas (Grand Rapids: Baker Academic, 2016), 257–73.

12. Pedagogically, even these questions are helpful in unpacking what is going on in a particular passage.

first five books of the Bible), recognizing that these texts were also a significant influence on ethics in the Western intellectual tradition. Like they did with the other primary sources, he and his students pored over these texts in a concerted effort to discover what wisdom they might contribute to the questions of ethics (what is the good life, what does it mean to be human, how do we live for the common good, etc.?). One product of decades of reading the Torah in this way is a commentary Kass wrote on the book of Exodus: *Founding God's Nation: Reading Exodus* (similarly, see also his commentary on Genesis: *The Beginning of Wisdom: Reading Genesis*).[13] Kass assumes that Exodus has relevance (i.e., it offers wisdom) in the public realm today, and so the kinds of questions he brings to the text yield insights into politics, leadership and governance, economic and labor practice, agriculture, law, ritual, science, art, time, and more – all in a way that is surprisingly relevant. Kass asks good questions, and he attentively listens to the text to hear what instruction it has to offer.[14]

Consider, for instance, the wisdom for art and artists that Kass draws from the implementation of Yahweh's instructions for the building of the tabernacle (Exodus 31). After elaborate details for the tabernacle have been given, Kass considers the following questions most pertinent: "Who among this collection of ex-slaves, experienced only in making and laying brick and mortar for Pharaoh, can execute these elaborate instructions for an edifice of such beauty and elegance? How can these craftsmen be found, and who will find them? And how will they be able to do the necessary work?"[15] These seem the most obvious questions that this particular part of Exodus elicits, and we expect Exodus 31 will answer, but Kass does not stop there:

> In addition to providing answers to these questions, we also expect that the Lord's account will address, at least indirectly, the place of art and artists in the way of life He is initiating in Israel, as well as our lingering questions about human making. Can artistic genius flourish in Israel without giving free rein to the artists' pride-filled and glory-seeking propensities? Can the artist of the beautiful lead people to the divine, or will he instead encourage deification of his art – and himself? How do the reasoning and know-how of the craftsman relate to biblical wisdom and to knowledge of law, morals, and God?[16]

---

13. Leon Kass, *Founding God's Nation: Reading Exodus* (New Haven: Yale University Press, 2021); Leon Kass, *The Beginning of Wisdom: Reading Genesis* (New York: Free Press, 2003).

14. For a reflection on Kass's hermeneutic for reading the texts of the Bible, see David J. H. Beldman, "Living with the Text: Leon Kass's Model for Attentive Listening to the Bible," *The Biblical Mind*, April 21, 2021, https://hebraicthought.org/leon-kass-model-attentive-listening-bible/.

15. Kass, *Founding God's Nation*, 515.

16. Kass, *Founding God's Nation*, 515.

From the calling and commissioning of Bezalel and Oholiab (Exodus 31:1–6), Kass draws out deep truths about the role of the artist and of art more generally, along with what he calls "artisan wisdom."[17] In sum, "This analysis of the surface of the text returns us to the deeper questions about the place of art and artists under God's Way . . . the true artist is God's divinely inspired co-creator, not a freelancer seeking fame for himself. The artists are God's prophets for the eyes. The beauty they cultivate becomes the skin of the good and the holy. And they help complete God's Creation by producing for it the hallowed place where man and God may meet and know each other."[18] Who would have expected such insights to emerge from the commissioning of two craftsmen to engage in building the tabernacle?[19]

Kass makes this kind of hermeneutical move time and time again in his commentary, drawing wisdom about leadership today from the unique leadership formation of Moses, about the development of peoplehood and nationhood from the unique experience of the formation of Israel as a nation, and more. As an expert in ethics and a self-professed humanist scholar (i.e., a student devoted to the study of human affairs/nature), Kass brings his expertise and his "humanist" questions to the text of Exodus, providing surprisingly relevant results.

Second, Ellen Davis is an Old Testament scholar with an interest in how "biblical interpretation bears on the life of faith communities and their response to urgent public issues."[20] Her 2009 book, *Scripture, Culture, and Agriculture: An Agrarian Reading of the Bible*, includes a chapter called "Leaving Egypt Behind: Embracing the Wilderness Economy."[21] Davis examines the narrative of the divine gift of manna in Exodus 16 in such a way that it is a "paradigmatic account" of the contest between the vision for an agrarian economy (put forth as a model for God's people in Exodus and beyond) and the oppressive industrial economy represented by Pharaonic Egypt on the one hand and, by extension, Canaanite economic structures on the other.[22]

The contest between economic visions in Exodus centres around food, which according to Davis confirms the principle of all agrarian writers that

---

17. Kass, *Founding God's Nation*, 515–19.

18. Kass, *Founding God's Nation*, 519.

19. Further to this discussion of art and artists, it is worthwhile considering Kass's discussion on the role of song (i.e., poetry) and dance after God's victory over Pharaoh and his armies, and how in Exodus the former is the "song of death-dealing victory" (portrayed as a masculine expression) and the other is movement of life and love in peace (portrayed as a feminine response); see Kass, *Founding God's Nation*, 216–17.

20. This from Davis's Duke Divinity faculty profile webpage, https://divinity.duke.edu/faculty/ellen-davis.

21. Ellen F. Davis, *Scripture, Culture, and Agriculture: An Agrarian Reading of the Bible* (Cambridge: Cambridge University Press, 2009), 66–79.

22. Davis, *Scripture, Culture, and Agriculture*, 67.

"Eating is the most basic of all cultural and economic acts."[23] In the liminal space of the wilderness, Israel's first expression after giving effusive praise for Yahweh's deliverance and the destruction of Pharaoh and his armies (Exodus 15) is complaint about lack of food: "Would that we had died by the hand of the LORD in the land of Egypt, when we sat by the meat pots and ate bread to the full, for you have brought us out into this wilderness to kill this whole assembly with hunger" (Exod 16:3 ESV). Davis writes,

> I believe that . . . the manna story . . . is working consciously against this cultural background – working against it in the strong sense. That is, the biblical storyteller is imaginatively recreating social reality, painting a new picture of work in the field for those who have left Egypt behind . . . I read the manna story as a counternarrative that outlines a new moral economy of food production and distribution.[24]

What are the principles and features of this counternarrative? I will summarize some of the salient points that Davis draws out.

The distinct economic vision that the manna story engenders, first, regards eating as worship and even revealing true knowledge of God. Second, it places Israel in the status of the vulnerable (i.e., gleaners) in a way that should engender solidarity with the economically vulnerable even when they enter the promised land and are vouchsafed a fuller measure of self-sufficiency. Third, God puts restraints on the gathering of manna. As such, it becomes "evident that if adequate and even generous food supply may provide the occasion to know God (Exod 16:12), then *accurate* knowledge of God, the world, and our place in it – in short, wisdom – is available only to those who eat with restraint."[25] Fourth, restraint and Sabbath transform a vision of the world from nature (impersonal supply) to creation (divine gift) – according to Davis, "a distinction that must be observed in our economies, if it is to be meaningful at all."[26] Fifth, memory of the right things in the right way (not skewed by intellectual pride and lack of trust) is essential for a right understanding of reality and a proper grasp of the economy and food production in the wilderness and beyond.[27]

The brilliance of Davis's examination of the manna narrative in Exodus 16

23. Davis, *Scripture, Culture, and Agriculture*, 71.
24. Davis, *Scripture, Culture, and Agriculture*, 72.
25. Davis, *Scripture, Culture, and Agriculture*, 78 (emphasis original).
26. Davis, *Scripture, Culture, and Agriculture*, 78.
27. Davis, *Scripture, Culture, and Agriculture*, 79.

is the way she examines the text closely, the way she productively clarifies the manna account with other significant biblical texts (particularly Genesis 3), the way she negotiates the cultural values of the text with those of the surrounding ancient cultures, and the way she connects all of these with the industrial and agrarian economies at work in our world today. It may be worth noting that how Davis frames the economic practice of Israel in contrast to the economy of Egypt is remarkably similar to what Yoram Hazony does in the realm of politics and political practice in Israel against the backdrop of Egyptian (and Canaanite) political structures (a possible fourth example of the use of Exodus in the realm of political theorizing that I will leave to the reader to pursue).[28] Davis's theological/economic reflections on Exodus 16 by no means provide a full-orbed theory of economics or food production, but certainly provide an orientation to these matters that could contribute to scholarship in these areas.

Third, William Abraham, a theologian and analytic philosopher who specializes in epistemology, provides a final example of fruitfully bringing disciplinary questions to bear on Scripture. His *Divine Agency and Divine Action. Vol. IV: A Theological and Philosophical Agenda* includes a chapter titled "Divine Action and Skepticism in the Book of Exodus."[29] The chapter begins by positing that "human agents are complex truth-detecting organisms" and Abraham briefly lays out a vision for an integrated understanding of the way humans come to know truth. On this basis, he presents a proposal: "Suppose . . . that we read the book of Exodus with something akin to this vision of epistemology in hand. In other words, just as some readers, say Philo or Maimonides, read the text with certain metaphysical concerns in mind; or just as other readers, say, Yoram Hazony or liberation theologians, read the text with certain political concerns; I propose we read the text with certain epistemological concerns in mind."[30] What might inspire Abraham to consider Exodus (and not, for example, Joshua or the Song of Songs, or Obadiah, or the book of Acts) through the lens of epistemology? I suspect that for the average Bible reader, Exodus may not stand out as particularly concerned with matters of epistemology – in fact, average readers of the Bible may never have considered that Scripture says anything at all about epistemology. Abraham's expertise in philosophy, epistemology, and theology, *and* his experience and knowledge of the Bible has made him especially attuned both to what the Bible might have to say

28. See Yoram Hazony, "Does the Bible Have a Political Teaching?," *Hebraic Political Studies* 1 (2006): 137–61.

29. William J. Abraham, *Divine Agency and Divine Action. Vol. IV: A Theological and Philosophical Agenda* (Oxford: Oxford University Press, 2021), 97–110.

30. Abraham, *Divine Agency and Divine Action*, 98.

epistemologically and to those places of particular concentration with regard to epistemology (notably, the book of Exodus).[31]

Abraham notes that attention to geography reveals a three-fold structure of Exodus: (1) Israel in Egypt, (2) Israel leaving Egypt, and (3) Israel at Sinai. Reading epistemologically, this three-fold division could be rendered: (1) Israel as a thriving community with a certain identity rooted in God's dealings with Abraham, Isaac, and Jacob; (2) Israel lapsing into unbelief and despair; and (3) Israel recovering its identity and a renewed commitment to the God of the patriarchs.[32] Abraham's analysis of Exodus through the lens of epistemology fruitfully explores the role of divine encounter and speaking, providential and miraculous confirmation, and human testimony (God's dealings with the patriarchs); he examines the effect of trauma in trusting testimony and past experience (Pharaoh's strategy of slave labour and attempted genocide); he probes the intricate interrelationship between knowing and divine action in history (the plagues and Israel's deliverance); and he establishes the significance of memory (in the thick sense), embedded in ritual practice, for the sustaining of true knowledge and community identity.

This brief summary of some of the key points of Abraham's essay does not do justice to the many insights into Exodus. Of course, Abraham is not merely interested in shedding light on Exodus but is interested in how reading Exodus in this way may speak more broadly to matters of epistemology, particularly to a view of epistemology informed by Hebraic/biblical thought. He admits that current trends in philosophical epistemology have opened up a space for this kind of reading of Exodus, and clearly Exodus has something to offer contemporary discussions of epistemology.

ON THE USE OF THE BIBLE IN CHRISTIAN SCHOLARSHIP: REFLECTION AND PROSPECTION

Finally, I briefly sketch out a path forward in the use of the Bible in Christian scholarship that aims to be relevant to the current context.[33]

---

31. Abraham notes, "The initial motivation for this [i.e., reading Exodus with epistemological concerns in mind] is an important feature of the text itself, namely, the remarkable number of references to knowledge of God that show up"; Abraham, *Divine Agency and Divine Action*.

32. Abraham, *Divine Agency and Divine Action*, 98.

33. Admittedly, my own experience with and perspective on the problem is shaped by my own context, which is the orb of Christian (and broadly evangelical) liberal arts scholarship in the West. No doubt my proposals will speak most to the challenges in this context, but I hope will be relevant beyond that.

KNOWING THE FINE DETAILS

If we hope to make Scripture a regular and meaningful contribution to our scholarship, we need more robust biblical literacy. This requires habitual immersion, nourishment, and saturation in the Word of God. Scripture is like a deep well, and we draw from that well by means of rhythms of exposure to the proclamation of the Bible, participation in communal Bible study, and the practice of regular meditation on Scripture (in combination with other Christian practices and disciplines like prayer, the sacraments, fellowship with other believers, acts of mercy, etc.).[34] We will not make use of the Bible in our scholarship if we are ignorant of the contents of the Bible.

GRASPING THE BIG PICTURE

Biblical fluency and not just literacy is the goal, and this will have a significant impact on Christian scholarship. Thus, to complement our knowledge of the contents of the Bible we also need a framework (or frameworks) for grasping how the disparate pieces contribute to the symphony of Scripture as a whole. We want to be able to think with Scripture. Biblical theology is the term used for the discipline "that seeks to discern and articulate the unity of Scripture on the basis of terms and categories derived from the Bible itself."[35] The overarching framework of the Bible is that of a narrative, and the individual stories, poems, laws, genealogies, prophecies, letters, etc., contribute to and are clarified by the metanarrative of Scripture. In the realm of scholarship, knowing the content of Scripture will bring an awareness of those places in the Bible (and places of particular concentration in the Bible) that address matters relevant to a scholar's discipline. Grasping the big picture of Scripture will prevent a scholar from misapplying or distorting Scripture's teaching in one place by allowing it to speak in concert with other texts on the subject. We should not expect to find in the Bible a full-orbed theory of economics, or art, or politics, but, as the examples in this essay demonstrate, we can expect to find a biblical orientation to the objects of our intellectual inquiry.

---

34. Truthfully, some of these "vessels" for drawing from the well of Scripture can at times be deficient. Significant effort can go into drawing out the life-giving "water." We engage in these practices with the expectation of drinking deeply from Scripture, only to discover in the end that the "bucket" is riddled with holes, producing only a few drops and leaving us parched and unsatisfied. This unfortunate state of affairs is beyond the scope of this paper, but suffice it to say that we need to utilize and develop meaningful practices of Scripture engagement that allow us to draw deeply and regularly from that life-giving source.

35. David J. H. Beldman and Jonathan Swales, "Biblical Theology and Theological Interpretation," in Bartholomew and Thomas, *A Manifesto for Theological Interpretation*, 150.

UNEARTHING THE PUBLIC DIMENSION OF THE BIBLE[36]

Grasping the story of Scripture reveals that biblical faith extends to all areas of private and public life, and this will attune readers to Scripture's teaching on a surprisingly vast array of dimensions of reality. Kass, Davis, and Abraham provided a glimpse of just how fruitful reading the Bible with attention to its public teaching can be! Exemplary examples of this kind can provide a guide, and, when found, scholars should take the time to share, examine what makes such readings so fruitful, and provide forums to discuss and unpack these readings. Most Christians are not formed to read Scripture this way, and the retooling needed may be difficult, gradual, and will require a community moving in the same direction, which leads to the next point.

READING IN COMMUNITY

Christian scholarship that extensively engages with Scripture demands genuine, meaningful, and sustained collaboration between biblical scholars, theologians, and their colleagues in other disciplines. The task is far too demanding and vital to settle for anything less. Increasing disciplinary specialization and balkanization make cooperation of this kind all the more important. To reiterate, this is not to suggest that biblical scholars and theologians should dictate to their colleagues in other disciplines how to do their academic work. According to this collaborative vision, insights should flow in both directions. Not only can biblical scholars and theologians facilitate interdisciplinary engagement with Scripture, but scholars in other disciplines can enrich and illuminate aspects of biblical studies and theology. While the current academic context does not generally equip or even encourage scholars across the disciplinary spectrum to engage meaningfully with Scripture, it is equally the case that biblical scholars and theologians are not typically trained to engage with matters outside their disciplines. Cross-fertilization among colleagues could go a long way to better equip all of us for the demands of our callings. There is, of course, a place and much value in Christian scholars from the same discipline grappling with Scripture and issues in their subject areas.

SKETCHING A BIBLICAL THEOLOGY OF ONE'S OWN DISCIPLINE

Christian scholars would do well to develop for themselves a biblical accounting of their own discipline. The proper starting point would be to identify the places in Scripture (areas of concentration) that deal specifically with their area of study. These biblical texts could be the subject of some study,

36. See especially Bartholomew and Emerson, "Theological Interpretation for All of Life," 257–73.

utilizing the best resources from biblical scholarship. From there, a composite and emerging picture of the Bible's witness about a discipline could be sketched out. Of course this would not be easy, and some disciplines (e.g., psychology) may have more significant challenges than others (e.g., environmental studies). A "biblical theology" of one's discipline of this kind could be something a scholar could return to at various points in his/her career to strengthen and deepen.

SETTLING IN FOR THE LONG OBEDIENCE

Taking Scripture seriously in Christian scholarship is demanding and requires slow, careful, and attentive listening to the Bible. Moreover, it demands a paradigm shift for many of us in how we typically read the Bible. It is not easy, and may at times be painful! We should consider ourselves collectively on a journey of the long obedience, exploring the wonder of Scripture as we explore the wonder of our disciplines in light of Scripture.

PART IV

A Community of Stories

Since its inception, the SAHS, and now the Scripture Collective and the Kirby Laing Centre, has sought to do our scholarship in community, rooted in Christian spirituality. A rich and diverse community has developed in this process, and for this section we invited members of our community to reflect on the SAHS. Reflections are listed in alphabetic order.

CRAIG G. BARTHOLOMEW

I find it helpful to think of the Bible as the field in which is hid the pearl of great price. Biblical hermeneutics, at its best, helps us to dig so that we are most likely to emerge again and again with that pearl. From its inception, the aim of the SAHS has been to contribute to a renewal of academic biblical interpretation in order to give it a key role in that digging. The journey has been exhilarating but not always easy. So many different people and institutions have contributed along the way that it is impossible to mention them all here. Pieter Kwant, then of Paternoster, took on the project and brought on Zondervan Academic as our US partner. Two friends of mine, Gert Swart, a distinguished South African sculptor, and Zak Benjamin, a prominent South African artist, helped us weave art and imagination into our work, an emphasis that the Kirby Laing Centre continues to this day. Once our nine international consultations were complete, we began meeting around the annual SBL meeting each year. Later we developed a partnership with the IBR which continues to this day, now with four Seminars. A body of substantial literature has emerged from the SAHS as well as a deep intellectual community rooted in Christian spirituality. It is this unusual combination of scholarship, Bible, hermeneutics, community, and spirituality that catalyses the work we seek to do and makes it all so very exhilarating and worthwhile. New challenges and opportunities have emerged since the SAHS began some twenty-five years ago. The SAHS now has a home in the Scripture Collective of the Kirby Laing Centre along with our other three Seminars. The imperative to excavate the pearl of great price remains. My hope is that this volume will introduce new generations to our work and that they will join us in this journey which moves ever more deeply into the life of God himself as we attend to his Word together *coram Deo.*

Craig is the director of the Kirby Laing Centre for Public Theology in Cambridge, UK.

DAVID J. H. BELDMAN

My first "taste" of the Scripture and Hermeneutics Seminar was way back in 2005 at the consultation in Rome on canon and biblical interpretation at the Pontifical Institute. Having only just earned my undergraduate diploma (the ink was still drying when I hopped on a plane to Rome), I was a little overwhelmed (and, to be honest, a bit anxious) about being in the presence of top-notch scholars whom I had read for my theology courses. The papers and academic dialogue were rich and stimulating, but what I remember most about that trip was the sense of community – the participants ate together, prayed together, shared stories together, and (of course) engaged in scholarship together. Three particularly meaningful experiences stood out to me in this regard. First, after a long day of academic work all the participants gathered one night to hear a Roman Catholic archdeacon tell his story. I understand the Seminar had developed a tradition of this kind of storytelling . . . or was it testimony sharing? The archdeacon's story was interesting and meaningful, but not without heartache – it was a rich and inspiring moment. Second, I remember sitting down for a meal one evening at a table with a number of scholars. Tremper Longman (whom I knew then only by reputation) was at that table, and rather than talk about all the interesting and significant things he was working on, he very kindly and attentively asked all sorts of questions about me – my family, background, studies, etc. (Over the years I've observed Tremper extend this kindness to students and others again and again.) Third, on a free afternoon Stephen Chapman (aka "Chaps") took me and a handful of doctoral students on a guided tour of Rome. He brought us to many of the usual tourist stops and some out-of-the-way spots, carefully explaining the history, art, architecture, etc., of Rome. These examples of generous hospitality are, sadly, not always typical in academic contexts, but they are at the heart of the work of the Seminar and they are what the Seminar does well and regularly.

Of course the SAHS has contributed a significant amount of scholarly work since its inception some twenty-five years ago, which has made its mark on theology and biblical studies (and beyond)! Since 2000 the Seminar has met annually for academic consultations – the presentation of countless papers and engagement with those papers has had an impact. In its first ten years the Seminar published eight volumes of collected essays, each centering around a particular theme. The works continue to be read, referenced, and used in courses (*Out of Egypt* was an assigned text for a graduate course I took). Since then other publications have emerged, most notably *A Manifesto for Theological Interpretation*. At least as important as this scholarly output is the investment into the lives and vocations of countless "young" scholars over the years. It's hard for me to imagine the trajectory my own life and career would have taken had I not been inducted into this community, and I can't express just how grateful I am to have been a recipient of the Seminar's investment and generous hospitality. I've said before that the Seminar has offered a countercultural way of doing scholarship – one that isn't the easiest and is costly, but worth the cost.

David is scholar in residence at the Surge Network and directs the North American office of the Kirby Laing Centre.

AMBER L. BOWEN

I was first introduced to the Scripture and Hermeneutics Seminar as a very young student in grad school with aspirations of doing a PhD. Aside from the invaluable opportunity for a young student to hear from, be encouraged by, and dialogue with seasoned scholars, the SAHS community has been formative for me in key ways. My most vivid memory of the first seminar I attended was of Craig Bartholomew stating emphatically that Christian scholarship is best done in community. Doing so requires generous dialogue, as well as rejoicing with those who rejoice and weeping with those who weep. I was struck by how different this way of doing scholarship was compared to the broader academy and desired to adopt it as my own. Being part of this community over the years, I have had the opportunity to cultivate distinctly Christian practices in scholarship such as pursuing learning and creating as prayer, praise, confession, and offering. This vision and these practices allow scholarship to be just as edifying as it is rigorous, which is something that Christian scholars can and should offer a fragmented world.

Amber is assistant professor of philosophy and core studies at Redeemer University, Canada.

JEANNINE BROWN

The volumes on Scripture and Hermeneutics began to be published when I was in my early career in New Testament studies. I was very much drawn to their topics and themes, not least because I was longing for a deeper and wider conversation regarding how a thoughtful hermeneutic might impact various domains such as linguistics, biblical theology, and interdisciplinary work. The volumes being produced in the Scripture and Hermeneutics Series were addressing just these kinds of questions. Additionally, they were taking on these topics in a thoroughgoing way and with an array of voices at the table. I believe my favorite volume is the one focused on linguistics (*After Pentecost: Language and Biblical Interpretation*, 2001), and I still return to the essays in that volume from time to time. They provide both theory and practice in this important area of hermeneutical study. They also offer a significant contribution to a guild that can, at times, lapse into pre-Barr categories and related pitfalls for how we understand language and linguistics in biblical studies.

Jeannine is professor of New Testament at Bethel Seminary, USA.

SUSAN I. BUBBERS

As I reflect on my experiences with the SAHS in the context of the SBL sessions, the phrase that comes to mind is "a place." Every human heart yearns for a place to belong, to be accepted, and to be productive. And as an academic I needed a context, a place, to pursue research that was innovative, bridging the gap between academy and church. Especially when the SAHS launched the Scripture and Church Seminar, I found a place to thrive as both an academic and as a Christian minister. Since I was a scholar with two doctoral degrees, being an ordained woman, a Bible-believing Christian, and a person devoted to a life led by the Holy Spirit, it was no small thing to have found such a place. One of my areas of specialty is the intersection of biblical interpretation methodology, hermeneutics, and practical theology. Such interpretation is best done not only interculturally and interdenominationally, but also interpersonally. The Scripture Collective Seminars have given me both a place and people to help me do my best work.

Susan is dean of the ATLAS Theological Center and an Anglican priest at Celebration Anglican Fellowship, USA.

GARETH LEE COCKERILL

I had used the Scripture and Hermeneutics Series sponsored by the SAHS for many years with profit but with little knowledge of the community that produced these essays. Then in 2016, at Craig's invitation, I attended the annual dinner sponsored by the SAHS, the Scripture and Doctrine Seminar, and the Scripture and University Seminar. I wondered if there was any place for me within this fellowship. Thankfully, I discovered a community humbly devoted to the theological interpretation of Scripture and the relevance of God's truth for our contemporary world. I discovered a community that embraced the diversity of Christ's church while maintaining an unbending commitment to consensual Christian orthodoxy. I discovered a group of scholars who believed that good theology was the fruit of the Christian community worshipping, studying, and thinking together. I discovered a fellowship committed to mutual encouragement in the pursuit of truth rather than to professional competition. I found a group of joyful people who knew how to pray, joke, study Scripture, and discuss theology together. In sum, I found a community dedicated to pursuing the theological task of the church in a way that brought honor to the Lord Jesus Christ. Then I realized that I had been looking for this kind of community all my life.

Gareth is professor emeritus of New Testament and biblical theology at Wesley Biblical Seminary, USA, and an associate fellow at the Kirby Laing Centre for Public Theology in Cambridge, UK.

KATYA COVRETT

Shortly after I came to work at Zondervan in 2002, I started to attend the ETS/AAR/SBL academic conventions as part of my responsibilities. One of my most vivid recollections from the first SBL meeting I attended was the setup of the Scripture and Hermeneutics Series right in the middle of our booth. The exhibit hall tables were stacked high with the four already published volumes and a boatload of the newest volume five, *Out of Egypt*. When the exhibits opened and scholars poured in, the latest SAH Series volume was *the book* attendees would ask for by title.

This was my first introduction to the work of the SAHS. And it left an indelible impression on this young editor. For nearly a quarter of a century now, these invaluable seminars and their publications have fostered a robust intellectual community that is rooted in Christian commitment, deeply engaged with Scripture, and modelling a healthy ecumenical scholarly collaboration. We need more of this – now, it seems, more than ever – and I look forward to being a part of where the SAHS goes in the next twenty-five years!

Katya is associate publisher for Zondervan Academic in Grand Rapids, Michigan, USA.

A. J. CULP

I'm not sure what I expected, to be honest. But I was surprised by what I found. The Society of Biblical Literature Annual Meeting was large and anonymous, a mass of people moving here and there. All of them seemed so sure of who they were and where they were going, and they all appeared rather important too. Yet this wasn't what I found so jarring. What I found jarring was how the prevailing sentiment at a conference about Bible and theology was that true scholarship, or at least the kind that mattered, was done by bracketing one's faith tradition from scholarship. This seemed bizarre to me. The only reason any of us had come to this place was because the Bible had had a profound impact on our world and on us. Furthermore, the only reason for its profound impact was because it was a religious text.

So, when I was invited to the Scripture and Hermeneutics Seminar and its Annual Meal, I assumed it was more of the same. But it wasn't. What I found instead was a community of *Christian* scholars. People were humble and hospitable, charitable and kind, and generous and insatiably curious. And, more than anything, I remember the laughter. I remember a room filled with the most extraordinary mixture of sounds: profound scholarly discussion punctuated by bursts of laughter, followed by prayer and culminating in songs of worship. *This*, I thought to myself, is what I've been looking for.

A. J. is pastor of theological training at Lakewood Baptist Church in Gainesville, Georgia, USA.

MATTHEW EMERSON

I first encountered the SAHS community in early 2011, at the initial "Paideia Gathers" conference in Hamilton, Ontario. Amidst a blizzard, I tasted and saw what it meant for serious biblical scholarship to be considered in light of sincere faith in the risen Lord Jesus. Prior to attending I'd read many of the Scripture and Hermeneutics volumes, and at some point I got up the nerve to tell Craig ("Dr Bartholomew") how much those books meant to my intellectual and spiritual growth. He very kindly asked me why I had such an appreciation for them, and my response then reflects how I continue to feel about the SAHS (and, now, the rest of the Scripture Collective Seminars): they show me what real academic rigor looks like in the context of the church's worship of the triune God, the one God who has made himself known to us in the person of his Son, Jesus Christ. After that conference I was hooked, and have been privileged to attend and serve with the SAHS in the subsequent decade.

Matthew is dean of theology, arts, & humanities and professor of religion at Oklahoma Baptist University, USA.

ROSEMARY HALES

I was employed by the British and Foreign Bible Society, which became the leading partner in the Scripture and Hermeneutics project. As part of their contribution and support I was seconded as the administrative manager for the project, during which time I organised a series of seven consultations in different countries – Canada, England (2), Italy, Scotland, and the USA (2).

When I began working on the project, I found that the potential for community already existed among the academics gathering together, since some of them had previous or existing connections with one another. Although I am not an academic, I found I was warmly accepted and greeted with courtesy and friendliness. I was helped to feel that I belonged, which gave a sense of emerging community. A community working on one project can touch into, and in turn become touched by, other communities of like-minded and open-hearted people, and so it was in this case.

For several years the project was based in the UK, but its base (and I) was subsequently relocated to Canada, away from my own home in the UK. I remain deeply grateful to those within the community of Redeemer University, Canada, who embraced me, supported me with friendship, and gave gifts and loans of household items to help me establish a temporary home. They also provided me with timely warnings and advice when the Canadian winter weather (freezing rain, heavy snowfalls with occasional "whiteouts!," etc.) might otherwise have proved more than threatening!

During my time working on the project there were many other examples of kindness and community spirit, such as when a small group of students spontaneously and willingly volunteered to assist when an unexpected problem occurred at the start of one of the consultations, and also when a prominent academic through doggedness and perseverance dealt with a critical situation when the taxi driver did not know the way from the airport to our destination! On another occasion a delegate's wife kindly saved the day by offering to acquire an item which could not be purchased on the campus, where no public transport was available. Finally, a porter at a college kindly helped when various items were unexpectedly but suddenly required. All of these people were outside the central core of the academic community of the project, but all became connected with it – some over an extended period, others fleetingly in the moment. All were essential to the building and sense of community, and all were kind and caring and touched by a sense of human connection, belonging to something greater than ourselves.

Rosemary is the fellows administrator at the Kirby Laing Centre for Public Theology in Cambridge, UK.

MARY HEALY

At one of the first academic conferences I attended as a newly-minted doctor of biblical theology, a memorable incident occurred. During a discussion I made a passing reference to the "divine authorship of Scripture," and afterward was soundly rebuked by a senior colleague, who informed me that divine authorship is a matter of faith and as such has no place in the scientific study of Scripture. When I later attended my first SAHS gathering, at which Craig Bartholomew spoke eloquently about doing biblical scholarship "on the knees," it was like coming into the fresh open air after being in a stuffy basement. Our times of morning and evening prayer together were an especially blessed experience of ecumenical communion. As we sang traditional hymns, the participants would spontaneously break into harmony, worshiping the Lord with fervor and joy.

Mary is professor of Scripture at Sacred Heart Major Seminary in Detroit, Michigan, USA, and a member of the Pontifical Biblical Commission.

DAVID LYLE JEFFREY

During the first week of June 2006, we at Baylor were privileged to host the eighth annual symposium of the Scripture and Hermeneutics Seminar. Fully aware that conservative biblical scholarship was under some duress, our colleagues were delighted to discover and get to know fellow Christians from many other universities and across several denominations. A highlight of that meeting was common worship of evangelical, Reformed, and Catholic scholars. The rich blessing of convivial friendship was added to many excellent and memorable papers, often leading to fresh and productive collaborations.

David is distinguished senior fellow at the Baylor Institute for Studies in Religion; emeritus distinguished professor of literature and the humanities at Baylor University, USA; and guest professor at Peking University, China.

JIM KINNEY

The Scripture and Hermeneutics Seminar has been a great source of enrichment for me, both personally and professionally. Some of the earliest SAHS gatherings produced insights and friendships that remain vital to me. I could say many good things about the SAHS, but I especially appreciate the group's commitment to scholarship in service of the church catholic and to scholarly rigor practiced in community, shaped by collegiality and Christian virtue.

I recall one meeting that featured a presentation by a Catholic archbishop. Afterward the attendees, representing a variety of Christian traditions, joined to sing a classic hymn, thereby linking the work of the Seminar to the life of the church in all places and times.

At another meeting, two scholars vigorously debated an exegetical point. After much back and forth with little movement on either side, they concluded that it was their differing ecclesiological commitments that kept them from seeing eye to eye on this point. Having achieved this clarity, they agreed to disagree and the conversation was able to move forward constructively. I'm ever grateful for the self-awareness and humility modelled by those two eminent scholars. Their honesty and Christian virtue showed the SAHS at its best.

Jim is executive vice president of academic publishing at Baker Publishing Group, USA.

TREMPER LONGMAN

I remember well the event that brought me into the SAHS community. In 2005, Craig invited me to participate in the Canon Criticism and Theological

Interpretation Conference held at the Pontifical Biblical Institute in Rome. Craig asked me to give a paper on canon and biblical wisdom to an invited group of twenty Catholic and twenty Protestant scholars (published as "Reading Wisdom Canonically" in *Canon and Biblical Interpretation*). This was a wonderful and learning experience that stayed with me as we shared our ideas to a group that knew the importance of interpreting Scripture in its canonical context, while differing in important nuances. I remember being kindly but firmly told that I needed to pay more attention to the Wisdom of Solomon and Ecclesiasticus in my work on wisdom. I took this to heart in my later book, *The Fear of the Lord Is the Beginning of Wisdom* (Baker, 2017).

But even more encouraging than the conference were the meals and the conversations with other participants. I knew some of them well, but others I met for the first time, leading to continuing relationships. Perhaps most memorable in that regard was a long walk along the Appian Way (a rather busy road, we found out) to the catacombs with Stephen Chapman. Later on he and I, along with Nathan MacDonald, edited the Siphrut series (Eisenbrauns/Penn State University Press).

Some years later Craig, Heath Thomas, and I (while president of the Institute of Biblical Research) formed a relationship that allowed the SAHS community to enter fully into the life of the IBR and (more selfishly important to me) enabled members of the IBR to participate in the life of the SAHS community, including the fabulous and utterly fun Saturday night dinners.

The SAHS has created a community of incredibly bright scholars, mostly young but also including a number of us older types. We encourage each other towards excellent scholarship addressed to other scholars, pastors, and even laypeople. Over the past twenty-five years, the SAHS community under the leadership of Craig and others has contributed to the kingdom of God in immeasurable ways. I have personally benefited greatly through my friendships and scholarly interaction with the community, and I look forward to what God has to bring to our common future.

Tremper is distinguished scholar and professor emeritus of biblical studies at Westmont College, USA.

RYAN O'DOWD

I attended my first SAHS consultation in Boston in 2002, invited by my soon-to-be doctoral supervisor Craig Bartholomew. I arrived to find myself the only grad student among dozens of established scholars: Plantinga, Thiselton, Sundberg, Wolters . . . I eventually worked up the nerve to ask what I quickly realized was a naïve and embarrassing question on the floor of the consultation – a mistake that turned out for my good. I was awakened to a richness of theological and philosophical reflection that I never imagined possible. For grad students who would attend consultations with me in subsequent years, the SAHS afforded the rare privilege of learning from the collegial dialogue of godly and intelligent women and men. The SAHS also provided gifts of friendship. Following my callow question that first year, Tremper Longman and Doug Green consoled me over an afternoon pint at the pub, blessing me with friendships that last to this day. In subsequent years David Moessner would give me a guided tour of the Vatican Museum; in Oxford Scott Hahn would tutor me in the beauty of ancient liturgies; Chris Wright would share pastoral and parental advice on a bus; and Edith Humphrey would bless several grad students with wise counsel for life and scholarship over a bottle of wine. I formed friendships with most of those grad students and with so many more who offered us their companionship. With deepest gratitude.

Ryan is rector at Bread of Life Anglican Church in Ithaca, New York, and senior fellow at Chesterton House, Cornell University, USA.

WILLIAM OLHAUSEN

I first met Craig Bartholomew in 1998. He was giving a lecture to his old seminary (Oxford's Wycliffe Hall), where I was just finishing my training for the Anglican ordained ministry. Craig's lecture was on hearing God's address in Scripture and his theme was inspired by verse 19 of Psalm 78: "Can God really spread a table in the wilderness?" Craig's high view of Scripture and his strong commitment to the doctrine of creation not only foregrounded hermeneutic questions but also helped me to make new intellectual connections. This would, in time, also facilitate new friendships.

Craig invited me to carry his bags for the second Scripture and Hermeneutics consultation held in Cambridge in 1999. The papers from this gathering would become the first volume of the eight-volume Scripture and Hermeneutics Series, entitled *Renewing Biblical Interpretation*. The ethos of the Seminar began to take shape in Cambridge. Emerging scholars could cut their teeth, learn from more established scholars, and begin to find their own specific vocation between academy and church.

Over the course of later consultations and subsequent gatherings of the Seminar at the SBL Annual Meeting, I have met many more scholars and scholar-pastors. The ever-expanding vision and implications for how God's Word is relevant to the whole of life continues to nourish my discipleship and inform my ministry. Allowing our Christian commitments and presuppositions to shape our work and, in turn, to do such work in community where we can remains a godly challenge to the prevailing academic culture in much of the Western world. It is also an antidote to those who remain suspicious of academic biblical studies and theology! Finally, I have always appreciated the ecumenical spirit in which the Seminar operates. This has been especially important for ministry and mission in Ireland.

William is rector of St Matthias' Church in the parish of Killiney/Ballybrack in South County Dublin, Ireland.

MURRAY RAE

Participation in the Scripture and Hermeneutics Seminar has been an immense privilege especially because of the contribution the Seminar has made to a renewal of confidence in the claim that God speaks through the text of Scripture. For all the insight that can be gained through rigorous critical attention to a text's literary and linguistic features, the historical circumstances that gave rise to its production and transmission, its form, and its redaction history, it is nevertheless possible to engage expertly in these spheres of inquiry and still miss the one thing that is most important. It is the one thing that Søren Kierkegaard spoke of so eloquently: the text is addressed to you! The Bible does have prominence, and has attracted the attention of the academy only because down through the ages countless people of faith have discovered it to be an instrument through which God speaks to his people. Without that claim of faith, the Bible would surely by now have become a relic that would be only of marginal interest to the academy. Many scholars, especially younger ones, are now encouraged by the SAHS to regain the confidence to advance this claim of faith within the academy, and to undertake their scholarly labours as an act of service to the church. I am grateful for all that the SAHS has contributed to this progression in the work of Christian scholarship.

Murray is professor of theology at the University of Otago, New Zealand.

MICHAEL RHODES

The 2014 Scripture and Hermeneutics Seminar was the first Society of Biblical Literature event I attended. I was in my last year of an MA program and showed up in San Diego to decide whether to pursue a PhD in biblical studies. Both the meeting itself and the annual feast with those involved convinced me that the answer was *yes*. I did want to keep studying Scripture academically, and the SAHS simultaneously introduced me to a community that I wanted to study Scripture *with*. This was not only because of the richness of the presentations and the strange, subversive practice of beginning an SBL session with prayer and song. The people were also a significant factor. At that first conference I heard Craig Bartholomew, my future PhD supervisor, speak, as he so often does, about theological interpretation aimed at all of life. I also met friends like Ryan O'Dowd, who rigorously edited my first attempt at submitting something for publication, and Jamie Grant, who coached me through my first time teaching the Psalms. In the back row of a later SAHS gathering, I somewhat accidentally started talking ritual with Dru Johnson, whose friendship changed my work and my life for the better. When the COVID-19 pandemic kept the annual SAHS gathering from happening, I realized just how much it meant to me. Since 2014 attending the SAHS has become a sort of pilgrimage for me, a ritual return to the relationships that have helped me listen to Scripture as God's address. May the Lord bless the SAHS, establishing it always as a place of pilgrimage and a community of pilgrims seeking the highways that lead "further up and further in" to the Lord's kingdom.

Michael is lecturer in Old Testament at Carey Baptist College, New Zealand.

SANDRA RICHTER

My involvement with the Scripture and Hermeneutics Seminar at the SBL Annual Meeting has embodied one of those rare academic experiences that bring both challenge and joy. Here I am invited into pointed debates regarding the challenge of new data and failed paradigms; I learn from those whose disciplines expand and chasten mine; and I engage in honest conversations with like-minded scholars engaging critical issues of faith and history. And all of this occurs in the context of joyful and allied community. This Seminar and its related functions have become one of my favorite parts of the Annual Meetings.

Sandra is the Robert H. Gundry Chair of Biblical Studies at Westmont College, USA.

LUKE STAMPS

What is so remarkable about the Scripture Collective is just how rare it is. Here you will find serious, discipline-shaping scholarship under the banner of Christ's loving lordship. Here is a fellowship of scholars committed to academic rigor in a liturgical frame. The communal solidarity of the Scripture Collective is disarming (and not a little disorienting) in an academic world so often shaped by self-promotion and isolation. This is a place where the accomplishments of graduate students are celebrated with the same exuberance as the career capstones of the most senior scholars. It is difficult to explain until you experience it for yourself.

Luke is the chair of the Herschel H. Hobbs School of Theology and Ministry at Oklahoma Baptist University, USA.

ANTHONY C. THISELTON

After Pentecost: Language and Biblical Interpretation (published in 2001) was the second volume of the eight-volume Scripture and Hermeneutics Series. My memory of hermeneutics goes beyond 2001 to the 1960s, when I regularly collaborated with my colleague Colin Brown. Our discussions turned often on academic strategy. Colin was primarily concerned with history; my interest then, and ever since, was with language. I am reminded that this volume was generously dedicated to me "in recognition of his work in biblical hermeneutics," which above all concerns interpreting concepts and language.

Speech acts stands at the centre of this. In *After Pentecost* Kevin Vanhoozer, Dan Stiver, Nicholas Wolterstorff, and I, along with others, directly address this subject. Scripture constitutes a storehouse of the promises of God, and my memory of our early seminars concerns exchanges of views on this subject. God's speech is also his act. We also shared thoughts on Derrida and postmodernism with Craig Bartholomew and others from Cheltenham and Gloucester College. It became clear that biblical hermeneutics was emphatically interdisciplinary and, not least, included linguistic philosophy. What I engaged with in 2001 has remained my primary focus until today.

Anthony is emeritus professor of Christian theology at the University of Nottingham, UK.

HEATH THOMAS

A passion for the possible captures my experience with the Scripture and Hermeneutics community. I was introduced to the work of the Seminar in 2003, where its transdisciplinary nature and interest in laying bare philosophical foundations of biblical studies resonated with my own interests. I stepped into the community at the Oxford and Rome consultations and fell headlong down the rabbit hole! But rather than entering Wonderland, I discovered horizons of possibility. I found that academic study of the Bible, the ancient Near East, the Greco-Roman world, and theology was possible and done best in community. And what a community! It was possible to interact with, and learn from, world-class scholars as well as mature and younger academics from Africa, Asia, Europe, and North and South America. We saw these folk go for the jugular of an argument without going for the jugular of a person, and the consultations modelled this well (even in sharp discussions!). Refreshingly, I found it was possible to rise above the political and ecumenical scuffles one finds in North America and engage pioneering and creative work that matters. I never got the sense that I did not belong or could not meet the demands of the work, even if I strained to understand a quarter of the conversation in the consultations I attended and needed to return to German, French, or ancient languages to catch up on the discussion from the day before! I found it was possible to find a supportive community that encouraged me to believe that I could do scholarly work at a high level. Crucially, the Seminar community (and especially Craig Bartholomew) helped me discover that it is possible – even necessary – to see my scholarship bent in service of Christ and the church for the good of the world. I am grateful.

Heath is the president of Oklahoma Baptist University, USA.

KEVIN VANHOOZER

It was my privilege to present, along with Anthony Thiselton and Nick Wolterstorff, a paper on speech-act theory at the first Scripture and Hermeneutics Seminar meeting at Cheltenham in 1998. Up until that time, I was under the impression that most biblical scholars called theologians like me "Not My People" (cf. Hos 1:9), for our tribes approached the task of biblical interpretation with different tools and priorities. However, twenty-five years and many Seminar meetings later, there is now a vibrant academic, interdisciplinary, and Christian community that has broken down the dividing wall of disciplinary hostility in order to pursue together the task of reading the Bible theologically, as Scripture: "You Are My People" (cf. Hos. 2:23). I am very grateful to Craig Bartholomew for his trans-Atlantic perseverance to organize follow-up conferences, and to all those who have contributed to subsequent Scripture and Hermeneutic Seminar meetings, the published results of which proudly occupy more than twelve inches of premium bookshelf space in my living room. These eight volumes are a standing testimony to what I believe to be one of the signal events in biblical scholarship at the turn of the millennium.

Kevin is research professor of systematic theology at Trinity Evangelical Divinity School, USA.

MICHAEL WAGENMAN

During a particularly challenging time in my career, I discovered the Scripture and Hermeneutics Seminar (and the other Seminars within the Kirby Laing Centre that are known together as the "Scripture Collective") at the Annual Meeting of the Society for Biblical Literature. Here was a group of openly committed Christians (of various denominations and even including those of other faith backgrounds), and yet they weren't walled off in their own holy huddle but fully engaged in rigorous scholarly work at the highest level. Neither were they ivory tower types; they've clearly kept their sleeves rolled up, since the committee members and each year's presenters have been not only stellar scholars but often seasoned practitioners on the ground. In this way, what I have discovered at the SAHS is a beautiful embodiment of what it means to be a human being, not just a believer or a scholar. Thus, for me the SAHS has been an inspiring, provocative, and healing community in which to pursue my own academic work. I am grateful for the spirit, the hospitality, and the joy that dwells in its midst.

Michael is senior research fellow and director of the Scripture Collective at the Kirby Laing Centre for Public Theology in Cambridge, UK, and chaplain and member of the graduate faculty at Western University in London, Ontario, Canada.

PAUL WILLIAMS

The royal charter that articulates the founding mission of the British and Foreign Bible Society declares that it is to promote the "wider circulation and use" of the Bible throughout the world. During the post-war period, and especially under the influence of Lesslie Newbigin and others, we began to realise that Britain and the wider Western world was once again a mission field in this regard. We thus needed to find new ways to increase confidence in the Bible and its use in all spheres of life, whether in the church or wider society.

It is for that reason that the Bible Society was delighted to support and help fund the Scripture and Hermeneutics Seminar in its execution of nine international Seminars and the publication of the eight-volume Scripture and Hermeneutics Series. The Bible Society also seconded Rosemary Hales to administer the project. We are glad to see that the Series remains in print, and are delighted to see it given fresh life through this rich and creative volume produced under the auspices of the Kirby Laing Centre.

On a more personal note, I have benefited personally from this early work without realising its provenance, as I was inspired by the Series to explore the relation between Scripture and economics in a thesis supervised by Dr Bruce Waltke at Regent College back in 1994. Thank you, everyone, for curating such a powerful resource for the church – it's as important and relevant now as it was when it started.

Paul is the chief executive of the British and Foreign Bible Society, UK.

LUCAS GLEN WISLEY

The first time I attended one of the Scripture and Hermeneutics Seminar meetings was in 2010 while a seminary student. Attending large conferences as a student can be intimidating, but I was immediately struck by the warmth and encouragement that the community shared with one another. One story that comes to mind was my first SAHS dinner, where I had the privilege to be seated next to Steve Dempster. Steve sat and engaged with me in conversation about our love for the Old Testament, and he provided much encouragement for me in my studies. As a student I had read and admired Steve's work, and I was struck by the fact that he didn't rush off to be with the many other scholars at the meal but spent time encouraging a student whom he had never met. For me this memory captures the Christian ethos of the community – the desire to encourage and spur one another on to pursue faithful and excellent work. And, many years later, that ethos hasn't changed.

Lucas is lecturer in Old Testament studies at the Bible College of South Australia.

CHRIS WRIGHT

"Let us pray." With those words Professor C. F. D. (Charlie) Moule began every lecture on New Testament theology in my undergraduate studies at the University of Cambridge Divinity School in the late 1960s. He was the only lecturer in the department who prayed before lecturing on the Scriptures, effectively turning the hour into an act of worship – which, in some ways, it was; such was the richness and nourishing content of his deep devotional reflection on the biblical texts we studied. We could tell that, for all the academic rigour of Dr Moule's renowned scholarship, this was more than an academic exercise for him. The fact that he was exceptional, and that so much of my theological study at the undergraduate and doctoral level was done in an atmosphere of rigorous exclusion of God from the discourse (as a living present reality, distinct from an "object" or "character" in the text), were major reasons why my own sense of personal calling shifted from thinking I should teach theology in a university department to choosing the path of theological education within the confessional context of church and seminary.

How refreshing it was, therefore, to be invited by Craig to join the SAHS meetings in Rome and St Andrews, as well as at the SBL Annual Meeting, and to participate in theological interaction of the highest academic quality. It was so wonderful to be enveloped in meaningful times of prayer and liturgy with a community of faith and friendship. Along with the joy of the friends that I have made through the SAHS, these meetings have been one of the most encouraging features of belonging to this group and doing theology together as believers, disciples, and worshippers of the living God of the Bible.

Chris is the global ambassador of Langham Partnership, UK.

Contributors to Parts I, II, and III

Craig G. Bartholomew is the director of the Kirby Laing Centre for Public Theology in Cambridge. Some twenty-five years ago he started the SAHS in partnership with the Bible Society when he was at the University of Gloucestershire. Craig is the author of many books, most recently *The Doctrine of Creation* (co-authored with Bruce Ashford) and *The God Who Acts in History: The Significance of Sinai*.

David J. H. Beldman (PhD, University of Bristol) is scholar in residence at the Surge Network and directs the North American office of the Kirby Laing Centre. He is an Old Testament scholar with an interest in historical narrative, wisdom, and the Pentateuch. He has published a number of essays, three books on Judges, including a commentary (Eerdmans, 2020) and a popular introduction (Lexham, 2017), and co-edited *Hearing the Old Testament: Listening for God's Address* (Eerdmans, 2012) and *A Classified Bibliography on Ecclesiastes* (T&T Clark, 2019).

Amber L. Bowen (PhD, University of Aberdeen) is assistant professor of philosophy and core studies at Redeemer University in Ancaster, Ontario. Co-editor of the forthcoming volume *Theology and Black Mirror*, Bowen has also published essays on Søren Kierkegaard, Michel Henry, Jean-Yves Lacoste, and other topics in phenomenological approaches to philosophy of religion in *The International Journal of Philosophy and Theology*, *Religions*, and *The Journal of Religious Ethics*. She is currently working on a book dealing with postcritical hermeneutics that is being funded by a grant from the Templeton Foundation as part of the Widening Horizons in Philosophical Theology project at the University of Saint Andrews.

Susan I. Bubbers is dean of the Center for Anglican Theology, Orlando, Florida. Ordained an Anglican priest in 1995, she has served as a parish rector and university chaplain. Her education includes a DMin in spiritual formation and a PhD in eucharistic theology. She has taught in seminaries and authored several articles and the monograph *A Scriptural Theology of Eucharistic Blessings* (T&T Clark, 2013). She is also a fellow of the Oxford Centre for Animal Ethics.

Havilah Dharamraj (PhD in Old Testament, University of Durham) is the head of the Department of Biblical Studies at the South Asia Institute for Advanced Christian Studies in Bangalore, India. She has a special interest in biblical narrative and poetry. Besides teaching and writing narrative theology, she encourages students to rediscover the traditional Indian forms of storytelling for use in ministry. Her other area of interest is the discipline of comparative literature, studying the Bible alongside the sacred texts of South Asian religions.

Bo H. Lim is professor of Old Testament at Seattle Pacific University. He teaches and writes on the topics of OT prophetic literature, theological interpretation, missional hermeneutics, and Asian American biblical interpretation. His publications include a commentary on *Hosea* (THCOT, Eerdmans, 2015) and essays in *The Oxford Handbook of the Minor Prophets* (2021), the *T&T Clark Handbook of Asian American Biblical Hermeneutics* (2019), and *Interpreting the Old Testament Theologically* (Zondervan, 2018). Dr Lim co-chairs the Theological Interpretation of Scripture Seminar at the Society of Biblical Literature and serves on the editorial board of the *Journal of Theological Interpretation*.

William Olhausen studied theology at Wycliffe Hall in Oxford and has been ordained in the Anglican Church since 1998. Since 2011, he has served as a parish minister in the Diocese of Dublin, Ireland. He holds a PhD in hermeneutics from Liverpool University and is a part-time member of faculty at the Church of Ireland Theological Institute. He is also a committee member of the Scripture and Hermeneutics Seminar and a trustee of the Kirby Laing Centre for Public Theology in Cambridge.

Murray Rae is professor of theology at the University of Otago, New Zealand. His research interests include the work of Søren Kierkegaard, theological hermeneutics, Māori engagements with Christianity, and theology and architecture. His publications include *Architecture and Theology: The Art of Place* (Baylor University Press, 2018), *Christian Theology: The Basics* (London: Routledge, 2015), *Kierkegaard and Theology* (London: Continuum, 2010), *History and Hermeneutics* (London: T&T Clark, 2005), and *Kierkegaard's Vision of the Incarnation* (Oxford: Clarendon, 1997).

Andrew Sackin-Poll is a final-year doctoral student in the French Section at the University of Cambridge and a translator of numerous French philosophical and theological texts, including works by Jean-Louis Chrétien, Emmanuel Falque, Michel Henry, and François Laruelle. His doctoral research explores new possibilities for the epic narrative form in modern French literature during our century of global challenges.

J. Aaron Simmons is professor of philosophy at Furman University and senior research fellow at the Kirby Laing Centre for Public Theology in Cambridge. Working primarily in phenomenology, existentialism, and philosophy of religion, he is the author of *God and the Other* (Indiana University Press), co-author of *The New Phenomenology* (Bloomsbury), and has edited volumes such as *Christian Philosophy* (Oxford University Press) and *Kierkegaard's God and the Good Life* (Indiana University Press).

Anthony C. Thiselton is emeritus professor of Christian theology in the University of Nottingham. Before that he was principal of St John's College, University of Durham. He is also emeritus professor of Christian theology in the University of Chester and emeritus canon theologian of Leicester and of Southwell and Nottingham. He was a member of the Church of England General Synod for fifteen years and is a fellow of the British Academy.

John Wyatt is emeritus professor of neonatal paediatrics at University College London (UCL) and was a consultant neonatologist in central London for more than twenty-five years. He led an internationally recognised multidisciplinary research group at UCL and pioneered new protective treatments for brain-injured babies. He is current president of the Christian Medical Fellowship, chair of John Stott's literary executors, and a senior research fellow at the Kirby Laing Centre for Public Theology. His book *Matters of Life and Death: Human Dilemmas in the Light of the Christian Faith* has been translated into more than ten languages.

Appendix

KIRBY LAING CENTRE FOR PUBLIC THEOLOGY IN CAMBRIDGE, UK

The Kirby Laing Centre (KLC) became a fully independent UK charity on 1 January 2021. We are a research centre in *public theology*, with the latter understood as Christian research across the disciplines oriented towards the question "How then should we live?" Our delightful offices are on the second floor of the old convent of Margaret Beaufort Institute, a Catholic women's house some fifteen minutes' walk from the centre of Cambridge. The KLC is an Associate Member of the Cambridge Theological Federation.

Our ethos is distinctive. Central to the KLC is intellectual community and we seek to ground this in Christian spirituality. Our desire is to do work for the glory of God and in the service of the church and the world.

In our view the Bible is central to public theology. This is reflected in our Scripture Collective, directed by Rev Dr Michael Wagenman. The Scripture Collective now houses four Seminars: The Scripture and Hermeneutics Seminar, the Scripture and Doctrine Seminar, the Scripture and Church Seminar (practical theology), and the Scripture and University Seminar. Each Seminar has its own committee and chair/s.

The origins of our Scripture Collective are found in the Scripture and Hermeneutics Seminar, which, in 2022, celebrates its 25th anniversary. This first volume in the KLC's new series with Zondervan Academic marks this anniversary. We are delighted to have a formal publishing partnership with Zondervan Academic, and already the first three volumes in this series, to be published in time for the annual AAR/SBL meetings each year, are in the pipeline.

The KLC is a growing community, and we invite you to become part of it. You can sign up for our emails and see who we are and what we are up to on our website at www.kirbylaingcentre.co.uk

Rev Dr Craig G. Bartholomew

Director, Kirby Laing Centre, October 2021

BRITISH AND FOREIGN BIBLE SOCIETY

The British and Foreign Bible Society (BFBS) was founded in 1804 by Thomas Charles, William Wilberforce, and other members of the Clapham Sect. We exist to promote the widest possible distribution and use of the Bible throughout the world. We do this through translation, publishing, distribution, literacy, Bible engagement, and advocacy throughout all spheres of society. We work with all Christian traditions.

Throughout the nineteenth century, the BFBS helped establish a worldwide Bible Society network. Over 150 societies now operate in over 200 territories under the umbrella of United Bible Societies (UBS). The BFBS continues to operate worldwide in partnership with members of the UBS.

We believe that the global church faces a crisis of Bible confidence in the midst of a growing opportunity and openness to the Bible in multiple contexts. Our vision is to see Christians confident in the Bible in all aspects of life, to see a changed conversation about the Bible in wider society, and to see the transformation that the Bible brings when it is embodied in our lives, relationships, and communities.

We seek to work with the highest possible standards of academic and research excellence with respect to the Bible and to societies and cultures around the world. This requires an attitude of deep listening to Scripture as well as to our varied and distinctive audiences. Our interventions always seek to help people and communities engage the Bible more deeply for themselves and experience the reality of Jesus, to which the Scripture leads.

We are delighted to continue our association with the Scripture and Hermeneutics Seminar through an ongoing partnership with the Kirby Laing Centre for Public Theology. The KLC is now administering our research grant programme, intended to support research into the relationship between the Bible and contemporary life. For further information on the Bible Society's work, see www.biblesociety.org.uk.

Professor Paul S. Williams
Chief executive, British and Foreign Bible Society